Springer Series on Ethics, Law, and Aging

Marshall B. Kapp, JD, MPH, Series Editor

Marshall B. Kapp was educated at Johns Hopkins University (B.A.), George Washington University (J.D., With Honors), and Harvard University School of Public Health (M.P.H.). He is the Frederick A. White Distinguished Professor of Service at Wright State University School of Medicine, where he holds faculty appointments in the Departments of Community Health and Psychiatry and serves as Director, Office of Geriatric Medicine and Gerontology. He is also a member of the adjunct faculty at the University of Dayton School of Law. He is a Fellow of the Gerontological Society of America and the American College of Legal Medicine.

—

Lessons in Law and Aging

A Tool for Educators and Students

Marshall B. Kapp, JD, MPH

 Springer Publishing Company

Springer Publishing Company, Inc.
536 Broadway
New York, NY 10012-3955

Acquisitions Editor: Helvi Gold
Production Editor: Jean Hurkin-Torres
Cover design by Susan Hauley

01 02 03 04 05 / 5 4 3 2 1

Library of Congress Cataloging-in-Publication Data

Kapp, Marshall B.
    Lessons in law and aging : a tool for educators and students /
      Marshall B. Kapp.
        p. cm. — (Springer series on ethics, law, and aging)
    Includes bibliographical references and index.
    ISBN 0-8261-1411-3
    1. Aged—Legal status, laws, etc.—Study and teaching—United
States I. Title. II. Series.
KF277.A35 K37 2001
344.73'0326'0711—dc21

                                       2001018394

Printed in the United States of America by Sheridan Press.

Contents

Acknowledgments

As always, I acknowledge with thanks the excellent assistance of the professional staffs of the Fordham Health Sciences Library at Wright State University and the Zimmerman Law Library at the University of Dayton School of Law. Christina Dewitt provided her usual fine secretarial services. I also thank the various Wright State University and University of Dayton students who served (often without full informed consent) as experimental human subjects while I tried much of the teaching material contained in this book out on them.

Copyright holders of the following works permitted portions of them to be included in this book:

Opinion 2.24, Impaired Drivers and Their Physicians, Code ofMedical Ethics, American Medical Association, copyright 2000.

Marshall B. Kapp, *'A Place Like That': Advance Directives and Nursing Home Admissions,* 4 Psychology, Public Policy, and Law 805-828 (1998), Copyright 1998 by the American Psychological Association. Reprinted with permission.

Marshall B. Kapp, *Quality of Care and Quality of Life in Nursing Facilities: What's Regulation Got to Do With It?* 31 Mc George Law Review 707-731 (2000). Reprinted by permission of the McGeorge Law Review. All rights reserved.

Marshall B. Kapp, *Physicians' Legal Duties Regarding the Use of Genetic Tests to Predict and Diagnose Alzheimer Disease,* 21 Journal of Legal Medicine (2000). Reprinted in part with permission.

Preface

Law as a process both for embodying and exhibiting important social attitudes and for effecting actions by society exerts a tremendous impact on the daily lives of older people and those around them. There is an increasing—and inevitable—effort in educational institutions and programs in the United States and elsewhere to incorporate a discussion of legal issues into gerontology-related courses at the undergraduate, graduate, and professional school levels. Sometimes this material is taught by attorneys, but often nonattorney faculty are thrust into this role. My experience in 1999 in preparing a Law and Aging addition to the Association for Gerontology in Higher Education (AGHE) Brief Bibliography Series confirmed my impression that teaching materials on legal issues suitable for classroom use in gerontology-related courses are very sparse and underdeveloped. This textbook intends to fill this identified gap by providing an organized collection of materials that can be used for educational purposes at various levels and by instructors with or without prior legal teaching expertise and experience.

I hope this text will be useful for lecture courses, seminars, and tutorials at various levels for students in the fields of social work, nursing, sociology, psychology, health and human services administration, philosophy (including ethics), and medicine who are interested in aging. Each chapter provides (as relevant and available) excerpts from selected statutes and regulations, judicial opinions, and literature, as well as commentary on these materials, discussion questions and hypothetical cases, and suggestions of other information sources for the teacher and student. The goal is to inform and sensitize those who will deal professionally with older persons about some of the current and potentially emerging legal issues they may encounter in providing services to elderly persons and to help them grapple intelligently with legal issues and the responsibilities they impose.

Abbreviations

ADA	Americans With Disabilities Act
ADEA	Age Discrimination in Employment Act
APS	Adult Protective Services
C.F.R.	Code of Federal Regulations
CCAC	Continuing Care Accreditation Commission
CCRC	Continuing Care Retirement Community
CoP	Condition of Participation
DHHS	Department of Health and Human Services
DNR	Do Not Resuscitate
DPOA	Durable Power of Attorney
FDA	Food and Drug Administration
Fed. Reg.	Federal Register
FHA	Fair Housing Act
FHAA	Fair Housing Act Amendments
FLSA	Fair Labor Standards Act
HCFA	Health Care Financing Administration
HHA	Home Health Agency
HIPAA	Health Insurance Portability and Accountability Act
IEC	Institutional Ethics Committee
IP	Independent Provider
IRB	Institutional Review Board
JCAHO	Joint Commission on Accreditation of Healthcare Organizations
LAR	Legally Authorized Representative
LSMT	Life-Sustaining Medical Treatment
NAMI	National Alliance for the Mentally Ill
NBAC	National Bioethics Advisory Commission

NCQA	National Committee for Quality Assurance
NIH	National Institutes of Health
OASDI	Old Age, Survivors, and Disabilities Insurance
OBRA	Omnibus Budget Reconciliation Act
OHRP	Office of Human Research Protection
OIG	Office of Inspector General
OSHA	Occupational Safety and Health Administration
POA	Power of Attorney
PA	Prospective Authorization
PAS	Physician-Assisted Suicide
PRO	Peer Review Organization
PVS	Persistent Vegetative State
SA	State Survey Agency
SOM	State Operations Manual
SSA	Social Security Administration
SSI	Supplemental Security Income
U.S.C.	United States Code
UR	Utilization Review
VA	Veterans Affairs

A Note on Legal Citations and Legal Sources

LEGAL CITATIONS

Legal citations for statutes and regulations generally take the form of: Volume, Name of Publication (abbreviated), Section or Part, and Year. Thus, for example, 42 U.S.C. § 1395 (1999) (the Medicare statute) is found at Volume 42 of the United States Code, Section 1395, with the most recent publication of that Section in 1999. In some situations, such as citation to the Federal Register or Congressional Record, the page number rather than section number is given.

Citations to judicial opinions in litigated cases take the form: name of case, volume, name of official reporter system (abbreviated), first page of opinion plus page(es) of material specifically quoted or referred to, and year. For state court cases, there is usually a parallel citation to the state Reporter system. For instance, *Kapp v. The World*, 290 A.2d 450, 400 N.J. 100 (1998) refers to a case that can be found in Volume 290 (Second Series), beginning at page 450 of the Atlantic Reporter system or Volume 400, beginning at page 100 of the New Jersey Reporter system. For federal cases: F. Supp. refers to the Federal Supplement Reporter system (i.e., federal district or trial court opinions); F., F.2d, or F.3d refers to opinions by Federal Circuit Courts of Appeals; and U.S. or S.Ct. refers to opinions by the United States Supreme Court.

Legal citations to published articles usually take the form: Volume, name of publication, beginning page and page number(s) of material specifically quoted or referred to, and date. A reference to Marshall B. Kapp, *A Brilliant Idea,* 125 Harvard Law Review 400 (1999) thus could be found in Volume 125 of the Harvard Law Review beginning at page 400 and published in 1999.

For further information about legal citation forms, consult the latest edition of *The Bluebook: A Uniform System of Citation,* published by the Harvard Law Review Association, Cambridge, MA.

LEGAL SOURCES

Copies of any of the legal sources cited throughout this text may be obtained by teachers and students for free. Hard copies of all federal and state statutes and regulations, as well as federal case reports and case reports from one's particular state (and often from other states as well), may be found at local law libraries (located in law schools and federal and county courthouses) and most decent size public and college libraries. Federal laws may also be obtained by contacting one's Congressional representative, and state laws may be obtained from one's state representative. Law libraries are the best place to find law review articles; articles usually may be ordered through a college's interlibrary loan system.

Statutes and regulations also are easily obtainable on the world wide web. Federal judicial opinions are available at www.uscourts.gov/link. Materials from individual states generally are available at www.state.[abbreviation of specific state].us. Other valuable "web portals" for obtaining primary materials include www.law.cornell.edu and www.findlaw.com. Valuable government links include www.gpo.gov/su_docs (for Code of Federal Regulations and Federal Register), www.gao.gov. (for reports of the General Accounting Office), www.hcfa.gov (for materials of the Health Care Financing Administration, including the Medicare and Medicaid laws and interpretations), and www.medicare.gov (Medicare materials).

General web sites of interest to teachers and students of law and aging include: www.uslaw.com, www.nih.gov/sigs/bioethics, www.law.uh.edu/healthlaw, www.lawlib..slu.edu/healthcenter/research, www.cornell.edu/ethics, www.bioethics.georgetown.edu, and www.healthlawyers.org.

For further background on legal research, see Colleen K. Pauwels, Linda K. Fariss, & Keith Buckley, *Legal Research: Traditional Sources, New Technologics,* Bloomington, IN: Phi Delta Kappa Educational Foundation (1999).

1

Discrimination Based on Age

TYPES OF AGE DISCRIMINATION

Discrimination on the basis of chronologic age may either benefit or disadvantage specific older persons. **Positive benefits** may be given to individuals on the basis of their having achieved a certain number of years of life, while those same benefits are withheld from younger persons. Examples of favorable treatment based on older age include: eligibility for Medicare; eligibility for Social Security retirement payments; reduced prices on many consumer goods and services (for example, the Ohio Department of Aging operates the Golden Buckeye Card Program for individuals age 60 and over, *www.state.oh.us/age/Buckeye*); preferential breaks on state property, income, and sales taxes and federal capital gains taxes on the sale of a residence; and eligibility for free services such as Meals on Wheels and legal services under the Older Americans Act (OAA), 42 U.S.C. § 3001 *et. seq.*

Discussion Question

Is it fair to treat older individuals more favorably than others solely on the basis of their age? What rationales support or attack such favorable discrimination? What actual evidence undergirds these rationales? See Robert B. Hudson (Guest ed.), *The Future of Age-Based Public Policy*, XIX Generations 1–78 (Fall 1995); Marshall B. Kapp, *Taking a Long Term View of Long-Term Care: 'Right' Sizing Terms of the Discussion*, 1 Quinnipiac Health Law Journal 123–137 (1997); Andrew E. Scharlach & Lenard Kaye (eds.), Controversial Issues in Aging 58–68. Boston: Allyn and Bacon (1997).

Age discrimination that **disadvantages** older persons may take place in a variety of contexts. Discrimination **against** the aged may entail differential, adverse treatment involving (among other things): employment, education, consumer transactions, transportation, and other public accommodations, recreational opportunities, and housing.

AGE DISCRIMINATION IN EMPLOYMENT

The main law pertaining to age discrimination in employment is the federal *Age Discrimination in Employment Act (ADEA)* passed by Congress in 1967, Public Law 90-202, codified at 29 U.S.C. §§ 621-634, with implementing regulations at 29 C.F.R. § 1625. Since this law regulates the actions of employers, employment agencies, and labor organizations that are engaged in various kinds of businesses, the authority of Congress to enact the ADEA is found in the U.S. Constitution, Article 1, Section 8:

> The Congress shall have the power to regulate **commerce** with foreign nations, and among the several states . . .

An important part of the history leading up to Congress' enactment of the ADEA was Congress' passage 3 years earlier of the Civil Rights Act of 1964, pertaining to discrimination on the basis of race. In enacting the ADEA, Congress expressly intended "to promote employment of older persons based on their ability rather than age; to prohibit arbitrary age discrimination in employment; to help employers and workers find ways of meeting problems arising from the impact of age on employment." 29 U.S.C. § 621(b).

Who Is Covered by the ADEA?

In its present form, the ADEA protects any "individual [**age 40 or older**] employed by any employer." 29 U.S.C. §§ 630(f), 631.

Discussion Question

Is 40 the appropriate age for declaring someone old enough to deserve special protection against age discrimination in employment? Should the age threshold be set higher? Lower? Should there even be any specific age indicated in the statute? See Bryan B. Woodruff, *Unprotected Until Forty: The Limited Scope of the Age*

Discrimination in Employment Act of 1967, 73 Indiana Law Journal 1295 (1998).

However, the ADEA expressly omits from its protections persons elected to public office, the personal staff of elected officials, elected officials' appointees on the policy-making level, and their immediate advisers with respect to the exercise of the constitutional or legal powers of the office, 29 U.S.C. § 630(f). Additionally, since the ADEA only protects "employees," individuals who are considered **owners or partners** of a business are not protected by the law. The statute also allows an employer to enforce **mandatory retirement** at age 65 for employees in certain executive or high policy making positions, 29 U.S.C. § 631(c), and permits state and local governments to "refuse to hire or to discharge any individual because of such individual's age if such action is taken with respect to the employment of an individual as a **firefighter** or as a **law enforcement officer** and [certain other conditions are met]." 29 U.S.C. § 623(i).

Discussion Question

What are the possible rationales for these omissions and exceptions? Do you find these rationales convincing? What criteria should we use to decide if a person is a partner or owner, rather than an employee, of a business?

The ADEA's restrictions against age discrimination apply to **employers** (defined as an industry with 20 or more employees), **employment agencies,** and **labor organizations.** In 1974, Congress amended the ADEA to apply its provisions expressly to **state governments** and their political subdivisions (e.g., counties and cities), in addition to the private employers who were covered already. In *Kimel v. Florida Board of Regents,* a group of faculty members and librarians employed by state universities in Alabama and Florida sued their respective employers under the ADEA, alleging that they as employees had been deprived because of their age of pay increases or promotions. The U.S. Supreme Court ruled that an ADEA claim was barred or invalidated under the Eleventh Amendment of the U.S. Constitution.

According to the majority opinion in *Kimel v. Florida Board of Regents,* 120 S. Ct. 631 (2000):

. . . [F]or over a century now, we have made clear that the Constitution does not provide for federal jurisdiction over suits against nonconsenting States. . . .

Section 5 of the Fourteenth Amendment, however, does grant Congress the authority to abrogate [i.e., overrule] the States' sovereign immunity [against lawsuits] . . . Accordingly, the private petitioners in these cases may maintain their ADEA suits against the States of Alabama and Florida if, and only if, the ADEA is appropriate legislation under § 5 . . .

The Fourteenth Amendment provides, in relevant part: Section 1. No State shall make or enforce any law which shall abridge the privileges or immunities of citizens of the United States; nor shall any State deprive any person of life, liberty, or property, without due process of law; nor deny to any person within its jurisdiction the equal protection of the laws . . .

Section 5. The Congress shall have power to enforce, by appropriate legislation, the provisions of this article. . . .

[W]e conclude that the ADEA is **not** "appropriate legislation" under § 5 of the Fourteenth Amendment. Initially, the substantive requirements the ADEA imposes on state and local governments are disproportionate to any unconstitutional conduct that conceivably could be targeted by the Act. We have considered claims of unconstitutional age discrimination under the Equal Protection Clause three times. In all three cases, we held that the age classifications at issue did not violate the Equal Protection Clause. Age classifications, unlike governmental conduct based on race or gender, cannot be characterized as so seldom relevant to the achievement of any legitimate state interest that laws grounded in such considerations are deemed to reflect prejudice and antipathy. Older persons, again, unlike those who suffer discrimination on the basis of race or gender, have not been subjected to a history of purposeful unequal treatment. Old age does not define a discrete and insular minority because all persons, if they live out their normal life spans, will experience it. Accordingly, as we recognized [in earlier cases], age is not a suspect classification under the Equal Protection Clause.

States may discriminate on the basis of age without offending the Fourteenth Amendment if the age classification in question is rationally related to a legitimate state interest. The rationality commanded by the Equal Protection Clause does not require States to match age distinctions and the legitimate interests they serve with razorlike precision . . . In contrast, when a State discriminates on the basis of race or gender, we require a tighter fit between the discriminatory means and the legitimate ends they serve . . . Under the Fourteenth

Amendment, a State may rely on age as a proxy for other qualities, abilities, or characteristics that are relevant to the State's legitimate interests. The Constitution does not preclude reliance on such generalizations. That age proves to be an inaccurate proxy in any individual case is irrelevant . . .

Our examination of the ADEA's legislative record confirms that Congress' 1974 extension of the Act to the States was an unwarranted response to a perhaps inconsequential problem. Congress never identified any pattern of age discrimination by the States, much less any discrimination whatsoever that rose to the level of constitutional violation . . . A review of the ADEA's legislative record as a whole, then, reveals that Congress had virtually no reason to believe that state and local governments were unconstitutionally discriminating against their employees on the basis of age . . . In light of the indiscriminate scope of the Act's substantive requirements, and the lack of evidence of widespread and unconstitutional age discrimination by the States, we hold that the ADEA is **not** a valid exercise of Congress' power under § 5 of the Fourteenth Amendment. The ADEA's purported abrogation of the States' sovereign immunity is accordingly invalid.

In terms of legal process, the *Kimel* case illustrates the doctrine of **judicial review.** Under this doctrine, a court may invalidate on constitutional grounds a statute enacted by a legislature and signed by the jurisdiction's chief executive. For example, here the Court overturned a provision of the ADEA because Congress lacked authority under the U.S. Constitution to enact that provision. Besides examining statutes in light of compliance with the U.S. Constitution, a court also may invalidate a state statute on the grounds that it violates the pertinent **state** constitution.

Discussion Questions

Do you agree with the Court's reasoning in *Kimel?* Is age discrimination in employment really deserving of less scrutiny and protection than discrimination based on race and gender? Is the Court accurate or overly complacent about the prevalence and seriousness of age discrimination in employment practiced by state and local governments? Is age really an accurate enough proxy for characteristics that are legitimately relevant to employment that state and local employers should be allowed to lump employees together according to age categories, or should the law mandate a more individualized approach?

What Conduct Is Prohibited by the ADEA?

29 U.S.C. § 623 Prohibition of Age Discrimination:

(a) It shall be unlawful for an **employer**—
(1) to fail or refuse to hire or to discharge any individual or otherwise discriminate against any individual with respect to his compensation, terms, conditions, or privileges of employment, because of such individual's age;
(2) to limit, segregate, or classify his employees in any way which would deprive or tend to deprive any individual of employment opportunities or otherwise adversely affect his status as an employee, because of such individual's age; or
(3) to reduce the wage rate of any employee in order to comply with this chapter.
(b) It shall be unlawful for an **employment agency** to fail or refuse to refer for employment, or otherwise to discriminate against, any individual because of such individual's age, or to classify or refer for employment any individual on the basis of such individual's age.
(c) It shall be unlawful for a **labor organization**—
(1) to exclude or to expel from its membership, or otherwise to discriminate against, any individual because of his age;
(2) to limit, segregate, or classify its membership, or to classify or fail or refuse to refer for employment any individual, in any way which would deprive or tend to deprive any individual of employment opportunities or otherwise adversely affect his status as an employee or as an applicant for employment, because of such individual's age;
(3) to cause or attempt to cause an employer to discriminate against an individual in violation of this section.

***

(e) It shall be unlawful for an employer, labor organization, or employment agency to print or publish, or cause to be printed or published, any **notice or advertisement** relating to employment by such an employer or membership in or any classification or referral for employment by such a labor organization, or relating to any classification or referral for employment by such an employment agency, indicating any preference, limitation, specification, or discrimination, based on age.

Discussion Questions

1. Typical of the way that many statutes and regulations are written, the obligations imposed on employers, employment agencies,

and labor organizations by the ADEA are phrased in negative terms, as "Thou Shalt Not" commandments. Should the law go farther than just prohibiting age discrimination in employment? Should the law impose some sort of positive affirmative action requirements on employers, employment agencies, and labor organizations regarding older employees? See Andrew E. Scharlach and Lenard W. Kaye (Eds.), *Controversial Issues in Aging,* 34–44. Boston: Allyn and Bacon (1997).

2. One of the purposes of the ADEA is to prohibit (with limited exceptions noted earlier) mandatory retirement policies based on age. Despite this prohibition, the actual retirement age of American workers continues to decrease. Should we enact laws intended to encourage (i.e., provide incentives for) individuals to take more advantage of the ADEA and stay in the workplace longer? See U.S. General Accounting Office, Social Security Reform: Implications of Raising the Retirement Age, GAO/HEHS-99-112 (1999).

What Defenses May be Asserted Against an Accusation of an ADEA Violation?

29 U.S.C. § 623(f):

> It shall **not** be unlawful for an employer, employment agency, or labor organization—
>
> (1) to take any action otherwise prohibited [by the ADEA] where age is a **bona fide occupational qualification** reasonably necessary to the normal operation of the particular business, or where the differentiation is based on **reasonable factors other than age,** or where such practices involve an employee in a workplace in a **foreign country,** and compliance with [the ADEA] would cause such employer, or a corporation controlled by such employer, to violate the laws of the country in which such workplace is located;
>
> (2) to take any action otherwise prohibited under [the ADEA]—
>
> (A) to observe the terms of a **bona fide seniority system** that is not intended to evade the purposes of [the ADEA], except that no such seniority system shall require or permit the **involuntary retirement** of any individual [age 40 or above] because of the age of such individual; or
>
> (B) to observe the terms of a **bona fide employee benefit plan**—
>
> (i) where, for each benefit or benefit package, the actual amount of payment made or cost incurred on behalf of an older

worker is no less than that made or incurred on behalf of a younger worker; or

(ii) that is a **voluntary early retirement incentive plan** consistent with the relevant purpose [of the ADEA]; or

(3) to discharge or otherwise discipline an individual for **good cause.**

Discussion Questions

1. Would it be lawful under the ADEA for a company, during a plant closing and downsizing, to give younger workers more severance pay than older co-workers? See Wall Street Journal B5 (Aug. 18, 1999).

2. Would it be lawful under the ADEA for an employer to offer its Medicare-eligible (i.e., over 65) retirees health insurance coverage that is inferior to coverage offered to retired employees not eligible for Medicare (i.e., under 65)? See *Erie County Retirees Association v. County of Erie,* 220F.3d 193 (3d Cir. 2000).

3. Would it be lawful under the ADEA for a health plan to pay more to physician-recruits who are in their early years of practice than to those who have been practicing longer? See *Wall Street Journal* B8 (Dec. 20, 1999).

4. What roles might be played by health care and human service professionals in helping to determine whether a valid defense to an ADEA claim exists in a particular case? What particular kinds of expertise might such professionals bring to this inquiry?

Burden of Proof

In *Reeves v. Sanderson Plumbing Products, Inc.,* 120 S. Ct. 2097 (2000), the U.S. Supreme Court held that a plaintiff asserting an ADEA claim need not prove by direct evidence (i.e., a "smoking gun") illegal intent on the part of the employer.

("[W]hen all legitimate reasons for rejecting an applicant have been eliminated as possible reasons for the employer's actions, it is more likely than not the employer, who we generally assume acts with *some* reason, based his decision on an impermissible consideration"). Thus, a plaintiff's prima facie case, combined with sufficient evidence to find that the employer's asserted justification is false, may permit the trier of fact to conclude that the employer unlawfully discriminated.

This is not to say that such a showing by the plaintiff will *always* be adequate to sustain a jury's finding of liability. Certainly there will be instances where, although the plaintiff has established a prima facie case and set forth sufficient evidence to reject the defendant's explanation, no rational factfinder could conclude that the action was discriminatory. For instance, an employer would be entitled to judgment as a matter of law if the record conclusively revealed some other, nondiscriminatory reason for the employer's decision, or if the plaintiff created only a weak issue of fact as to whether the employer's reason was untrue and there was abundant and uncontroverted independent evidence that no discrimination had occurred.

* * * *

Whether judgment as a matter of law is appropriate in any particular case will depend on a number of factors. Those include the strength of the plaintiff's prima facie case, the probative value of the proof that the employer's explanation is false, and any other evidence that supports the employer's case and that properly may be considered on a motion for judgment as a matter of law. (Citations omitted)

Discussion Questions

1. Do you agree with the *Reeves* decision? Does it unfairly expose employers to liability based on circumstantial or inferential, rather than direct, evidence? On the other hand, would requiring production of direct evidence of the employer's intent to discriminate based on age impose an impossible hurdle for plaintiffs?

2. How can a plaintiff in an ADEA lawsuit establish the "prima facie" (on its face) case of discrimination required by *Reeves*?

It is undisputed that petitioner satisfied this burden here: (i) at the time he was fired, he was a member of the class protected by the ADEA ("individuals who are at least 40 years of age"), (ii) he was otherwise qualified for the position of Hinge Room supervisor, (iii) he was discharged by respondent, and (iv) respondent successively hired three persons in their thirties to fill petitioner's position. (Citations omitted)

What Remedies Are Available Under the ADEA for an ADEA Violation?

An individual alleging unlawful discrimination under the ADEA must first file a charge with the federal Equal Employment Opportunity Commission (EEOC), *www.eeoc.gov*, which decides whether or not to bring a civil action on the individual's behalf. If the EEOC declines to bring a lawsuit, "Any person aggrieved may bring a civil action in any [federal] court of competent jurisdiction for such legal or equitable relief as will effectuate the purposes of [the ADEA]." 29 U.S.C. § 626 (c)(1). Legal relief could include money damages for back pay (e.g., lost wages after an illegal firing or failure to hire) or front pay (e.g., anticipated future lost wages due to an illegal firing). When money damages are sought, the plaintiff has a right to a jury trial on any factual issues. When a jury finds that the discriminatory actions of the employer, employment agency, or labor organization were **"willful,"** *McGinty v. State of New York,* 193 F.3d 64 (2d Cir. 1999), it may impose double the actual amount of damages. Equitable relief could include court orders (injunctions) directing the defendant to take some action other than paying money damages (e.g., to promote or reinstate) to the aggrieved individual.

Legal representation of individuals alleging unlawful age discrimination ordinarily is by private attorneys, especially since a court has authority to award reasonable attorneys' fees to a prevailing plaintiff's attorney at the expense of the losing defendant. Regarding the availability of legal services relating to age discrimination, see *www.aoa.dhhs.gov.*

State Remedies

Virtually every state has enacted its own counterpart to the ADEA. Even if individuals, like the state employees in *Kimel* (discussed above), are precluded from suing in federal court for age discrimination under the ADEA, they may try to vindicate their rights in state court under their own state statute. Additionally, some state age discrimination statutes impose broader protections for the employee than the ADEA does. See: Alaska Stat. Ann.§18.80.010 *et seq.* (1998); Ariz. Rev. Stat. Ann. §41-1401 *et seq.* (1999); Ark. Code Ann. §§21-3-201, 21-3-203 (1996); Cal. Govt. Code Ann. §12900 *et seq.* (West 1992 and Supp. 1999); Colo. Rev. Stat. §24-34-301 *et seq.* (1998); Conn. Gen. Stat. §46a-51 *et seq.* (1999); Del. Code Ann., Tit. 19, §710 *et seq.* (Supp. 1998); Fla. Stat. Ann. §§112.044, 760.01 *et seq.* (1997 and Supp. 1998); Ga. Code Ann. §45-19-21 *et seq.* (1990 and Supp. 1996); Haw. Rev. Stat. §378-1 *et seq.* (1993 and Cum. Supp. 1998); Idaho Code §67-5901 *et seq.* (1995 and Supp. 1999); Ill. Comp.

Stat., ch. 775, §5/1-101 *et seq.* (1998); Ind. Code §22-9-2-1 *et seq.* (1993); Iowa Code §216.1 *et seq.* (1994 and Supp. 1999); Kan Stat. Ann. §44-1111 *et seq.* (1993 and Cum. Supp. 1998); Ky. Rev. Stat. Ann. §344.010 *et seq.* (Michie 1997 and Supp. 1998); La. Rev. Stat. Ann. §23.311 *et seq.* (West 1998); *id.*, §51:2231 *et seq.* (West Supp. 1999); Me. Rev. Stat. Ann., Tit. 5, §4551 *et seq.* (1998-1999 Supp.); Md. Ann. Code, Art, 49B, §1 *et seq.* (1998 and Supp. 1999); Mass. Gen. Laws §151:1 *et seq.* (West 1997 and Supp. 1998); Mich. Comp. Laws §37.2101 *et seq.* (West 1985 and Supp. 1999); Minn. Stat. §363.01 *et seq.* (1991 and Supp. 1999); Miss. Code Ann. §25-9-149 (1991); Mo. Rev. Stat. §213.010 *et seq.* (1994 and Cum Supp. 1998); Mont. Code Ann. §49-1-101 *et seq.* (1997); Neb. Rev. Stat. §48-1001 *et seq.* (1998); Nev. Rev. Stat. §613.310 *et seq.* (1995); N.H. Rev. Stat. Ann. §354-A:1 *et seq.* (1995 and Supp. 1998); N. J. Stat. Ann. §§10:3-1, 10:5-1 *et seq.* (West 1993 and Supp. 1999); N. M. Stat. Ann. §28-1-1 *et seq.* (1996); N.Y. Exec. Law §290 *et seq.* (McKinney 1993 and Supp. 1999); N.C. Gen. Stat. §126-16 *et seq.* (1999); N.D. Cent. Code §14-02.4-01 *et seq.* (1997 and Supp. 1999); Ohio Rev. Code Ann. §4112.01 *et seq.* (1998); Okla. Stat., Tit. 25, §1101 *et seq.* (1991 and Supp. 1999); Ore. Rev. Stat. §659.010 *et seq.* (1997); 43 Pa. Cons. Stat. §951 *et seq.* (1991 and Supp. 1999); R. I. Gen. Laws §28-5-1 *et seq.* (1995 and Supp. 1997); S. C. Code Ann. §1-13-10 *et seq.* (1986 and Cum. Supp. 1998); Tenn. Code Ann. §4-21-101 *et seq.* (1998); Tex. Lab. Code Ann. §21.001 *et seq.* (1996 and Supp. 1999); Utah Code Ann. §34A-5-101 *et seq.* (Supp. 1999); Vt. Stat. Ann., Tit. 21, §495 *et seq.* (1987 and Supp. 1999); Va. Code Ann. §2.1-116.10 *et seq.* (1995 and Supp.1999); Wash. Rev. Code §49.60.010 *et seq.* (1994); W. Va. Code §5-11-1-*et seq.* (1999); Wis. Stat. Ann. §111.01 *et seq.* (West 1997 and Supp. 1998); Wyo. Stat. Ann. §27-9-101 *et seq.* (1999).

Age Discrimination in Employment Under the Americans With Disabilities Act (ADA)

Most of the lawsuits brought by older persons claiming illegal discrimination in employment are brought under the ADEA or its state counterparts. However, many older workers or job applicants may also fall within the protections of the Americans With Disabilities Act (ADA). Title I of the ADA, 42 U.S.C. § 12112 (a), prohibits private and public employers with 25 or more employees from discriminating:

against **a qualified individual** with a disability because of the disability of such individual in regard to job application procedures, the hiring, advancement, or discharge of employees, employee compensation, job training, and other terms, conditions, and privileges of employment.

Unlike the ADEA, which only requires equal treatment for older workers, the ADA imposes **affirmative** obligations on employers regarding employment of the disabled. Specifically, the ADA, 42 U.S.C. § 12112 (b)(5) defines unlawful discrimination to include:

(A) not making **reasonable accommodations** to the known physical or mental limitations of an otherwise qualified individual with a disability who is an applicant or employee, unless [the employer] can demonstrate that the accommodation would impose an **undue hardship** on the operation of the business of [the employer]; or
(B) denying employment opportunities to a job applicant or employee who is an otherwise qualified individual with a disability, if such denial is based on the need [of the employer] to make reasonable accommodation to the physical or mental impairments of the employee or applicant.

The ADA, 42 U.S.C. § 12102 (2), protects persons with a disability, which means, with respect to an individual—

(A) a physical or mental impairment that substantially limits one or more of the major life activities of such individual;
(B) a record [i.e., a history] of such an impairment; or
(C) being regarded [by others] as having such an impairment.
Implementing regulations for Title I of the ADA are found at 29 C.F.R. Part 1630.

Many older persons would qualify as persons with a disability so defined. See, e.g., Edward F. Ansello & Nancy N. Eustis (guest eds.), *Aging and Disabilities: Seeking Common Ground*, XVI Generations 1–99 (Winter 1992); Robert J. Riekse & Henry Holstege, *Growing Older in America*, 65–113. New York: McGraw-Hill (1996).

In March 1999, the EEOC issued guidelines to assist employers in complying with the ADA (available at *www.eeoc.gov/docs/accommodation*). See also Constance K. Hood, *Age Discrimination in Employment and the Americans with Disabilities Act: "A Second Bite at the Apple,"* 6 Elder Law Journal 1–30 (1998).

DISCRIMINATION IN PUBLIC SERVICES
AND ACCOMMODATIONS

Older individuals who qualify as persons with disabilities are also protected by Titles II and III of the ADA. These titles relate to, respectively, discrimination by public and private entities.

Title II, 42 U.S.C. § 12132, provides:

> . . . [N]o **qualified individual** with a disability shall, by reason of such disability, be excluded from participation in or be denied the benefits of the services, programs, or activities of a public entity [defined in § 12131(1) as any department or agency of a state or local government], or be subjected to discrimination by any such entity.
>
> § 12131(2) defines "qualified individual with a disability" to mean:
>
> . . . an individual with a disability who, with or without **reasonable modifications** to rules, policies, or practices, the removal of architectural, communication, or transportation **barriers,** or the **provision of auxiliary aids and services,** meets the **essential eligibility requirements** for the receipt of services or the participation in programs or activities provided by a public entity.

A major U.S. Supreme Court decision interpreted Title II of the ADA in 1999. In *Olmstead v. L.C.*, 119 S.Ct. 2176, the state of Georgia was sued by two women whose disabilities include mental retardation and mental illness. Both women lived in state owned and operated institutions, despite the fact that their treatment professionals had determined that they could be appropriately served in a community setting. The plaintiffs asserted that their continued institutionalization was a violation of their right under the ADA, 28 C.F.R. §35.130(d), to live "in the most integrated setting appropriate to the needs of qualified individuals with disabilities." The Court found that "Unjustified isolation . . . is properly regarded as discrimination based on disability." It observed that "institutional placement of persons who can handle and benefit from community settings perpetuates unwarranted assumptions that persons so isolated are incapable or unworthy of participating in community life" and "confinement in an institution severely diminishes the everyday life activities of individuals, including family relations, social contacts, work options, economic independence, educational advancement, and cultural enrichment."

Discussion Question

How well does this reasoning apply to frail, debilitated older individuals? Is living and receiving services in the home always really less restrictive, segregated, and isolated for such individuals than living in a long-term care facility surrounded by other people? Is a frail elder living alone at home, ambulating poorly, really "participating in community life" more than he or she would be in a long-term care facility with planned activities?

Under *Olmstead,* states are required to provide community-based services for persons with disabilities who would otherwise be entitled to institutional services when: (1) the state's treatment professionals reasonably determine that such placement is appropriate; (2) the affected persons do not oppose such placement; and (3) the placement can be reasonably accommodated, taking into account the resources available to the state and the needs of others who are receiving state-supported disability services. The Court cautioned, however, that nothing in the ADA condones termination of institutional settings for persons unable to handle or benefit from community settings. Moreover, the state's responsibility, once it provides community-based treatment to qualified persons with disabilities, is not unlimited.

Under the ADA, states are obligated to "make reasonable modifications in policies, practices, or procedures when the modifications are necessary to avoid discrimination on the basis of disability, unless the public entity can demonstrate that making the modifications would fundamentally alter the nature of the service, program, or activity," 28 CFR §35.130(b)(7). The Supreme Court indicated that the test as to whether a modification entails "fundamental alteration" of a program takes into account three factors: the cost of providing services to the individual in the most integrated setting appropriate; the resources available to the state; and how the provision of services affects the state's ability to meet the needs of others with disabilities. According to the Court, a state can establish compliance with Title II of the ADA if it demonstrates that it has:

- a comprehensive, effectively working plan for placing qualified persons with disabilities in less restrictive settings, and
- a waiting list that moves at a reasonable pace not controlled by the state's endeavors to keep its institutions fully populated.

Discussion Question

What are the likely practical ramifications of *Olmstead* for long-term care in your jurisdiction? Will it lead to a depopulation of your state's nursing homes?

Title III of the ADA, 42 U.S.C. § 12182, prohibits discrimination by public accommodations:

> (a) No **individual** shall be discriminated against on the basis of dis-ability in the full and equal enjoyment of the goods, services, facili-ties, privileges, advantages, or accommodations of any place of public accommodation by any person who owns, leases (or leases to), or operates a place of public accommodation.

Under 42 U.S.C. § 12181 (7), the following private entities are con-sidered public accommodations: places of lodging; establishments serving food or drink; places of exhibition or entertainment; places of public gathering; sales or rental establishments; service establish-ments (including professional offices of attorneys and health care providers); stations used for public transportation; places of public display or collection; places of education; social service center estab-lishments; and places of exercise or recreation. Moreover, under 42 U.S.C. § 12184 (a):

> No individual shall be discriminated against on the basis of disability in the full and equal enjoyment of specified public transportation services provided by a private entity that is primarily engaged in the business of transporting people . . .

Title III imposes **affirmative** obligations on private entities. 42 U.S.C. § 12182 (b)(2) requires places of public accommodation to:

> (ii) make **reasonable modifications** in policies, practices, or procedures, when such modifications are necessary to afford [covered] goods, services, facilities, privileges, advantages, or accommodations to indi-viduals with disabilities, unless such entity can demonstrate that mak-ing such modifications would **fundamentally alter the nature** of such goods, services, facilities, privileges, advantages, or accommodations;
>
> (iii) **take such steps as may be necessary** to ensure that no individual with a disability is excluded, denied services, segregated or otherwise be treated differently than other individuals because of the absence of **auxiliary aids and services,** unless the entity can demonstrate that taking such steps would **fundamentally alter the nature** of the good,

service, facility, privilege, advantage, or accommodation being offered or would result in an **undue burden;**

(iv) **remove architectural barriers,** and **communication barriers** that are structural in nature, in existing facilities, and **transportation barriers** in existing vehicles and rail passenger cars used by an establishment for transporting individuals . . . [**New** construction and alterations in public accommodations are dealt with in § 12183.];

(v) where an entity can demonstrate that the removal of a barrier under clause (iv) is **not readily achievable,** [the entity must] make such goods, services, facilities, privileges, advantages, or accommodations available through **alternative methods** if such methods are **readily achievable.**

However, 42 U.S.C. § 12182 (b)(3) provides:

Nothing in [Title III] shall require an entity to permit an individual to participate in or benefit from the goods, services, facilities, privileges, advantages and accommodations of such entity where such individual poses a **direct threat** to the health or safety of others. The term "direct threat" means a **significant risk** to the health or safety of others **that cannot be eliminated** by a modification of policies, practices, or procedures or by the provision of auxiliary aids or services.

Discussion Question

Describe a situation in which an older person might pose such a direct threat to others.

For further reading, see, e.g., American Association of Retired Persons, Implementation of the Americans With Disabilities Act, PF 4886(492)-D14717. Washington, DC (1992).

DISCRIMINATION IN HOUSING

Discrimination Against Frail and Disabled Elders

The housing rights of persons with disabilities, including older Americans, are covered by Titles II (public services) and III (public accommodations and services rendered by private entities) of the ADA, described above, as well as by § 504 of the Rehabilitation Act, 29 U.S.C. § 794. The 1988 Fair Housing Act Amendments (FHAA) also address persons with disabilities. 50 U.S.C. §§ 3604 makes it illegal:

(f) (1) To discriminate in the sale or rental, or to otherwise make unavailable or deny, a dwelling to any buyer or renter because of a handicap of—

(A) that buyer or renter;

(B) a person residing in or intending to reside in that dwelling after it is so sold, rented, or made available; or

(C) any person associated with that buyer or renter,

(2) To discriminate against any person in the terms, conditions, or privileges of sale or rental of a dwelling, or in the provision of services or facilities in connection with such dwelling, because of a handicap of—

(A) that person; or

(B) a person residing in or intending to reside in that dwelling after it is so sold, rented, or made available; or

(C) any person associated with that person

(3) For purposes of this subsection, discrimination includes—

(A) a refusal to permit, at the expense of the handicapped person, reasonable modifications of existing premises occupied or to be occupied by such person if such modifications may be necessary to afford such person full enjoyment of the premises except that, in the case of a rental, the landlord may where it is reasonable to do so condition permission for a modification on the renter agreeing to restore the interior of the premises to the condition that existed before the modification, reasonable wear and tear excepted;

(B) a refusal to make reasonable accommodations in rules, policies, practices, or services, when such accommodations may be necessary to afford such person equal opportunity to use and enjoy a dwelling . . .

Discussion Questions

1. If someone owns private property, should the federal government have authority to restrict what the property owner can do (in terms of sale or rental) with that property? Should government have the authority to impose affirmative accommodation requirements on the property owner?

2. Assuming government has the authority to set conditions on the sale or rental of property, is it good policy to prohibit discrimination against the handicapped in this regard? For antidiscrimination purposes in the housing context, should a handicap be treated the same way we treat race, color, religion, sex, familial status, and national origin?

3. Should the frail elderly be considered "handicapped" for purposes of the FHAA? See *Casa Marie, Inc. v. Superior Court of Puerto Rico,* 752 F. Supp. 1152, 1168 (D.P.R. 1990).

Age-Segregated Housing

The FHAA, § 23.05(b)(1), restrict the right to live in adults-only housing to prevent discrimination in the housing marketplace against families with children. However, the FHAA provide an exception (i.e., permits adults-only housing) for "housing for older people," which is defined in three ways:

1. Housing provided by federal or state programs which the federal housing Secretary identifies as being designed for elderly persons.
2. Housing intended for, and solely occupied by, persons age 62 and over.
3. Housing "intended and operated for occupancy by at least one person age 55 or over per unit," provided
   a. Eighty percent of the units must be occupied by someone age 55 or over;
   b. Management must publish and follow policies which demonstrate intent to provide housing for persons age 55 and over.

In the Housing for Older Persons Act of 1995, 42 U.S.C. § 3607(b)(2)(C), Congress set out a four-prong, fact-based test to be employed when making a determination of whether a housing complex is legitimately exempt from the FHAA under the "housing for older persons" exemption.

Discussion Questions

1. Do you agree that adults-only housing should be permitted if one of these three conditions is met? Should we permit adults-only housing even if those conditions were not satisfied, that is, Should we repeal the FHAA provisions against age-segregated housing?
2. Why should we permit age-segregated housing under any circumstances, when the law does not permit segregated housing on the basis of race, religion, or national origin?

2

The Right to Make Decisions: Informed Consent and Refusal

The relationship between older individuals and the health care and human service professionals who seek to provide them with services has legal, ethical, and moral dimensions. Respect for the person's right to make choices is the legal and ethical nucleus of that relationship.

Informed consent doctrine reflects the basic ethical responsibility to pay attention to the personal autonomy of the individual. Autonomy stems from the Greek for "self-law or rule" and stands for the idea of determining the details of one's own life. The legal system enforces the person's prerogative to control his or her own body and the right to be protected against unwanted intrusions. As stated in Judge Cardozo's famous proclamation, "Every human being of adult years and sound mind has a right to determine what shall be done with his own body; and a surgeon who performs an operation without his patient's consent commits an assault for which he is liable in damages." *Schloendorf v. Society of New York Hospitals,* 211 N.Y. 125, 105 N.E.2d 92 (1914).

Many professionals mistakenly believe that, once properly informed consent for a service has been obtained, they are then completely immune from any potential legal liability, even if substandard care is rendered. In actuality, there is a clear analytical distinction between lawsuits (a) based on lack of effective consent and (b) those based on the other malpractice theories of negligence for substandard care and breach of contract. A person never consents to receive substandard care; consent always implies permission to be given care of an acceptable professional level. Thus, if the care rendered falls below that level, the patient's consent is no defense to a claim of malpractice. Conversely, proper or even exceptionally fine care is no defense to a lawsuit based on lack of informed consent; the wrong in that case is not the quality of performance but rather the violation of the person's right to self-determination.

LEGAL THEORY

Most professional liability lawsuits today alleging lack of informed consent are based on the civil tort of negligence. In most cases, some bare form of consent to the services in question generally is present. A modern negligence inquiry focuses on whether that consent contains all of the elements necessary to make it legally effective. Specifically, a plaintiff alleging negligence must show that the professional was negligent (i.e., unintentionally failed to perform according to minimally acceptable professional standards) in fulfilling his or her duties toward that plaintiff. The professional owes the patient or client fiduciary, or trust, obligations to act in good faith and in the best interests of the patient or client. The imposition of fiduciary responsibility is the law's way of trying to rectify the disparity in power between the knowledgeable professional and the unknowledgeable, dependent patient/client. These fiduciary responsibilities include the assurance that any consent given to proposed medical interventions contains certain vital elements discussed below. Failure to assure the presence of these elements constitutes a violation of the professional's fiduciary duties and an act of negligence.

Discussion Question

Is it fair to impose fiduciary or trust obligations on health and human service professionals, when we do not impose that level of responsibility on members of most other occupations? Do you agree with the presumption that health and human service professionals, mainly because of their superior knowledge and skills, wield inordinate power over their patients or clients and that the law must correct that power imbalance?

The remedy ordinarily available to the wronged patient in a negligence suit claiming lack of valid consent is an award of monetary damages. Compensation of the victim for losses suffered is the primary goal of contemporary tort law. Thus, persons able to show the violation of their rights under the informed consent doctrine may collect damages from the offending party(ies) for actual out-of-pocket expenses occasioned by the risk that materialized but about which they were not forewarned. Plaintiffs also may be entitled to damages for the pain and suffering resulting from the unconsented-to intrusion.

Failure to obtain the patient's or client's informed consent could conceivably lead to other sanctions against the offending health or human service professional. To the extent that hospital or nursing home bylaws require compliance with the doctrine of informed consent, a professional might lose staff privileges or be subject to other institutional sanctions for failing to obtain informed consent. Similarly, a health or human service professional might be subject to penalties by state licensing authorities if the relevant licensing statute or regulations make it an offense to fail to obtain informed consent.

Vermont Statutes § 18-1852:

> (a) The general assembly hereby adopts the "Bill of rights for Hospital patients" as follows:
> ***
> (3) The patient has the right to obtain, from the physician coordinating his or her care, complete and current information concerning diagnosis, treatment, and any known prognosis in terms the patient can reasonably be expected to understand.
> ***
> (4) Except in emergencies, the patient has the right to receive from the patient's physician information necessary to give informed consent prior to the start of any procedure or treatment, or both. Such information for informed consent should include but not necessarily be limited to the specific procedure or treatment, or both, the medically significant risks involved, and the probable duration of incapacitation. Where medically significant alternatives for care or treatment exist, or when the patient requests information concerning medical alternatives, the patient has the right to such information. The patient also has the right to know the name of the person responsible for the procedures or treatment, or both.
> (5) The patient has the right to refuse treatment to the extent permitted by law. In the event the patient refuses treatment, the patient shall be informed of the medical consequences of that action and the hospital shall be relieved of any further responsibility for that refusal.
> ***

(b) Failure to comply with any provision of this section may constitute a basis for disciplinary action against a physician . . . A complaint may be filed with the board of medical practice.

In a particularly rare and egregious situation of treating a patient without first obtaining informed consent, a professional could be subjected to prosecution for criminal battery.

Discussion Question

Is it appropriate or excessive to expose a professional who fails to obtain proper informed consent to loss of hospital or nursing home privileges, a punishment that could jeopardize the professional's livelihood? To disciplinary action (e.g., licensure suspension)? To criminal prosecution?

An individual may give consent to medical or social service interventions by stating it directly, either orally or in writing. Formal consent, through spoken or written words, is "express." The legal significance of written consent forms is discussed below.

There are plenty of situations in which consent is not explicitly put into words, but the individual nonetheless consents to the intervention. A patient's or client's consent may be implied from the circumstances. Specifically, through actions the person may manifest a desire to receive the intervention by voluntarily submitting to it in a manner that the professional reasonably relies on to conclude that the procedure is authorized. Implied consent is not an exception to the general informed consent principle. The only difference between implied and express consent is that in the former the individual's permission may be given by actions rather than by spoken or written words. Authorization comes by compliance, but only after the professional has assured that the essential preconditions for such compliance have been satisfied.

Discussion Question

Describe some situations involving services to older persons that might lend themselves to implied rather than express consent.

As a general rule, each health care or human service professional must obtain consent to the particular health care or social service intervention, or part thereof, that he or she expects to provide. Although the process of informing the patient/client certainly may be shared among members of the service team, the legal responsibility to ascertain that informed consent has taken place ultimately rests with the professional in charge of delivering the service.

Some jurisdictions place exclusive responsibility for obtaining consent, at least for medical interventions, on the treating physician. Ohio Rev. Code § 2317.54:

> No hospital, home health agency, or provider of a hospice care program shall be held liable for a physician's failure to obtain an informed consent from his patient prior to a surgical or medical procedure or course of procedures, unless the physician is an employee of the hospital, home health agency, or provider of a hospice care program.

Kelly v. Methodist Hospital, 444 Pa. Super. 427, 664 A.2d 148 (1995):

> . . . we find compelling reasons for not imposing upon hospitals the duty of obtaining informed consent. It is the surgeon and not the hospital who has the education, training and experience necessary to advise each patient of risks associated with the proposed surgery. Likewise, by virtue of his relationship with the patient, the physician is in the best position to know the patient's medical history and to evaluate and explain the risks of a particular operation in light of the particular medical history. Appellants' attempt to impose upon a hospital the duty not only to ensure that physicians obtain informed consent but also to draft the substantive information to be disclosed, ignores these unique aspects of the physician-patient relationship. Moreover, we are unable to conceive of how a hospital could draft, in laundry-list fashion, the substantive information to be disclosed for each surgery as it relates to each patient. Thus, the approach suggested by appellants would prove not only improvident but unworkable as well.

In other jurisdictions, however, when care is given within a facility or through an agency, legal responsibility for assuring the validity of patient or client consent may be shared between the facility or agency, on one side, and the caring professional, on the other. *Keel v. St. Elizabeth Medical Center,* 842 S.W.2d 860 (Ky. 1992).

Discussion Questions

1. Should the facility or organization share exposure to liability if valid informed consent for a particular intervention has not been

obtained? On what grounds? Conversely, is it fair to let the facility or organization entirely off the legal "hook"?

2. What can a facility or organization do, proactively, to manage this legal risk?

ELEMENTS OF VALID CONSENT

The first requirement for a valid legal consent is that the patient's participation in the decision-making process and the ultimate decision regarding care must be voluntary—without undue elements of force, fraud, deceit, duress, overreaching, or other ulterior form of constraint or coercion. Every choice made by a competent adult is legally presumed to be voluntary, and the burden of rebutting or disproving that presumption falls on a complaining patient or the patient's surrogate.

Discussion Questions

1. Give examples of scenarios in which the voluntariness of an older person's consent to particular medical or human services interventions might be questioned. Is such questioning likely to happen more or less frequently when older persons are involved?

2. At what point does the advice, encouragement, and cajoling of family members or health care and human service professionals turn into undue coercion or duress? How can others be supportive of the older person without becoming overbearing?

3. What can health care and human service professionals do to maximize the voluntariness of their older patients' or clients' decisions?

The second essential element for valid decision making is that the patient's choice be informed. For the individual to issue a "knowing" or "intelligent" consent or refusal, the health care or human services professional must disclose sufficient information.

Discussion Questions

1. What are the ethical justifications underlying this legal doctrine?

2. What are the therapeutic justifications underlying this legal doctrine?

There are basically two legal standards detailing the amount and type of information that the professional should convey to the patient or client. The disclosure standard currently enforced in the majority of American jurisdictions is referred to as the "reasonable professional" or "community" standard.

New Hampshire Statutes § 507-C:2:

> II. . . . where the plaintiff claims that a medical care provider failed to supply adequate information to obtain the informed consent of the injured person:
>
> (a) The plaintiff shall have the burden of proving by affirmative evidence, consisting of expert testimony of a competent witness or witnesses, . . . that the medical care provider did not supply that type of information regarding the treatment, procedure or surgery as would customarily have been given to a patient in the position of the injured person or other persons authorized to give consent for such a patient by other medical care providers with similar training and experience at the time of the treatment, procedure or surgery.

Vermont Statutes § 12-1909:

> (a) For the purpose of this section "lack of informed consent" means:
>
> (1) The failure of the person providing the professional treatment or diagnosis to disclose to the patient such alternatives thereto and the reasonably foreseeable risks and benefits involved as a reasonable medical practitioner under similar circumstances would have disclosed, in a manner permitting the patient to make a knowledgeable evaluation.

Under this test, the adequacy of disclosure is judged against the amount and type of information that other reasonable, prudent professionals would have disclosed to patients under similar conditions. When proof is adduced that the customary practice within the professional community, at least for a respectable minority if not the majority of the profession, would be to withhold particular facts from the patient or client, a defense is established in a professional standard jurisdiction. However, the professional is always obligated to respond honestly to a patient's or client's specific questions. Vermont Statutes § 12-1909 (d): "A patient shall be entitled to a reasonable answer to any specific question about foreseeable risks and benefits, and a medical practitioner shall not withhold any requested information . . ."

Almost half of the states have officially accepted a more expansive standard of information disclosure: the "reasonable patient" or "material risk" standard. *Canterbury v. Spence,* 464 F.2d 772 (D.C. Cir. 1972):

> In our view, the patient's right of self-decision shapes the boundaries of the duty to reveal. That right can be effectively exercised only if the patient possesses enough information to enable an intelligent choice. The scope of the physician's communications to the patient, then, must be measured by the patient's need, and that need is the information material to the decision. Thus the test for determining whether a particular peril must be divulged is its materiality to the patient's decision: All risks potentially affecting the decision must be unmasked. And to safeguard the patient's interest in achieving his own determination on treatment, the law must itself set the standard for adequate disclosure.
>
> Optimally for the patient, exposure of a risk would be mandatory whenever the patient would deem it significant to his decision, either singly or in combination with other risks. Such a requirement, however, would summon the physician to second-guess the patient, whose ideas on materiality could hardly be known to the physician. That would make an undue demand upon medical practitioners, whose conduct, like that of others, is to be measured in terms of reasonableness. Consonantly with orthodox negligence doctrine, the physician's liability for nondisclosure is to be determined on the basis of foresight, not hindsight; no less than any other aspect of negligence, the issue on nondisclosure must be approached from the viewpoint of the reasonableness of the physician's divulgence in terms of what he knows or should know to be the patient's informational needs . . .
>
> From these considerations we derive the breadth of the disclosure of risks legally to be required. The scope of the standard is not subjective as to either the physician or the patient; it remains objective with due regard for the patient's informational needs and with suitable leeway for the physician's situation. In broad outline, we agree that a risk is thus material when a reasonable person, in what the physician knows or should know to be the patient's position, would be likely to attach significance to the risk or cluster of risks in deciding whether or not to forego the proposed therapy.

Discussion Questions

1. Ideally, shouldn't the reasonable professional/community standard lead to the same practice as the reasonable patient/material risk standard? In other words, shouldn't the information that a

reasonable patient would deem material to the patient's decision in any particular case be precisely the same information that good, prudent professionals ordinarily would share with their patients in such cases? Why, then, does the law distinguish between these two informational standards? See Michael J. Barry, *Involving Patients in Medical Decisions: How Can Physicians Do Better?* 282 Journal of the American Medical Association 2356–2357 (1999); Clarence H. Braddock, Stephan D. Fihn, Wendy Levinson, Albert R. Jonsen, & Robert A. Pearlman, *How Doctors and Patients Discuss Routine Clinical Decisions: Informed Decision Making in the Outpatient Setting*, 12 Journal of General Internal Medicine 339–345 (1997).

2. What are the practical barriers to fuller communication of information between health care and human service professionals and their patients or clients or their surrogates? How can those barriers be addressed successfully?

3. What are the arguments for and against the reasonable professional/community standard of information disclosure versus the reasonable patient/materiality standard? What values and assumptions underlie each of these standards?

4. From a risk management perspective, shouldn't the health care or human services professional always err on the side of providing more, rather than less, information? See T. Elaine Adamson, Jeanne M. Tschann, David S. Gullion, & Andrew A. Oppenberg, *Physician Communication Skills and Malpractice Claims: A Complex Relationship*, 150 Western Journal of Medicine 356–360 (1989).

5. Is one or the other of these two informational standards better suited to older persons?

Several specific informational items are required to be disclosed as part of the consent process under either of the informational standards.

Iowa Code § 147.137:

Consent is valid only when the professional communicating with the patient "sets forth in general terms the nature and purpose of the procedure or procedures, together with the known risks, if any, of death, brain damage, quadriplegia, paraplegia, the loss or loss of function of any organ or limb, or disfiguring scars associated with such procedure or procedures, with the probability of each such risk if reasonably determinable."

Canterbury v. Spence:

The topics importantly demanding a communication of information are the inherent and potential hazards of the proposed treatment, the alternatives to that treatment, if any, and the results likely if the patient remains untreated. The factors contributing significance to the dangerousness of a medical technique are, of course, the incidence of injury and the degree of the harm threatened.

Discussion Questions

1. What else would you add to the list of informational items to be shared with the patient as part of the informed consent process? How about relevant financial costs? See Michael S. Wilkes & David L. Schriger, *Caution: The Meter is Running-Informing Patients About Health Care Costs,* 165 Western Journal of Medicine 74–79 (1996). Any financial incentives (e.g., because of managed care) of the care provider? See *Pegram v. Herdrich,* 120 S. Ct. 2143 (2000) (holding that health maintenance organizations may offer physicians financial bonuses to hold down health care costs).

2. How should the professional calculate at what point a potential risk is significant enough that the patient should be warned about it under the reasonable professional and the reasonable patient standards of disclosure?

3. Should health care or human service professionals give advice to their patients or clients about choosing among alternative interventions? Don't individuals, especially older persons, want and expect such advice as part of the professional relationship? On the other hand, can't advice turn into coercion or undue influence, especially for vulnerable older persons? See Timothy E. Quill & Howard Brody, *Physician Recommendations and Patient Autonomy: Finding a Balance Between Physician Power and Patient Choice,* 125 Annals of Internal Medicine 763–769 (1996).

4. Is it realistic to expect nonprofessionally educated patients or clients, especially the elderly ones, to adequately understand, assimilate, and mentally process the often extensive and detailed information that must be disclosed? How can we accurately measure how much information a person actually has understood? Does "informed" consent equate with "understanding" consent? Should we insist on "understanding," not just "informed," consent? See *Daum v. SpineCare Med. Group,* 52 Cal.App.4th 1285, 61 Cal. Rptr.2d 260

(1997): ". . . the medical profession must conform its methods of disclosure to the needs and understanding of patients." See also Donna A. Wirshing, William C. Wirshing, Stephen R. Marder, Robert P. Liberman, & Jim Mintz, *Informed Consent: Assessment of Comprehension,* 155 American Journal of Psychiatry 1508–1511 (1998); Jay Katz, *Informed Consent—Must It Remain a Fairy Tale?* 10 Journal of Contemporary Health Law and Policy 69–91 (1994).

5. Should we worry that the mandated disclosure of information will frighten away individuals from agreeing to undergo clinically or socially indicated interventions? Is the root of most refusals of care too much, or too little, shared information? See Robert Chaplin & Andrew Kent, *Informing Patients About Tardive Dyskinesia: Controlled Trial of Patient Education,* 172 British Journal of Psychiatry 78–81 (1998); Edward H. Wagner, Paul Barrett, Michael J. Barry, William Barlow, & Floyd J. Fowler, Jr., *The Effect of a Shared Decisionmaking Program on Rates of Surgery for Benign Prostatic Hyperplasia,* 33 Medical Care 765–770 (1995).

6. Should we worry that the mandated disclosure of information will cause patients to experience those side effects about which they were warned? See Geoffrey C. Lamb, Sandra S. Green, & James Heron, *Can Physicians Warn Patients of Potential Side Effects Without Fear of Causing Those Side Effects?* 154 Archives of Internal Medicine 2753–2756 (1994).

7. The informed consent doctrine applies to a wide variety of interventions besides medical procedures such as surgery or dialysis. For example, what specific information should the physician and pharmacist supply to a patient for whom the physician has prescribed a particular medication? See Betsy Sleath, Debra Roter, Betty Chewning, & Bonnie Svarstad, *Asking Questions About Medication: Analysis of Physician-Patient Interactions and Physician Perceptions,* 37 Medical Care 1169–1173 (1999); Louis A. Morris, Ellen R. Tabak, & Kathleen Gondek, *Counseling Patients About Prescribed Medication,* 35 Medical Care 996–1007 (1997). What about screening for asymptomatic diseases? See Andrew M.D. Wold & Daniel M. Becker, *Cancer Screening and Informed Patient Discussions: Truth and Consequences,* 156 Archives of Internal Medicine 1069–1072 (1996).

Even if a patient or client can establish the absence of informed consent, no civil recovery can be had unless the plaintiff can also prove that the professional's failure to inform properly was a proximate, or direct, cause of the injury suffered. Put differently, if the person (or a "reasonable" person in the same set of circumstances) would have proceeded with the intervention anyway, he or she cannot subsequently complain about a risk that he or she (or a "reasonable" person) would have found unpersuasive. Vermont Statutes § 12-1909:

(c) It shall be a defense to any action for medical malpractice based upon an alleged failure to obtain such an informed consent that:
***
(2) The patient assured the medical practitioner he would undergo the treatment, procedure or diagnosis regardless of the risk involved, or the patient indicated to the medical practitioner that he did not want to be informed of the matters to which he would be entitled to be informed; or
***
(4) A reasonably prudent person in the patient's position would have undergone the treatment or diagnosis if he had been fully informed.

Mustacchio v. Parker, 535 So.2d 833 (La. Ct. App.2d Cir. 1988):

The courts have adopted an objective test for determining causation. Under this test, the court examines whether a reasonable person in the patient's position would have consented to the operation if full disclosure had been made. Among the things to be considered in determining causation are the condition of the patient at the time of the decision, the necessity for the treatment, the seriousness of the undisclosed consequence, the likelihood of the consequence occurring, and the measures available for the correction of the consequence if it should occur. (Citations omitted)

Discussion Question

Do you agree with the requirement that there be proximate causation of injuries before recovery for lack of informed consent may occur? Why shouldn't violation of the patient's dignity by itself, regardless of its effect on the outcome of care, subject the inadequate, negligent communicator to liability?

The third essential element of legally valid consent is that the person must be mentally (both cognitively and emotionally) capable of giving valid consent or refusal regarding personal matters. See *Greynolds v. Kurman,* 91 Ohio App.3d 389 (1993). Every adult human being is presumed to be decisionally capable, and that presumption is rebutted or done away with only when a judge expressly rules that the individual is incompetent.

Vermont Statutes § 14-3075:

(a) When a ward whose right to consent to surgery or other medical procedure has not been restricted pursuant to . . . [a guardianship order] is admitted to a hospital for nonemergency surgery or other nonemergency medical procedures requiring consent, the treating physician shall determine if the person's physical condition is such that the person has sufficient capacity to make a responsible decision. If the person has such capacity, his informed consent shall be obtained before such surgery or medical procedure is performed. In such cases, the ward's consent shall be determinative and no other consent is necessary.

(b) When a ward whose right to consent to surgery or other medical procedures has been restricted pursuant to . . . [a guardianship order] is admitted to a hospital for nonemergency surgery or other nonemergency medical procedures requiring consent, the guardian may give such consent upon the advice of the treating physician and after obtaining permission of the probate court, after hearing, upon such notice as the court may direct.

A major problem is the older patient who is incapacitated in clinical fact (*de facto* incompetent) but who has not been so adjudicated in a court of law (*de jure* incompetent) and for whom no guardian has been formally appointed. The topic of formal and informal surrogate decision making for decisionally incapable older persons is discussed in chapters 3 and 7.

Discussion Questions

1. Discuss the pros and cons of insisting on absolute legal certainty, to be sought through initiation of formal guardianship proceedings, for every patient needing medical attention for whom competence to consent or refuse is questionable.

2. In assessing a person's capacity to make particular decisions, what specific questions should the assessor ask? See Daniel C. Marson, Lauren Hawkins, Bronwyn McInturff, & Lindy E. Harrell, *Cognitive Models That Predict Physician Judgments of Capacity to Consent in Mild Alzheimer's Disease,* 45 Journal of the American Geriatrics Society 458–464 (1997); Marshall B. Kapp, *Assessment of Competence to Make*

Medical Decisions, in The Practical Handbook of Clinical Gerontology 174–187 (Laura L. Carstensen, Barry A. Edelstein, & Laurie Dornbrand, eds.), Thousand Oaks, CA: Sage Publications (1996).

3. Describe the components of an ideal capacity assessment process and who should be involved in conducting the assessment. See Rodney R. Baker, Peter A. Lichtenberg, & Jennifer Moye, *A Practice Guideline for Assessment of Competency and Capacity of the Older Adult,* 2 Professional Psychology: Research and Practice 149–154 (1998).

4. What is the proper role of standardized testing in the capacity assessment process? See Kathleen C. Glass, *Redefining Definitions and Devising Instruments: Two Decades of Assessing Mental Competence,* 20 International Journal of Law and Psychiatry 5–33 (1997); Marshall B. Kapp & Douglas Mossman, *Measuring Decisional Capacity: Cautions on the Construction of a 'Capacimeter',* 2 Psychology, Public Policy, and Law 73–95 (1996); Daniel C. Marson, Kellie K. Ingram, Heather A. Cody, & Lindy E. Harrell, *Assessing the Competency of Patients With Alzheimer's Disease Under Different Legal Standards,* 52 Archives of Neurology 949–954 (1995).

5. What special training do, or should, health care and human service professionals receive to prepare them to assess decisional capacity among their patients or clients?

EXCEPTIONS TO INFORMED CONSENT
REQUIREMENTS

A number of well-recognized exceptions exist to the general informed consent requirements. They are all applicable, in appropriate circumstances, to older persons.

First, informed consent is not required in certain instances in which interventions are directed or authorized by law. These include actions performed pursuant to the authority of police officers or public health officials. Connecticut Statutes § 19a-265:

> (c) If any town, city or borough director of health determines that the public health is substantially and imminently endangered by a person with or suspected of having active tuberculosis, he may take the following actions as reasonably necessary to protect the public health: (1) Issue a warning stating the person should have a physician's examination for tuberculosis to a person who has active tuberculosis or who is suspected of having active tuberculosis when that

person is unable or unwilling voluntarily to submit to such examination despite demonstrated efforts to educate and counsel the person about the need for such examination; (2) issue a warning stating that the person should complete an appropriate prescribed course of medication for tuberculosis when that person has active tuberculosis but is unwilling or unable to adhere to an appropriate prescribed course of medication despite a demonstrated effort to educate and counsel the person about the need to complete the prescribed course of treatment and the offering of such enablers and incentives as are reasonably appropriate to facilitate the completion of treatment by that person; (3) issue a warning stating that the person should follow a course of directly observed therapy for tuberculosis that should be given in such a manner as shall minimize the time and financial burden on the person given that person's individual circumstances, when that person has active tuberculosis, has been nonadherent to treatment for it and is unwilling or unable otherwise to adhere to an appropriate prescribed course of medication for tuberculosis despite a demonstrated effort to educate and counsel the person about the need to complete the course of treatment and the provision of such enablers and incentives to the person as are reasonably appropriate to facilitate the completion of treatment by that person; (4) issue an emergency commitment order which shall extend for no more than ninety-six hours that authorizes the removal to or detention in a hospital or other medically-appropriate setting of a person: (A) Who has active tuberculosis that is infectious or who presents a substantial likelihood of having active tuberculosis that is infectious based upon epidemiologic, clinical, radiographic evidence and laboratory test results; (B) who poses a substantial and imminent likelihood of transmitting tuberculosis to others because of his or her inadequate separation from others, based on a physician's professional judgment using recognized infection control principles; (C) who is unwilling or unable to behave so as not to expose others to risk of infection from tuberculosis despite a demonstrated effort to educate and counsel the person about the need to avoid exposing others and required contagion precautions; (D) who has expressed or demonstrated an unwillingness to adhere to the prescribed course of treatment that would render the person noninfectious despite being educated and counseled about the need to do so and being offered such enablers and incentives as are reasonably appropriate to facilitate the completion of treatment; and (E) for whom emergency commitment is the least restrictive alternative to protect the public health. When issuing an emergency commitment order, the director of health may direct a police officer or other designated transport personnel to immediately transport the person with tuberculosis as so ordered by the director of health. The police officer shall take into custody and isolate the person in such a manner as required by the director of health.

Discussion Questions

1. What is the policy rationale for the state's police power authority to enforce mandatory intervention in this sort of circumstance? Do you agree with that rationale?

2. What due process rights, if any, should be afforded a person refusing intervention in this sort of situation?

Second, an emergency exception applies when (a) immediate medical treatment is required to preserve life or to prevent a serious, perhaps permanent impairment to health, but (b) consent cannot be obtained from the patient (or from someone else empowered to authorize treatment on the patient's behalf), and (c) there is no credible indication that the treatment would be refused were the patient then able to make his or her own wishes known.

Discussion Question

When an older person presents to health care professionals in need of treatment, what should those health care professionals do prior to relying on the emergency exception and dispensing with the usual informed consent process?

Third, a person, even though still mentally competent, may waive or give up the right to informed consent and delegate decision-making authority to the service provider or someone else. When such a waiver is made voluntarily, knowingly, and competently, it authorizes the service provider or designated third party to act without the patient's or client's own permission for each specific intervention.

Discussion Questions

1. What is the ethical foundation for legally permitting individuals the opportunity to waive their right to informed consent?

2. Why might a person, particularly an older person, want to waive the right of informed consent and have someone else make decisions about various kinds of interventions? See Marshall B. Kapp, *Medical Empowerment of the Elderly*, 19 Hastings Center Report 5–7 (1989). What cultural factors might come into play in this context?

Is the American commitment (some characterize it as an "obsession") to personal autonomy universally shared? See Elysa Gordon, *Multiculturalism in Medical Decisionmaking: The Notion of Informed Waiver,* XXIII Fordham Urban Law Journal 1321–1362 (1996).

3. Waiver of the right to informed consent, especially in the case of older persons, is often done tacitly rather than explicitly or formally, especially when adult children are involved. How can health and human service professionals verify that waiver of decisionmaking authority was the real intent of the older patient or client? What are the pros and cons of requiring that all delegations of authority be formalized and written?

4. How can health and human services professionals help prevent the waiver doctrine, especially in the case of older persons ("I'm sure that old Mrs. Jones wouldn't want to be burdened with that difficult decision"), from being relied on so readily that it rapidly becomes the exception that swallows the rule?

Fourth, the most controversial exception to compliance with informed consent requirements is the doctrine of "therapeutic exception" or "therapeutic privilege." In the medical context, the defense of therapeutic privilege to a claim of nondisclosure of material information about a patient's diagnosis, prognosis, or treatment is applicable when, in the health care professional's good faith judgment, disclosure would be likely to complicate or hinder necessary treatment, cause severe psychological harm, and be so upsetting as to render a rational decision by the patient impossible.

New Hampshire Statutes § 332-I:2:

> The patient shall be fully informed by a health care provider of his or her medical condition, health care needs, and diagnostic test results, including the manner by which such results will be provided and the expected time interval between testing and receiving results, *unless medically inadvisable and so documented in the medical record,* and shall be given the opportunity to participate in the planning of his or her total care and medical treatment, to refuse treatment, and to be involved in experimental research upon the patient's written consent only. (Emphasis added)

Nishi v. Hartwell, 52 Haw. 188, 473 P.2d 116 (1970), *overruled on other grounds, Carr v. Strode,* 904 P.2d 489 (Haw. 1995):

Dr. Scully performed the procedure pursuant to consent signed by Dr. Nishi and Mrs. Nishi, concededly with professional competence. However, after the procedure was completed, Dr. Nishi was paralyzed from the waist down and had no control of his bowel and bladder. It is admitted that this condition occurred as a side effect of Urokon, the contrast medium which Dr. Scully used in the procedure. Neither Dr. Hartwell nor Dr. Scully apprised Dr. Nishi of the danger before he submitted himself to the procedure, although both were aware of the existence of such collateral hazard.

***

The doctrine of informed consent imposes upon a physician a duty to disclose to his patient all relevant information concerning a proposed treatment, including the collateral hazards attendant thereto, so that the patient's consent to the treatment would be an intelligent one based on complete information.

However, the doctrine recognizes that the primary duty of a physician is to do what is best for his patient and that a physician may withhold disclosure of information regarding any untoward consequences of a treatment where full disclosure will be detrimental to the patient's total care and best interest.

In this connection, it is also recognized that no hard and fast rule can be stated as to the circumstances which will excuse withholding of full disclosure and as to the kind of information to be withheld, and that each case will depend on its particular facts.

***

We . . . hold that . . . the medical standard so established was that a competent and responsible medical practitioner would not disclose information which might induce an adverse psychosomatic reaction in a patient highly apprehensive of his condition. (Citations omitted)

Discussion Questions

1. Is the therapeutic privilege exception a way to encourage compassion and benevolence toward vulnerable patients, or is it an invitation to unbridled paternalism by health care professionals?

2. Is this an exception that threatens to swallow the rule (of informed consent)? How can that outcome be prevented?

3. Is the widening access of patients to their own medical records likely to affect health care professionals' use of the therapeutic privilege exception to withhold material information from patients?

4. From a risk management perspective, what steps should a health care professional take prior to treating a patient on the basis of the therapeutic privilege exception to informed consent?

Finally, a health care professional is not required to disclose information about which the particular patient is already aware from past experience. The exception also applies to information that is so broadly known that the average, or "reasonable," patient would be aware of it.

SIGNIFICANCE OF CONSENT FORMS

As discussed in chapter 8, a written consent form ordinarily is legally required when a proposed intervention is part of a biomedical or behavioral research protocol. By contrast, it is the exceptional circumstance when written consent is legally required for a diagnostic or therapeutic intervention. Massachusetts Statutes § 111-70E:

> Every patient or resident of a facility shall be provided by the physician in the facility the right:
>
> ***
>
> (h) in the case of a patient suffering from any form of breast cancer, to complete information on all alternative treatments which are medically viable.
>
> Except in cases of emergency surgery, at least ten days before a physician operates on a patient to insert a breast implant, the physician shall inform the patient of the disadvantages and risks associated with breast implantation. The information shall include, but not be limited to, the standardized written summary provided by the department. The patient shall sign a statement provided by the department acknowledging the receipt of said standardized written summary. . . . The department of public health shall:
>
> (1) develop a standardized written summary, as set forth in this paragraph in layman's language that discloses side effects, warnings, and cautions for a breast implantation operation within three months of the date of enactment of this act;
>
> (2) update as necessary the standardized written summary;
>
> (3) distribute the standardized written summary to each hospital, clinic, and physician's office and any other facility that performs breast implants; and
>
> (4) provide the physician inserting the breast implant with a statement to be signed by the patient acknowledging receipt of the standardized written summary.

Washington Administrative Code § 246-100-207:

(4) Persons subject to regulation [as insurers] and requesting an insured, subscriber, or potential insured or subscriber to furnish the results of an HIV test for underwriting purposes, as a condition for obtaining or renewing coverage under an insurance contract, health care service contract, or health maintenance organization agreement shall:

***

(b) Obtain informed specific written consent for an HIV test.

Discussion Question

Why have some states singled out interventions such as breast implantation and HIV testing for written informed consent requirements, while not requiring written informed consent for the vast majority of medical (or human service) interventions?

Health care delivered within facilities of the U.S. Department of Veterans' Affairs is governed by 38 C.F.R. § 17.32:

(d) *Documentation of informed consent.* (1) The informed consent process must be appropriately documented in the medical record. In addition, signature consent is required for all diagnostic and therapeutic treatments or procedures that:
(i) Require the use of sedation:
(ii) Require anesthesia or narcotic analgesia:
(iii) Are considered to produce significant discomfort to the patient:
(iv) Have a significant risk of complication or morbidity;
(v) Require injections of any substance into a joint space or body cavity: or (vi) Involve testing for Human Immunodeficiency Virus (HIV).

Discussion Question

Do you agree with this regulation in terms of the types of interventions singled out for written consent forms? Are there interventions you would add to or subtract from this list? What valid purpose is served by requiring written consent forms for certain interventions but not others?

Even when a written consent form has been signed by the patient or client, there are numerous ways for its legitimacy to be attacked.

Discussion Question

What are some of the claims that patients/clients or their advocates might make to attack the legitimacy of a signed consent form?

In spite of the fact that written consent forms are neither usually legally mandated nor impervious to legal attack even when they have been created, many health care professionals, facilities, and agencies widely use written consent forms in their everyday clinical practice. To some extent, this results from a common confusion between form and the substance of the consent process. See Alan Meisel & Mark Kuczewski, *Legal and Ethical Myths About Informed Consent,* 156 Archives of Internal Medicine 2521–2526 (1996). Nevertheless, appropriate use of written consent forms in clinical practice can serve a variety of valuable purposes.

First, the regular use of written consent forms is required by standards of the Joint Commission on Accreditation of Healthcare Organizations (JCAHO). The significance of JCAHO accreditation is discussed in chapter 4. Second, the written consent form can and should serve as a valuable source of information and education for the patient or client and family. Handled properly, the written form can become an integral part of the professional/patient relationship and can perform a cognitive as well as therapeutic function for the patient or client and family.

Discussion Question

How can consent forms be best written, presented, and supplemented so as to maximize their educational and therapeutic potential for patients/clients and their families?

Third, a written consent form does provide some measure of legal protection for health and human service professionals. Although it does not by itself constitute the totality of the required consent, the written form ordinarily does have status as an important piece of proof or evidence that the required process of communication took place. Iowa Statutes § 147.137:

> A consent in writing to any medical or surgical procedure or course of procedures in patient care which meets the requirements of this section shall create a presumption that informed consent was given. A consent in writing meets the requirements of this section if it:
>
> 1. Sets forth in general terms the nature and purpose of the procedure or procedures, together with the known risks, if any, of death, brain damage, quadriplegia, paraplegia, the loss or loss of function of any organ or limb, or disfiguring scars associated with such procedure

or procedures, with the probability of each such risk if reasonably determinable.

2. Acknowledges that the disclosure of that information has been made and that all questions asked about the procedure or procedures have been answered in a satisfactory manner.

3. Is signed by the patient for whom the procedure is to be performed, or if the patient for any reason lacks legal capacity to consent, is signed by a person who has legal authority to consent on behalf of that patient in those circumstances.

Once a presumption has been created that informed consent took place, the burden of proof then shifts to the patient to rebut or overcome that presumption by persuasively showing that one or more of the essential elements of consent were missing. *Hiddings v. Williams,* 578 So.2d 1192 (La. Ct. App. 5 Cir. 1991):

> When the form is signed the patient is presumed to have understood and agreed to encounter whatever risk a reasonable person, in what the doctor knows or should have known to be the patient's position, would have apprehended from the written form. The statutory presumption of "consent" to encounter risks adequately described in the form is rebuttable, by showing that the consent was induced by misrepresentation, that is, that it was uninformed. (Citations omitted)

Discussion Questions

1. How should a health care or human services professional, facility, or agency decide whether or not to use written consent forms for any particular intervention?

2. What can be done to prevent privately practicing professionals or facility or agency staff from elevating the importance of getting written consent forms signed by patients or clients or their surrogates over that of assuring that a proper process of communication has occurred?

3. What can be done by health and human services professionals, facilities, and agencies to maximize the risk management value of written consent forms?

3

Legal Interventions for Incapacitated Older Adults

Ordinarily, the person who will be most directly affected by any particular decision about health care, finances, social services, residential issues, or other personal matters is the person who gets to make that decision. There may be times, however, when that individual is not capable of making and expressing difficult personal choices. *State of Tennessee v. Northern,* 563 S.W. 2d 197, 210 (Tenn. 1978):

> If . . . this patient could and would give evidence of a comprehension of the facts of her condition and could and would express her unequivocal desire in the face of such comprehended facts, then her decision, however unreasonable to others, would be accepted and honored by the Courts and her doctors. The difficulty is that she cannot or will not comprehend the facts.

In such instances, the legal system may need to intervene on behalf of the incapacitated individual. This may be accomplished through a variety of legal devices that vary in terms of their invasiveness into personal autonomy. These legal mechanisms include involuntary commitment to a public mental institution (or to a private institution that is licensed by the state to accept involuntarily committed mental patients), involuntary guardianship, adult protective services, representative payeeships, and ordinary (POA) and durable powers of attorney (DPOA). (POAs and DPOAs are discussed in chapter 7).

Incapacity to make and express valid decisions is a problem that affects older persons in disproportionate terms. The extent of mental disorders in old age, representing decrements in both intellectual and emotional functioning, is considerable. For some older persons, mental dysfunction may be a carryover from earlier life. See Matthew P. Janicki & Arthur J. Dalton, Dementia, Aging, and Intellectual Disabilities: A Handbook, Philadelphia: Brunner/Mazel (1999); Stanley S. Herr & Germain Weber (eds.), Aging, Rights and Quality of Life: Prospects for Older People with Developmental Disabilities, Baltimore: Brookes Publishing Company (1999). For most older persons, though, mental health problems develop later in life as a result of organic brain disorders (primary degenerative disorders or multiinfarct dementia), paranoid disorders, drug reactions, excessive use of alcohol, or as the by-product of various physical illnesses. These problems may take the form of cognitive impairment (dementia) in memory, attention, or information processing; emotional liability (psychosis) often manifested as aggression; or pseudodementia (depression).

Discussion Question

Discuss the social attitudes that make us unwilling to tolerate (and therefore more willing to intervene legally regarding) the same silly decision in an eighty-year old that we would much more readily condone in a person half that age. Why are older women more likely than older men to be found in need of protective legal intervention?

INVOLUNTARY COMMITMENT

Involuntary commitment sometimes is referred to as involuntary institutionalization, involuntary hospitalization, or civil commitment (to distinguish it from the criminal commitment that follows a finding of incompetence to stand trial or a verdict of not guilty by reason of insanity in a criminal proceeding). It is a legal intervention that disproportionately affects older persons.

Discussion Question

Why do you think the elderly are disproportionately represented among the involuntarily committed persons?

Voluntary

Before discussing involuntary commitment, it must be noted that a person may gain admission to a public mental institution through a process of voluntary hospitalization. In theory, this represents the free, competent, informed choice of the patient, but the "voluntary" label may be misleading. In practice, it is likely that many individuals (especially older persons) presenting themselves for admission to public mental health institutions, usually under threat of involuntary commitment if they do not cooperate, will have substantially impaired mental competence and voluntariness. It is also suspect whether material risks and alternatives will have been adequately explained to most mental institution applicants. Thus, the similarities between voluntary and involuntary admission generally are more important than the distinctions.

Zinermon v. Burch, 494 U.S. 113 (1990):

Respondent Darrell Burch brought this suit under 42 U.S.C. § 1983 against the 11 petitioners, who are physicians, administrators, and staff members at Florida State Hospital (FSH) in Chattahoochee, and others. Respondent alleges that petitioners deprived him of his liberty, without due process of law, by admitting him to FSH as a "voluntary" mental patient when he was incompetent to give informed consent to his admission. Burch contends that in his case petitioners should have afforded him procedural safeguards required by the Constitution before involuntary commitment of a mentally ill person, and that petitioners' failure to do so violated his due process rights****

Burch apparently concedes that, if Florida's statutes were strictly complied with, no deprivation of liberty without due process would occur. If only those patients who are competent to consent to admission are allowed to sign themselves in as "voluntary" patients, then they would not be deprived of any liberty interest at all. And if all other patients-those who are incompetent and those who are unwilling to consent to admission-are afforded the protections of Florida's involuntary placement procedures, they would be deprived of their liberty only after due process.

***

Burch . . . was admitted by signing forms applying for voluntary admission. He alleges, however, that petitioners violated this statute in admitting him as a voluntary patient, because they knew or should have known that he was incapable of making an informed decision as to his admission. He claims that he was entitled to receive the procedural safeguards provided by Florida's involuntary placement procedure, and that petitioners violated his due process rights by failing to initiate this procedure.

***

The very risks created by the application of the informed-consent requirement to the special context of mental health care are borne out by the facts alleged in this case. It appears from the exhibits accompanying Burch's complaint that he was simply given admission forms to sign by clerical workers, and, after he signed, was considered a voluntary patient. Burch alleges that petitioners knew or should have known that he was incapable of informed consent. This allegation is supported, at least as to petitioner Zinermon, by the psychiatrist's admission notes, described above, on Burch's mental state. Thus, the way in which Burch allegedly was admitted to FSH certainly did not ensure compliance with the statutory standard for voluntary admission.

***

The Florida statutes, of course, do not allow incompetent persons to be admitted as "voluntary" patients. But the statutes do not direct any member of the facility staff to determine whether a person is competent to give consent, nor to initiate the involuntary placement procedure for every incompetent patient. A patient who is willing to sign forms but incapable of informed consent certainly cannot be relied on to protest his "voluntary" admission and demand that the involuntary placement procedure be followed. The staff are the only persons in a position to take notice of any misuse of the voluntary admission process, and to ensure that the proper procedure is followed.

Florida chose to delegate to petitioners a broad power to admit patients to FSH, i.e., to effect what, in the absence of informed consent, is a substantial deprivation of liberty. Because petitioners had state authority to deprive persons of liberty, the Constitution imposed on them the State's concomitant duty to see that no deprivation occurs without adequate procedural protections.

Discussion Questions:

1. Did the Supreme Court impose an unreasonable burden on state officials in *Zinermon*?

2. Some commentators have suggested that voluntary admission to public mental institutions is a charade that should be abolished, and that all admissions ought to be processed as involuntary instead, with procedural protections required accordingly. Do you agree? What purposes are served by maintaining a voluntary admission status?

3. What are the possible implications, if any, of the *Zinermon* decision for "voluntary" admissions to nursing homes? See Chapter 4.

Involuntary

Every state has statutory and constitutional authority to exercise its inherent police power to protect the general health, safety, welfare, and morals of the community by confining in public mental health facilities those individuals who, by reason of mental illness, pose an imminent, serious threat of danger to others. Many jurisdictions require some concrete evidence of this likelihood, in the form of an articulated threat, an overt act, or the prior infliction of physical damage on another person.

The state also may act on the basis of its inherent *parens patriae* authority, which is the state's power to protect those individuals who cannot protect themselves. Basing an involuntary commitment on the *parens patriae* rationale requires a determination that the person is mentally incapable of providing for his or her own minimal life requirements (in some jurisdictions, stated as being "gravely disabled").

A variety of procedural safeguards characterize the civil commitment process.

Idaho Code § 66-329:

> (g) An opportunity to be represented by counsel shall be afforded to every proposed patient, and if neither the proposed patient nor others provide counsel, the court shall appoint counsel . . .
>
> ***
>
> (j) The proposed patient, the applicant, and any other persons to whom notice is required to be given shall be afforded an opportunity to appear at the hearing, to testify, and to present and cross-examine witnesses. The proposed patient shall be required to be present at the hearing unless the court determines that the mental or physical state of the proposed patient is such that his presence at the hearing would be detrimental to the proposed patient's health or would unduly disrupt the proceedings. A record of the proceedings shall be made as for other civil hearings. The hearing shall be conducted in as informal a manner as may be consistent with orderly procedure. The court shall receive all relevant and material evidence consistent with the rules of evidence.

Discussion Question

Why are these kinds of procedural safeguards necessary? Doesn't the presence of extensive due process requirements tend to equate civil commitment with criminal confinement? Is an emphasis on procedural safeguards and a vigorous adversarial atmosphere antitherapeutic for the patient? Doesn't the state have the best interests of the committed individual at heart?

In involuntary commitment proceedings, the state always bears the burden of proof. The constitutional minimum standard (*Addington v. Texas*, 99 S. Ct. 1804 (1979)), which has been implemented in most states, is reflected in Indiana Code § 12-26-2-5:

> (e) The petitioner is required to prove by clear and convincing evidence that:
> (1) the individual is mentally ill and either dangerous or gravely disabled; and
> (2) detention or commitment of that individual is appropriate.

"Clear and convincing" evidence translates roughly into 75 chances out of 100 that the individual meets the statutory criteria for involuntary commitment. A few states, though, have chosen to go beyond the constitutional minimum and adopt a "beyond a reasonable doubt" (approximately 90 to 95 chances out of 100) evidentiary test.

Discussion Questions

1. Why should involuntary commitment require a higher standard of proof than the one (a preponderance of the evidence, or more likely than not) used in ordinary civil cases such as professional malpractice litigation?

2. If a heightened burden of proof is appropriate for involuntary commitment, should it be "clear and convincing" evidence or evidence "beyond a reasonable doubt"? Is involuntary commitment more akin to a civil or a criminal law matter?

With the exception of only a very few states, involuntary commitment does not automatically equal a loss of all personal decision-making authority for the committed individual. Put differently, the substantive criteria for commitment are not synonymous with the criteria for a finding of incompetence to make medical or other decisions. Indiana Code § 12-26-2-8:

(a) Detention or commitment of an individual under this article does not deprive the individual of any of the following:
  (1) The right to do the following:
    (A) Dispose of property.
    (B) Execute instruments.
    (C) Make purchases.
    (D) Enter into contracts.
    (E) Give testimony in a court of law.
    (F) Vote.
  (2) A right of a citizen not listed in subdivision (1).
  (b) A procedure is not required for restoration of rights of citizenship of an individual detained or committed under this article.

The other side of the coin is that being found in need of guardianship does not necessarily mean that a person satisfies the legal criteria for involuntary commitment.

Under the Due Process clause of the U.S. Constitution's 14th Amendment, intrusions by the government into individual freedom must be based on the principle of least intrusive or least restrictive alternative available consistent with the purpose of the intrusion. Thus, there has been a trend in recent years toward outpatient involuntary commitment. Under this approach, an individual who is found to satisfy the criteria for commitment may be ordered by the court to comply with an outpatient treatment plan as a condition of not being placed involuntarily inside a public mental health institution.

Georgia Code § 37-3-90:

(a) When a physician or psychologist at a facility or on behalf of a facility determines and certifies under this article that there is reason to believe a patient admitted to or examined at the facility is a mentally ill person requiring involuntary treatment, that physician or psychologist shall further determine and certify whether there is reason to believe that patient is:
    (1) An inpatient or outpatient; and
    (2) If an outpatient, whether there is available outpatient treatment.
                                    ***
  (c) A person determined and certified to be:
    (1) An outpatient; and
    (2) A person for whom there is available outpatient treatment shall be considered to be in need of involuntary outpatient treatment and not involuntary inpatient treatment for purposes of further

proceedings under this article until such time as that person's status is determined to be otherwise pursuant to those proceedings.

Georgia Code § 37-3-1:

(.1) "Available outpatient treatment" means outpatient treatment, either public or private, available in the patient's community, including but not limited to supervision and support of the patient by family, friends, or other responsible persons in that community.

***

(10) "Least restrictive alternative," "least restrictive environment," or "least restrictive appropriate care and treatment" means that which is the least restrictive available alternative, environment, or care and treatment, respectively, within the limits of state funds specifically appropriated therefor.

***

(12.1) "Outpatient" means a person who is mentally ill and:

(A) Who is not an inpatient but who, based on the person's treatment history or current mental status, will require outpatient treatment in order to avoid predictably and imminently becoming an inpatient;

(B) Who because of the person's current mental status, mental history, or nature of the person's mental illness is unable voluntarily to seek or comply with outpatient treatment; and

(C) Who is in need of involuntary treatment.

(12.2) "Outpatient treatment" means a program of treatment for mental illness outside a hospital facility setting which includes, without being limited to, medication and prescription monitoring, individual or group therapy, day or partial programming activities, case management services, and other services to alleviate or treat the patient's mental illness so as to maintain the patient's semi-independent functioning and to prevent the patient's becoming an inpatient.

Georgia Code § 37-3-81.1

(a) . . . the court shall determine whether the patient is a mentally ill person requiring involuntary treatment and, if so, whether the patient is an inpatient or outpatient and, unless otherwise provided in this subsection, the type of involuntary treatment the patient should be ordered to obtain. At such hearing, if the court determines:

(2) That the patient is an outpatient, . . . whether there is available outpatient treatment for the patient which meets the requirements of the plan chosen by the court and whether the patient will likely obtain that treatment so as to minimize the likelihood of the patient's

becoming an inpatient. If the court determines that there is such available outpatient treatment which the patient will likely obtain so as to minimize the likelihood of the patient's becoming an inpatient, then the court shall order the patient to obtain that treatment and shall discharge the patient subject to such order . . .

Discussion Questions

1. From the perspectives of public policy and therapeutic care, respectively, what are the likely advantages and problems associated with outpatient commitment?

2. What particular benefits and/or difficulties might be encountered with outpatient commitment for older mentally ill individuals? What are the characteristics of older persons who might be viable candidates for outpatient commitment?

GUARDIANSHIP

Background

Every state has enacted statutes that empower the courts to appoint a surrogate decision maker with authority to make decisions on behalf of a mentally incompetent ward. The terminology for the court-appointed surrogate decision maker varies among jurisdictions; "guardian" is the most commonly used term, although "conservator" and other terms are employed in some places.

Guardianship statutes are an example of the state's inherent *parens patriae* power to protect those who cannot take care of themselves in a manner that society believes is appropriate. The origins of some form of guardianship based on the state's benevolence stretch back beyond 13th century England.

Discussion Question

Do you agree with the premise of the *parens patriae* power, namely, that society—acting through the state—has the inherent authority to step in and protect persons who cannot make appropriate decisions for themselves, even if that means protecting people from their own decisions and over their own objections? In such situations, does society have not only a right but a *duty* to intervene? At what point does the benevolence value of *parens patriae* become overbearing paternalism?

Like involuntary commitment, guardianship is a legal device that disproportionately affects older persons, especially those residing in institutions. Guardianship constitutes a major restriction on the fundamental liberties of the older man or woman concerned.

The terms "capable" or "having capacity" usually are used to describe individuals who, in a health care clinician's professional judgment, have sufficient functional ability to make their own choices. The terms "incompetent" or "incompetence" refer to a court's formal ruling on the decision-making status of an individual in the context of an official guardianship proceeding.

Every adult person is presumed to be legally competent to make personal decisions in life. This presumption may be overcome and a surrogate decision maker may be appointed only on a sufficient showing that the individual is mentally unable to participate authentically and self-sufficiently in a rational decision making process.

Role of the Courts

State guardianship statutes contain a two-pronged definition of competence. First, the individual must fall within a particular category such as old age, mental illness, or developmental disability. Second, the individual must be found to be impaired functionally—that is, unable to care appropriately for person or property—as a result of being within that category.

Texas Probate Code § 601 (13)(B):

> Incapacitated person means:
> an adult individual who, because of a physical or mental condition, is substantially unable to provide food, clothing, or shelter for himself or herself, to care for the individual's own physical health, or to manage the individual's own financial affairs.

Ohio Revised Code § 2111.01(D):

> Incompetent means any person who is so mentally impaired as a result of a physical or mental illness or disability, or retardation, or as a result of chronic substance abuse, that he is incapable of taking proper care of himself or his property or fails to provide for his family or others persons for whom he is charged by law to provide . . .

The requirement of functional impairment is emphasized in those states whose statutes restrict eligibility for guardianship to those who are "gravely disabled" or the equivalent. California

Welfare & Institutions Code § 5008(h):

> "Gravely disabled" means a condition in which a person, as a result of a mental disorder [or chronic alcoholism] is unable to provide for his or her basic personal needs for food, clothing, or shelter.

Discussion Question

In guardianship statutes, why can't incompetence be equated with a categoric condition (such as advanced years) alone? Wouldn't that approach be much more efficient in operating the guardianship system?

A court appoints a guardian (referred to in a few jurisdictions as a conservator or committee) as substitute decision maker for an incompetent person. The incompetent person for whom a guardian is appointed is a "ward," and the relationship between the guardian/conservator and ward is "guardianship" or "conservatorship."

There has been a strong movement since the late 1980s toward greatly strengthening the procedural protections available to prospective wards. California Welfare & Institutions Code § 5350(d):

> "The person for whom conservatorship is sought shall have the right to demand a court or jury trial on the issue whether he or she is gravely disabled."

Nevada Revised Statutes § 159.048:

> The [notice to a proposed ward] must state that the:
> 1. Proposed ward may be adjudged to be incompetent or of limited capacity and a guardian may be appointed for him;
> 2. Proposed ward's rights may be affected as specified in the petition;
> 3. Proposed ward has the right to appear at the hearing and to oppose the petition; and
> 4. Proposed ward has the right to be represented by an attorney, who may be appointed for him by the court if he is unable to retain one.

Nevada Revised Statutes § 159.0458:

> If an adult ward or proposed adult ward is unable to retain legal counsel and requests the appointment of counsel, at any stage of a proceeding for guardianship and whether or not he lacks or appears to lack capacity, the court shall, at or before the time of the next hearing, appoint an attorney who works for legal aid services, if available, or a private attorney to represent him. The attorney's fees must be paid from the estate of the ward or proposed ward to the extent possible.

Nevada Revised Statutes § 159.0535.1

If the proposed ward is in the state, he must attend the hearing unless the court for good cause excuses him from attending.

Discussion Questions

1. Why is there a trend toward guardianship reform in the direction of more procedural due process for prospective wards? What are the statutes' procedural protections intended to accomplish?

2. Are the various procedural protections now contained in guardianship statutes actually likely to achieve their goals or are they more a matter of form than substance?

3. Do the procedural requirements contained in contemporary guardianship statutes impose excessive and unnecessary impediments to protecting older individuals who really need external protection? According to Lawrence A. Frolik, *Guardianship Reform: When the Best Is the Enemy of the Good,* 9 Stanford Law & Policy Review 347–358 (1998):

> It may be that the problem with guardianship lies not with the statutes, nor even with the guardianship actors, i.e., the courts, the lawyers, the petitioners, and the guardians. It is possible that the reform goals of personal autonomy and dignity are so at odds with reality so as to be unattainable . . . By overreaching, by striving for perfection, we risk creating a system of guardianship that fails to offer the protection to the lives and property of older persons that was, after all, the reason for the creation of guardianship . . .

Do you share these worries? In setting guardianship policy, how much weight should be paid to the procedural hassles and burdens placed on well-meaning relatives and health and human service professionals?

In a majority of states, statutes allow for the relaxation of normal procedural requirements to permit the appointment of a temporary or emergency guardian when there is a immediate life-threatening situation. California Welfare & Institutions Code § 5352.1:

> The court may establish a temporary conservatorship for a period not to exceed 30 days and appoint a temporary conservator on the basis of the comprehensive report of the officer providing conservatorship investigation . . . or on the basis of an affidavit of the professional

person who recommended conservatorship stating the reasons for his recommendation, if the court is satisfied that such comprehensive report or affidavit show the necessity for a temporary conservatorship.

Except as provided in this section, all temporary conservatorships shall expire automatically at the conclusion of 30 days, unless prior to that date the court shall conduct a hearing on the issue of whether or not the proposed conservatee is gravely disabled . . .

If the proposed conservatee demands a court or jury trial on the issue whether he is gravely disabled, the court may extend the temporary conservatorship until the date of the disposition of the issue by the court or jury trial, provided that such extension shall in no event exceed a period of six months.

Nevada Revised Statutes § 159.052.2:

> If the court:
> (a) Finds reasonable cause to believe that the proposed ward is unable to respond to a substantial and immediate risk of financial loss or physical harm or to a need for immediate medical attention . . . the court may appoint a temporary guardian to serve for 10 days. The court shall limit the temporary guardian's powers to those necessary to assist in the emergency.

Discussion Question

What are the dangers associated with emergency guardianship statutes? How can these dangers be minimized?

The guardian who is appointed ordinarily is a private person (relative, friend, or attorney) or institution (bank or trust company); the majority of guardians are relatives of the ward. Many state statutes establish procedures for competent adults to nominate in advance the person they wish to serve as guardian for them in the event that guardianship is ordered, and the courts are required to give strong deference to these preferences.

Discussion Questions

1. What are the qualities or characteristics that a court should look for in identifying an appropriate guardian for an incompetent person?
2. Is it ever proper for a health or human service professional to serve in the formal capacity of guardian for an incompetent person under that professional's care? What are the problems entailed? In reality, don't health and human service professionals frequently

function as *de facto* surrogate decision makers for incapacitated elders who have no one else, even in the absence of *de jure* or formal authority? What is wrong with that practice?

3. Why might a person, while still capable of making such decisions, nominate a guardian in advance? What are the advantages and disadvantages of this approach, as compared to executing a durable power of attorney (DPOA)? As compared to doing nothing regarding advance planning?

In a growing number of cases, older individuals do not have any family members or friends who are willing and able to act as surrogate decision makers for them. In response to this social phenomenon, several states have devised some form of "public guardianship" system under which a government agency, acting either directly or through contract with a private not-for-profit or for-profit organization, functions in the guardian role for a ward who has no one else.

Utah Statutes § 62A-14-103 (1):

There is created within the department [of Human Services] the Office of Public Guardian which has the powers and duties provided in this chapter.

Utah Statutes § 62A-14-105:

(1) The office shall:
    (a) . . . develop and operate a statewide program to:
        (i) educate the public about the role and function of guardians and conservators; and
        (ii) serve as a guardian, conservator, or both for a ward upon appointment by a court when no other person is able and willing to do so and the office petitioned for or agreed in advance to the appointment;
    (b) possess and exercise all the powers and duties specifically given to the office by virtue of being appointed as guardian or conservator of a ward, including the power to access a ward's records;
    (c) review and monitor the personal and, if appropriate, financial status of each ward for whom the office has been appointed to serve as guardian or conservator;
    (d) train and monitor each employee and volunteer, and monitor each contract provider to whom the office has delegated a responsibility for a ward;
    (e) retain all court-delegated powers and duties for a ward;

(f) report on the personal and financial status of a ward as required by a court . . .

(g) handle a ward's funds in accordance with the department's trust account system;

***

(i) maintain accurate records concerning each ward, his property, and office services provided to him;

(j) make reasonable and continuous efforts to find a family member, friend, or other person to serve as a ward's guardian or conservator; ***

(2) The office may:

(a) petition a court . . . to be appointed an incapacitated person's guardian, conservator, or both after conducting a prepetition assessment . . .

(b) develop and operate a statewide program to recruit, train, supervise, and monitor volunteers to assist the office in providing guardian and conservator services;

(c) delegate one or more responsibilities for a ward to an employee, volunteer, or contract provider . . .

(d) solicit and receive private donations to provide guardian and conservator services under this chapter ***

Elsewhere, some private corporations offer their services as guardians directly to the courts, either for a fee or *pro bono.*

Discussion Questions

1. What are the advantages and disadvantages of relying on a public guardianship system to protect incompetent persons without family or friends?

2. What are the advantages and disadvantages of relying on private entities for guardianship services to protect incompetent persons without family or friends? What difference does it make if the guardianship entity is proprietary (for-profit) or not-for-profit? What difference does it make if the private entity is charging a fee for guardianship services or volunteering those services for free?

3. Besides supporting public and private entity guardianship services, in what other ways might we protect incompetent persons who lack relatives or friends to act in the role of surrogate decision maker?

A court may confer different types of powers on a guardian. Plenary power is complete authority over the ward's person and estate, encompassing virtually every element of the ward's life. Alternatively, guardianship powers may be restricted to control of the ward's estate. In this event, the guardian of the estate may make decisions only about the ward's financial assets—real and personal property—and income.

Utah Statutes § 75-5-312:

> (1) A guardian of an incapacitated person has only the powers, rights, and duties respecting the ward granted in the order of appointment . . .;
>
> (2) Absent a specific limitation on the guardian's power in the order of appointment, the guardian has the same powers, rights, and duties respecting the ward that a parent has respecting the parent's unemancipated minor child except that a guardian is not liable to third persons for acts of the ward solely by reason of the parental relationship. In particular, and without qualifying the foregoing, a guardian has the following powers and duties, except as modified by order of the court:
>
> (a) To the extent that it is consistent with the terms of any order by a court of competent jurisdiction relating to detention or commitment of the ward, the guardian is entitled to custody of the person of the ward and may establish the ward's place of abode within or without this state.
>
> (b) If entitled to custody of the ward the guardian shall provide for the care, comfort, and maintenance of the ward and, whenever appropriate, arrange for the ward's training and education. Without regard to custodial rights of the ward's person, the guardian shall take reasonable care of the ward's clothing, furniture, vehicles, and other personal effects and commence protective proceedings if other property of the ward is in need of protection.
>
> (c) A guardian may give any consents or approvals that may be necessary to enable the ward to receive medical or other professional care, counsel, treatment, or service.
>
> (d) If no conservator for the estate of the ward has been appointed, the guardian may:
>
> (i) institute proceedings to compel any person under a duty to support the ward or to pay sums for the welfare of the ward to perform that duty; or
>
> (ii) receive money and tangible property deliverable to the ward and apply the money and property for support, care, and education of the ward; but the guardian may not use funds from the ward's estate for room and board which the guardian, the guardian's spouse, parent, or child have furnished the ward unless a charge for the service is approved by order of the court . . .

A court may also appoint a *guardian ad litem* who has authority to represent the ward just in a particular legal proceeding, such as a petition for authority to terminate life-sustaining medical intervention.

Courts and legislatures traditionally have treated mental competence as an all-or-nothing concept, even though an older person's functional capacity may wax and wane from time to time and vary widely depending on the kind of choice facing the individual and various environmental factors. In recognition of this reality, all states now allow courts to grant "limited" or "partial" guardianship explicitly delineating the particular, limited types of decisions that the ward is incapable of making and over which the guardian may exercise surrogate authority, with remaining power residing with the ward. Limited or partial guardianship statutes may be permissive, allowing but not requiring courts to carefully tailor the guardian's powers to the ward's needs, or they may mandate that the guardian's powers be drawn as narrowly as possible.

Utah Statutes § 75-5-304:

(1) The court may appoint a guardian as requested if it is satisfied that the person for whom a guardian is sought is incapacitated and that the appointment is necessary or desirable as a means of providing continuing care and supervision of the incapacitated person.

(2) The court shall prefer a limited guardianship and may only grant a full guardianship if no other alternative exists. If the court does not grant a limited guardianship, a specific finding shall be made that nothing less than a full guardianship is adequate.

Discussion Questions

1. Should limited or partial guardianship statutes be permissive or mandatory for the courts?

2. Why haven't courts used the limited or partial guardianship power very much yet? What are the disadvantages or costs of this approach?

3. Do you interpret the modest use of limited or partial guardianships a positive or a negative thing?

In a disputed, adversarial guardianship proceeding, each side usually calls on expert medical and psychological professionals to present opinions about the nature and degree of the proposed ward's functional impairment. In practice, the medical and psychological evidence frequently becomes the primary, if not the sole, basis for adjudicating incompetence.

Discussion Question

Ideally, what special background and qualifications should medical and psychological professionals involved in guardianship assessments and adjudications possess? Should there be special mandatory legal standards to be met before a professional's expertise would be accepted as the basis for expressing an opinion in the guardianship context?

Any ward, but especially one for whom a plenary guardian is appointed, suffers a serious deprivation of decision-making authority. Among numerous other rights, a ward may lose the right to enter into a binding contract, to vote, to hold public office, to marry or divorce, to hold a license (such as a motor vehicle driver's license), to execute a will, to own and sell or give away real and personal property, and to sue and be sued in the courts. California Welfare & Institutions Code § 5357:

> [The court must decide] for or against the imposition of each of the following disabilities on the proposed conservatee:
> (a) The privilege of possessing a license to operate a motor vehicle.
> (b) The right to enter into contracts.
> (c) The disqualification of the person from voting . . .
> (d) The right to refuse or consent to treatment related specifically to the conservatee's being gravely disabled.
> (e) The right to refuse or consent to routine medical treatment unrelated to remedying or preventing the recurrence of the conservatee's being gravely disabled.
> (f) The disqualification of the person from possessing a firearm . . .

Discussion Questions

1. What legitimate social purposes are served by the deprivation of these rights of a ward?
2. What can health care and human service professionals do to minimize the extent to which a ward's rights are jeopardized?
3. Guardianship petitions usually are initiated by family members, health care institutions or other service providers, or financial institutions. What are the motivations of these various parties in seeking to have guardianship imposed on an older individual? To what extent is there likely to be divergence between expressed and actual motivations? Whose interests are really being served?

4. Even once a guardianship has been ordered, how can health and human service professionals help to assure that the ward has as much input into important decisions as possible?

Even when substantial mental impairment is detected in an older person, the ensuing result need not be a guardianship petition. Health care and human service professionals should work with the individual, family, and other involved parties and agencies to identify and explore available alternatives, in terms of substitute decision making arrangements and community resources, to divert persons away from the formal judicial system.

Discussion Questions

1. What relevant resources and services exist in your community that older persons with impaired mental capacity might be willing to accept voluntarily? Where would you look to find the answer to this question?

2. Possible alternatives to guardianship for financial matters might include a DPOA for finances, representative payeeship (see below), temporary or *ad litem* guardianship, *inter vivos* (while alive) trusts and other property transfers, insurers or guarantors for loans, and limited bank accounts (e.g., cosigners, ceiling amounts, and pour-over mechanisms). Discuss the pros and cons of these various options.

3. If less intrusive options do not work in a particular case, discuss the merits and disadvantages of benign neglect as an alternative to involuntary guardianship?

4. How should we determine whether a particular form of intervention is more or less intrusive or restrictive than guardianship for an older person with impaired capacity?

Once a guardianship has been imposed, the appointed guardian is expected to act in a fiduciary, or trust, manner. In other words, the guardian is always required to act in the best interests of the ward. After appointing a guardian, the court retains jurisdiction or power to oversee the guardian's conduct.

Discussion Question

What is the purpose of continuing court monitoring of guardians? Is such monitoring likely to be effective in achieving its goals?

A guardianship may be discontinued when it is no longer needed, and in some states (e.g., California Welfare & Institutions Code § 5362) the continued appropriateness of each guardianship must automatically be reviewed at set time intervals. To successfully terminate a guardianship, the party arguing for termination (almost always the ward) bears the burden of proving that competence has been restored and hence rebutting the presumption of incompetence that was created when the guardian was appointed.

Texas Probate Code § 672:

(a) A court in which a guardianship proceeding is pending shall review annually each guardianship in which the application to create the guardianship was filed after September 1, 1993, and may review annually any other guardianship to determine whether the guardianship should be continued, modified, or terminated.

Texas Probate Code § 694D:

(a) At a hearing on an application for complete restoration of a ward's capacity or modification of a ward's guardianship, the court shall consider only evidence regarding the ward's mental or physical capacity at the time of the hearing that is relevant to the restoration of capacity or modification of the guardianship, as appropriate.
(b) The party who filed the application has the burden of proof at the hearing.

Texas Probate Code § 694F:

(a) The court may not grant an order completely restoring a ward's capacity or modifying a ward's guardianship under an application filed under this code unless, in addition to other requirements prescribed by this code, the applicant presents to the court a written letter or certificate from a physician licensed in this state that is dated not earlier than the 120th day before the date of the filing of the application or dated after the date on which the application was filed but before the date of the hearing. The letter or certificate must:
(1) describe the nature and degree of incapacity, including the medical history if reasonably available, or state that, in the physician's opinion, the ward has the capacity to provide food, clothing, and shelter for himself or herself, to care for the ward's own physical health, and to manage the financial affairs of the ward;

(2) provide a medical prognosis specifying the estimated severity of any incapacity;

(3) state how or in what manner the ward's ability to make or communicate responsible decisions concerning himself or herself is affected by the person's physical or mental health;

(4) state whether any current medication affects the demeanor of the ward or the ward's ability to participate fully in a court proceeding;

(5) describe the precise physical and mental conditions underlying a diagnosis of senility, if applicable; and

(6) include any other information required by the court.

Discussion Questions

1. Should the continuing need for a guardianship automatically be reviewed periodically? If so, how often?

2. What should be the burden of proof for termination of a guardianship? Does this evidentiary burden rest properly on the party arguing for termination? What evidence should be considered relevant in this context?

ADULT PROTECTIVE SERVICES (APS)

Based on their *parens patriae* power to protect those who cannot protect themselves, the states have used the legislative process to create a wide variety of programs under the general rubric of APS. The basic definition of this concept is a system of preventive and supportive services for older persons living in the community to enable them to maintain independent living and avoid abuse and exploitation. APS programs are characterized (ideally) by the coordinated delivery of services to adults at risk and the actual or potential authority to provide substitute decision making regarding those services.

The services feature consists of an assortment of health, housing, and social interventions. In a good APS system, these services are coordinated by a caseworker/organizer (variously termed case manager, care manager, or care coordinator) who is responsible for assessing an individual's needs and bringing together the available responses.

Ohio Revised Code § 5101.60:

(N) "Protective services" means services provided by the county department of human services or its designated agency to an adult

who has been determined by evaluation to require such services . . .
Protective services may include, but are not limited to, case work services, medical care, mental health services, legal services, fiscal management, home health care, homemaker services, housing-related
services, guardianship services, and placement services as well as the
provision of such commodities as food, clothing, and shelter.

The second component of an APS system is authority to intervene on behalf of the client. Ordinarily, the client (if mentally able)
will voluntarily grant the helping agency permission to deliver services. However, if the client refuses offered assistance while still
needing it, the legal system may be invoked to authorize appointment of a substitute decision maker over the client's objections.
Ohio Revised Code § 5106.62:

> The county department of job and family services shall be
> responsible for the investigation of all reports . . . and for evaluating
> the need for and, to the extent of available funds, providing or
> arranging for the provision of protective services. The department
> may designate another agency to perform the department's duties
> under this section.
>
> ***
>
> Investigation of the need for protective services shall include a
> face-to-face visit with the adult who is the subject of the report,
> preferably in the adult's residence, and consultation with the per-
> son who made the report, if feasible, and agencies or persons who
> have information about the adult's alleged abuse, neglect, or
> exploitation.
>
> The department shall give written notice of the intent of the inves-
> tigation and an explanation of the notice in language reasonably
> understandable to the adult who is the subject of the investigation, at
> the time of the initial interview with that person.
>
> Upon completion of the investigation, the department shall deter-
> mine from its findings whether or not the adult who is the subject of
> the report is in need of protective services.

Ohio Revised Code § 5101.60:

> (H) "In need of protective services" means an adult known or sus-
> pected to be suffering from abuse, neglect, or exploitation to an
> extent that either life is endangered or physical harm, mental
> anguish, or mental illness results or is likely to result.

Discussion Questions

1. Do you agree with this typical definition of "in need of protective services"? Are there things you would add to, or subtract from, this definition? Is the definition broad enough to include all those individuals who ought to be included, yet precise enough to exclude those whose autonomous refusal of services ought to be respected? Does the definition leave too much discretion to the APS agency and/or the court?

2. In such statutory definitions of persons eligible for involuntary APS, "neglect" is always interpreted to include self-neglect by the individual. Do you agree that self-neglect should be a basis for forcing APS on a person over objection?

Some states deal with recalcitrant clients through the traditional methods of involuntary commitment or guardianship. Legislation has been enacted in many jurisdictions, however, that creates special procedures to secure court orders for various aspects of APS.

Ohio Revised Code § 5106.65:

> If the county department of human services determines that an adult is in need of protective services and is an incapacitated person, the department may petition the court for an order authorizing the provision of protective services. The petition shall state the specific facts alleging the abuse, neglect, or exploitation and shall include a proposed protective service plan. Any plan for protective services shall be specified in the petition.

These procedures are either in addition to, or in place of, the existing guardianship system. Before a court may order APS interventions over the client's objections, the client is entitled to certain due process protections.

Ohio Revised Code § 5101.66:

> Notice of a petition for the provision of court-ordered protective services . . . shall be personally served upon the adult who is the subject of the petition at least five working days prior to the date set for the hearing. . . . Notice shall be given orally and in writing in language reasonably understandable to the adult. The notice shall include the names of all petitioners, the basis of the belief that protective services are needed, the rights of the adult in the court proceedings, and the consequences of a court order for protective services. The adult shall

be informed of his right to counsel and his right to appointed counsel if he is indigent and if appointed counsel is requested. Written notice by certified mail shall also be given to the adult's guardian, legal counsel, caretaker, and spouse, if any, or if he has none of these, to his adult children or next of kin, if any, or to any other person as the court may require. The adult who is the subject of the petition may not waive notice as provided in this section.

Ohio Revised Code § 5101.67:

(A) The court shall hold a hearing on the petition . . . within fourteen days after its filing. The adult who is the subject of the petition shall have the right to be present at the hearing, present evidence, and examine and cross-examine witnesses. The adult shall be represented by counsel unless the right to counsel is knowingly waived. If the adult is indigent, the court shall appoint counsel to represent the adult. If the court determines that the adult lacks the capacity to waive the right to counsel, the court shall appoint counsel to represent the adult's interests.

(B) If the court finds, on the basis of clear and convincing evidence, that the adult has been abused, neglected, or exploited, is in need of protective services, and is incapacitated, and no person authorized by law or by court order is available to give consent, it shall issue an order requiring the provision of protective services . . .

Discussion Question

Is this panoply of procedural due process requirements really necessary to protect objecting individuals from having APS inflicted on them involuntarily? What other protections would you add? Or, do these requirements unduly interfere with the proper provision of APS to persons in need?

In most states, court orders for APS are only valid for a delimited period of time, after which they must be reviewed. Ohio Revised Code § 5101.67:

(E) A court order provided for in this section shall remain in effect for no longer than six months. Thereafter, the county department of job and family services shall review the adult's need for continued services and, if the department determines that there is a continued need, it shall apply for a renewal of the order for additional periods of no longer than one year each. The adult who is the subject of the court-ordered services may petition for modification of the order at any time.

Discussion Question

Why have legislatures limited the duration of court orders for APS? Do the benefits of automatic periodic review of court orders for APS outweigh the costs and inefficiencies that such review engenders?

If an APS agency believes that, in a particular situation, the usual legal process for obtaining court-ordered services for an objecting person will take too long, the agency may petition for permission to provide emergency services. Ohio Revised Code § 5101.69:

(A) Upon petition by the county department of human services, the court may issue an order authorizing the provision of protective services on an emergency basis to an adult. The petition for any emergency order shall include:

(1) The name, age, and address of the adult in need of protective services;

(2) The nature of the emergency;

(3) The proposed protective services;

(4) The petitioner's reasonable belief, together with facts supportive thereof, as to the existence of the circumstances described in divisions (D) (1) to (3) of this section;

(5) Facts showing the petitioner's attempts to obtain the adult's consent to the protective services.

***

(D) The court shall issue an order authorizing the provision of protective services on an emergency basis if it finds, on the basis of clear and convincing evidence, that:

(1) The adult is an incapacitated person;

(2) An emergency exists;

(3) No person authorized by law or court order to give consent for the adult is available or willing to consent to emergency services.

(E) In issuing an emergency order, the court shall adhere to the following limitations:

(1) The court shall order only such protective services as are necessary and available locally to remove the conditions creating the emergency, and the court shall specifically designate those protective services the adult shall receive;

(2) The court shall not order any change of residence under this section unless the court specifically finds that a change of residence is necessary;

(3) The court may order emergency services only for fourteen days. The department may petition the court for a renewal of the order for a fourteen-day period upon a showing that continuation of the order is necessary to remove the emergency.

(4) In its order the court shall authorize the director of the department or his designee to give consent for the person for the approved emergency services until the expiration of the order;

***

(F) If the department determines that the adult continues to need protective services after the order provided for in division (D) of this section has expired, the department may petition the court for an order to continue protective services, pursuant to section 5101.65 of the Revised Code. After the filing of the petition, the department may continue to provide protective services pending a hearing by the court.

Discussion Question

Do statutes empowering courts to order APS over objection on an emergency basis, without observing the due process protections required for a regular APS order, unduly jeopardize the civil liberties of an objecting potential client? What are some reasonable alternatives?

REPRESENTATIVE PAYEE PROGRAMS

Another way in which society may intervene in the life of an older individual without that person's permission and restrict decision-making authority is through the administrative appointment of a substitute payee for a person who is regularly receiving certain government benefit payments. The substitute check handler is called a fiduciary under the Department of Veterans Affairs (VA) program and a representative payee under other government programs.

Participating programs include pension and disability benefits from the VA (38 C.F.R. §§ 13.1-13.111), Department of Defense (37 U.S.C. §§ 601-604), Railroad Retirement Board (20 C.F.R. §§ 266.11-266.13), and Office of Personnel Management (for federal employees' retirement benefits) (5 U.S.C. § 8345[e]). Most significant, both economically and in terms of number of older people affected, are Old Age, Survivors, and Disability Insurance (OASDI) benefit payments under Title 2 of the Social Security Act (20 C.F.R. §§ 404.2001-404.2065) and Supplemental Security Income (SSI) benefit payments to the aged, blind, or disabled under Title 16 of the Social Security Act. Under Social Security retirement and disability benefit programs, over three million incapacitated adults have representative payees.

42 U.S.C. App., 20 C.F.R. § 404.2001 (OASDI):

(a) Explanation of representative payment. This subpart explains the principles and procedures that we [the Social Security Administration] follow in determining whether to make representative payment and in selecting a representative payee. It also explains the responsibilities that a representative payee has concerning the use of the funds he or she receives on behalf of a beneficiary. A representative payee may be either a person or an organization selected by us to receive benefits on behalf of a beneficiary. A representative payee will be selected if we believe that the interest of a beneficiary will be served by representative payment rather than direct payment of benefits. Generally, we appoint a representative payee if we have determined that the beneficiary is not able to manage or direct the management of benefit payments in his or her interest.

(b) Policy used to determine whether to make representative payment. Our policy is that every beneficiary has the right to manage his or her own benefits. However, some beneficiaries due to a mental or physical condition or due to their youth may be unable to do so. Under these circumstances, we may determine that the interests of the beneficiary would be better served if we certified benefit payments to another person as a representative payee.

(2) If we determine that representative payment is in the interest of a beneficiary, we will appoint a representative payee. We may appoint a representative payee even if the beneficiary is a legally competent individual. If the beneficiary is a legally incompetent individual, we may appoint the legal guardian or some other person as a representative payee.

(3) If payment is being made directly to a beneficiary and a question arises concerning his or her ability to manage or direct the management of benefit payments, we will, if the beneficiary is 18 years old or older and has not been adjudged legally incompetent, continue to pay the beneficiary until we make a determination about his or her ability to manage or direct the management of benefit payments and the selection of a representative payee.

42 U.S.C. App., 20 C.F.R. § 404.2010:

When payment will be made to representative payee (a) We pay benefits to a representative payee on behalf of a beneficiary 18 years old or older when it appears to us that this method of payment will be in the interest of the beneficiary. We do this if we have information that the beneficiary is—

(1) Legally incompetent or mentally incapable of managing benefit payments; or

(2) Physically incapable of managing or directing the management of his or her benefit payments.

42 U.S.C. App., 20 C.F.R. § 404.2020:

Information considered in selecting a representative payee

In selecting a payee we try to select the person, agency, organization or institution that will best serve the interest of the beneficiary. In making our selection we consider—
(a) The relationship of the person to the beneficiary;
(b) The amount of interest that the person shows in the beneficiary;
(c) Any legal authority the person, agency, organization or institution has to act on behalf of the beneficiary;
(d) Whether the potential payee has custody of the beneficiary; and
(e) Whether the potential payee is in a position to know of and look after the needs of the beneficiary.

42 U.S.C. App., 20 C.F.R. § 404.2021:

Order of preference in selecting a representative payee

As a guide in selecting a representative payee, categories of preferred payees have been established. These preferences are flexible. Our primary concern is to select the payee who will best serve the beneficiary's interest. The preferences are:
(a) For beneficiaries 18 years old or older, our preference is—
(1) A legal guardian, spouse (or other relative) who has custody of the beneficiary or who demonstrates strong concern for the personal welfare of the beneficiary;
(2) A friend who has custody of the beneficiary or demonstrates strong concern for the personal welfare of the beneficiary;
(3) A public or nonprofit agency or institution having custody of the beneficiary;
(4) A private institution operated for profit and licensed under State law, which has custody of the beneficiary; and
(5) Persons other than above who are qualified to carry out the responsibilities of a payee and who are able and willing to serve as a payee for a beneficiary; e.g., members of community groups or organizations who volunteer to serve as payee for a beneficiary.

Discussion Questions

1. The regulations give the Social Security Administration (SSA) a large amount of discretion in determining when OASDI benefits

should be paid to a representative payee, and who should act as the payee. Is this substantial degree of flexibility necessary and appropriate to allow the SSA to respond to the complexities of individual, unique cases, or does so much flexibility open the way for the SSA to be arbitrary, capricious, and unaccountable? If you wanted to tighten the regulations to restrict the degree of flexibility now held by the SSA, what specific changes in regulatory language would you make?

2. Do the representative payee regulations protect the class of persons who ought to be protected? Is that class of persons defined in these regulations too broadly? Too narrowly?

3. Do you agree with the order of preference for representative payee selection contained in the regulations? What changes, if any, would you make? Are there any categories of persons who should be ineligible to serve as representative payees?

42 U.S.C. App., 20 C.F.R. § 404.2025:

Information to be submitted by a representative payee

(a) Before we select a representative payee, the payee applicant must give us information showing his or her relationship to the beneficiary and his or her responsibility for the care of the beneficiary.

(b) Anytime after we have selected a payee, we may ask the payee to give us information showing a continuing relationship to the beneficiary and a continuing responsibility for the care of the beneficiary. If the payee does not give us the requested information within a reasonable period of time, we may stop paying the payee unless we determine that the payee had a good reason for not complying with our request, and we receive the information requested.

42 U.S.C. App., 20 C.F.R. § 404.2030:

Advance notice of the determination to make representative payment

(a) Generally, whenever we intend to make representative payment and to name a payee, we notify the beneficiary or the individual acting on his or her behalf, of our proposed actions. In this notice we tell the person that we plan to name a representative payee and who that payee will be. We also ask the person to contact us if he or she objects to either proposed action. If he or she objects to either proposed action, the person may—

(1) Review the evidence upon which the proposed actions will be based; and

(2) Submit any additional evidence regarding the proposed actions.

(b) If the person objects to the proposed actions, we will review our proposed determinations and consider any additional information given to us. We will then issue our determinations. If the person is dissatisfied with either determination, he or she may request a reconsideration.

(c) If the person does not object to the proposed actions, we will issue our determinations. If the person is dissatisfied with either determination, he or she may request a reconsideration.

Discussion Question

Are these procedural provisions sufficient to protect the due process rights of persons for whom a representative payee may be appointed? What procedural changes, if any, would you suggest in the current representative payee system to strengthen the protection of individual rights? Would the benefits of those enhanced protections be worth the costs?

42 U.S.C. App., 20 C.F.R. § 404.2035:

Responsibilities of a representative payee
A representative payee has a responsibility to—
(a) Use the payments he or she receives only for the use and benefit of the beneficiary in a manner and for the purposes he or she determines, under the guidelines in this subpart, to be in the best interests of the beneficiary;
(b) Notify us of any event that will affect the amount of benefits the beneficiary receives or the right of the beneficiary to receive benefits;
(c) Submit to us, upon our request, a written report accounting for the benefits received; and
(d) Notify us of any change in his or her circumstances that would affect performance of the payee responsibilities.

42 U.S.C. App., 20 C.F.R. § 404.2040:

Use of benefit payments
(a) **Current maintenance.** (1) We will consider that payments we certify to a representative payee have been used for the use and benefit of the beneficiary if they are used for the beneficiary's current maintenance. Current maintenance includes cost incurred in obtaining food, shelter, clothing, medical care, and personal comfort items.
***
(b) **Institutional care.** If a beneficiary is receiving care in a Federal, State, or private institution because of mental or physical incapacity, current maintenance includes the customary charges made by the

institution, as well as expenditures for those items which will aid in the beneficiary's recovery or release from the institution or expenses for personal needs which will improve the beneficiary's conditions while in the institution.

***

(c) Support of legal dependents. If the current maintenance needs of the beneficiary are met, the payee may use part of the payments for the support of the beneficiary's legally dependent spouse, child, and/or parent.

***

(d) Claims of creditor. A payee may not be required to use benefit payments to satisfy a debt of the beneficiary, if the debt arose prior to the first month for which payments are certified to a payee. If the debt arose prior to this time, a payee may satisfy it only if the current and reasonably foreseeable needs of the beneficiary are met.

42 U.S.C. App., 20 C.F.R. § 404.2045:

Conservation and investment of benefit payments

(a) General. After the representative payee has used benefit payments consistent with the guidelines in this subpart, any remaining amount shall be conserved or invested on behalf of the beneficiary. Conserved funds should be invested in accordance with the rules followed by trustees. Any investment must show clearly that the payee holds the property in trust for the beneficiary.

***

(b) Preferred investments. Preferred investments for excess funds are U.S. Savings Bonds and deposits in an interest or dividend paying account in a bank, trust company, credit union, or savings and loan association which is insured under either Federal or State law. The account must be in a form which shows clearly that the representative payee has only a fiduciary and not a personal interest in the funds. If the payee is the legally appointed guardian or fiduciary of the beneficiary, the account may be established to indicate this relationship. . . .

***

(c) Interest and dividend payment. The interest and dividends which result from an investment are the property of the beneficiary and may not be considered to be the property of the payee.

42 U.S.C. App., 20 C.F.R. § 404.2065:

Accounting for benefit payments

A representative payee is accountable for the use of benefits. We may require periodic written reports from representative payees. We may also, in certain situations, verify how a representative payee used the funds. A representative payee should keep records of what was done with the benefit payments in order to make accounting reports. We may ask the following questions—

(a) The amount of benefit payments on hand at the beginning of the accounting period;

(b) How the benefit payments were used;

(c) How much of the benefit payments were saved and how the savings were invested;

(d) Where the beneficiary lived during the accounting period; and

(e) The amount of the beneficiary's income from other sources during the accounting period.

Discussion Questions

1. Do the regulations give sufficient guidance to representative payees regarding the permissible use of benefit payments? Is the degree of flexibility given to representative payees in this regard insufficient, appropriate, or excessive?

2. Do you agree with the uses of benefits delineated in the regulations? What changes, if any, would you suggest?

3. How, if at all, would you change the regulatory requirements concerning the investment of excess funds?

4. Are the regulatory provisions regarding accounting for benefit payments sufficient to assure meaningful accountability? Is sufficient, relevant information being requested? What changes, if any, would you suggest to assure both the public and individual program beneficiaries that funds are being spent properly?

42 U.S.C. App., 20 C.F.R. § 404.2040a:

Compensation for qualified organizations serving as representative payees

(a) **General.** A community-based, nonprofit social service agency which meets the requirements set out in paragraph (b) of this section may request our authorization to collect a monthly fee from a beneficiary for providing representative payee services.

(b) **Organizations that may request compensation.** We will authorize an organization to collect a fee if all the following requirements are met.

(1) It is community-based, i.e., serves or represents one or more neighborhoods, city or county locales and is located within its service area.

(2) It is a nonprofit social service organization founded for religious, charitable or social welfare purposes and is tax exempt . . .

(3) It is bonded or licensed in the State in which it serves as representative payee.

(4) It regularly provides representative payee services concurrently to at least five beneficiaries. . . .

(5) It was in existence on October 1, 1988.

(6) It is not a creditor of the beneficiary.

Discussion Questions

1. What is the rationale for allowing certain organizations to serve as representative payees, rather than restricting eligibility to individuals?

2. What is the rationale for the restrictions placed on which organizations may serve in this capacity? Why shouldn't for-profit entities be permitted to serve as representative payees?

3. What potential abuses or conflicts of interest might be engendered by an organization serving as a representative payee?

One set of authors has described the representative payment system as "a giant, special purpose guardianship system," in which representative payees are "the guardians of property, not of the person, and limited guardians of only one species of property—funds derived from Social Security program benefits." Daniel L. Skoler & Amy L. Allbright, *Judicial Oversight of the Nation's Largest Guardianship System: Caselaw on Social Security Administration Representative Payee Issues*, 24 Mental and Physical Disability Law Reporter 169–174 (2000).

Discussion Question

Given the stakes and issues involved, is the current administrative structure for dealing with representative payees the most appropriate approach, or should such matters routinely be handled by the courts in the context of an adversary proceeding? What are the advantages and disadvantages of each approach, in terms of the respective interests of the public, individual program beneficiaries, and those providing goods and services to program beneficiaries?

4

Regulating Geriatric Services and Settings

INTRODUCTION

The various settings within which older persons receive services are regulated by a combination of: federal, state, and local statutes and regulations; voluntary accreditation standards; and common law litigation.

Marshall B. Kapp, *Key Words in Ethics, Law, and Aging: A Guide to Contemporary Usage,* New York: Springer Publishing Company (1995), pp. 69–70, 61:

> A **statute** is a law enacted by an elected legislature. On the federal level, statutes . . . are enacted by Congress, state legislatures enact state statutes (for example, professional licensure requirements), and city or county commissions or councils enact local statutes (also often called ordinances) (for instance, fire safety codes). Legislatures act on the basis of authority given to them by the U.S. Constitution, and are bound by the limits set in the Constitution. Statutes are compiled in volumes called codes. Statutes must be written and published so that affected people are put on notice regarding what is expected of them. When courts are called upon to interpret the meaning of a particular statute, these judicial decisions become part of statutory law. A statute may empower an administrative agency to create regulations that implement the intent of the law.
>
> A **regulation,** also know as a rule, is the form taken by administrative law. A regulation is enacted or promulgated by administrative (executive or independent) agencies, such as departments of health

or public welfare, pursuant to powers delegated by the legislature. Administrative laws contain the specific content of programs and activities that are authorized by statute. This characteristic can be seen, for example, in federal and state regulations that have been enacted to implement the broad Medicare and Medicaid statutes passed by the Congress and state legislatures. Rules and regulations have the full force of law behind them and, just like statutes, must be written, published, limited to future effect, and consistent with the Constitution (as well as the authorizing statute). Although there are certain constitutional limits to the amount of authority that a legislature may delegate to an administrative agency, it is the general practice of legislatures to give agencies the power to fill out with specifics the often empty shell of statutory programs. Administrative law also includes judicial decisions interpreting the meaning and effect of regulations.

Accreditation is the granting of approval or credentials (i.e., a stamp of approval) to an agency or facility, based upon that agency or facility demonstrating (usually by passing a specific survey or inspection) that standards prescribed by the accrediting body have been met. Accreditation is **voluntarily** sought by the agency or facility, rather than being required by the government, and the accrediting body (e.g., Joint Commission on Accreditation of Healthcare Organizations, JCAHO) is a **private** rather than governmental entity. There may be a financial incentive for an agency or facility to be accredited by a particular body; for example, the federal government "deems" accreditation of a hospital by the JCAHO to qualify that hospital for reimbursement under the Medicare program. Additionally, some states effectively delegate their hospital licensure function to the JCAHO by incorporating by specific reference JCAHO standards into the licensure statute.

HOSPITAL REGULATION

Federal Regulation

A major source of hospital regulation is the federal Conditions of Participation (CoPs) for Medicare and Medicaid payment. These CoPs for acute care hospitals are published at 42 C.F.R. Part 482. State survey agencies (SAs), under contract with the federal Health Care Financing Administration (HCFA), survey hospitals to assess compliance with the CoPs. The SAs conduct these surveys using the *State Operations Manual* (SOM) (HCFA Publication No. 7, available at *www.hcfa.gov/pubforms*).

As noted earlier, the federal government has given "deemed status" to the JCAHO, 42 C.F.R. § 488.5, meaning that if a hospital is accredited by the JCAHO according to its standards (Joint Commission on Accreditation of Healthcare Organizations, Accreditation Manual for Hospitals, Chicago (2000)), it is deemed to satisfy eligibility requirements to receive Medicare and Medicaid payments for patient care. A JCAHO accredited hospital is not routinely surveyed by the SA.

Discussion Questions

1. What are the purposes of hospital regulation? Why do hospitals need to be regulated by external bodies? Why isn't a combination of self-regulation and a competitive economic marketplace sufficient to assure safety and quality of care? Is external oversight of hospitals effective? See Department of Health and Human Services, Office of Inspector General, The External Review of Hospital Quality, OEI-01-97-00051-00053 (July 20, 1999).

2. Should not-for-profit hospitals, such as those that are religiously affiliated, be regulated differently than for-profit hospitals? See David A. Hyman, *Hospital Conversions: Fact, Fantasy, and Regulatory Follies,* 23 The Journal of Corporation Law 741–778 (1998).

3. Is it proper for the federal government to award "deemed status" to a private organization? What are the arguments for and against this regulatory option?

On July 2, 1999, HCFA published an Interim Final Rule to revise the Patients' Rights section of the hospital CoPs, 64 Fed. Reg. 36070:

§482.13 Condition of participation: Patients' rights.
A hospital must protect and promote each patient's rights.
(a) *Standard: Notice of rights.* (1) A hospital must inform each patient, or when appropriate, the patient's representative (as allowed under State law), of the patient's rights, in advance of furnishing or discontinuing patient care whenever possible.
(2) The hospital must establish a process for prompt resolution of patient grievances and must inform each patient whom to contact to file a grievance. The hospital's governing body must approve and be responsible for the effective operation of the grievance process and must review and resolve grievances, unless it delegates the responsibility in writing to a grievance committee. The grievance process must include a mechanism for timely referral of patient concerns

regarding quality of care or premature discharge to the appropriate Utilization and Quality Control Peer Review Organization. At a minimum:

(i) The hospital must establish a clearly explained procedure for the submission of a patient's written or verbal grievance to the hospital.

(ii) The grievance process must specify time frames for review of the grievance and the provision of a response.

(iii) In its resolution of the grievance, the hospital must provide the patient with written notice of its decision that contains the name of the hospital contact person, the steps taken on behalf of the patient to investigate the grievance, the results of the grievance process, and the date of completion.

(b) *Standard: Exercise of rights.* (1) The patient has the right to participate in the development and implementation of his or her plan of care.

(2) The patient or his or her representative (as allowed under State law) has the right to make informed decisions regarding his or her care. The patient's rights include being informed of his or her health status, being involved in care planning and treatment, and being able to request or refuse treatment. This right must not be construed as a mechanism to demand the provision of treatment or services deemed medically unnecessary or inappropriate.

(3) The patient has the right to formulate advance directives and to have hospital staff and practitioners who provide care in the hospital comply with these directives . . .

(4) The patient has the right to have a family member or representative of his or her choice and his or her own physician notified promptly of his or her admission to the hospital.

(c) *Standard: Privacy and safety.* (1) The patient has the right to personal privacy.

(2) The patient has the right to receive care in a safe setting.

(3) The patient has the right to be free from all forms of abuse or harassment.

(d) *Standard: Confidentiality of patient records.* (1) The patient has the right to the confidentiality of his or her clinical records.

(2) The patient has the right to access information contained in his or her clinical records within a reasonable time frame. The hospital must not frustrate the legitimate efforts of individuals to gain access to their own medical records and must actively seek to meet these requests as quickly as its recordkeeping system permits.

(e) *Standard: Restraint for acute medical and surgical care.* (1) The patient has the right to be free from restraints of any form that are not medically necessary or are used as a means of coercion, discipline, convenience, or retaliation by staff. The term "restraint" includes either a physical restraint or a drug that is being used as a restraint. A physical restraint is any manual method or physical or mechanical device, material, or equipment attached or adjacent to the patient's body that he or she cannot easily remove that restricts freedom of movement or normal access to one's body. A drug used as a restraint is a medication used to control behavior or to restrict the patient's freedom of movement and is not a standard treatment for the patient's medical or psychiatric condition.

(2) A restraint can only be used if needed to improve the patient's well-being and less restrictive interventions have been determined to be ineffective.

(3) The use of a restraint must be—

(i) Selected only when other less restrictive measures have been found to be ineffective to protect the patient or others from harm;

(ii) In accordance with the order of a physician or other licensed independent practitioner permitted by the State and hospital to order a restraint. This order must—

(A) Never be written as a standing or on an as needed basis (that is, PRN); and

(B) Be followed by consultation with the patient's treating physician, as soon as possible, if the restraint is not ordered by the patient's treating physician;

(iii) In accordance with a written modification to the patient's plan of care;

(iv) Implemented in the least restrictive manner possible;

(v) In accordance with safe and appropriate restraining techniques; and

(vi) Ended at the earliest possible time.

(4) The condition of the restrained patient must be continually assessed, monitored, and reevaluated.

(5) All staff who have direct patient contact must have ongoing education and training in the proper and safe use of restraints.

(f) *Standard: Seclusion and restraint for behavior management.* (1) The patient has the right to be free from seclusion and restraints, of any form, imposed as a means of coercion, discipline, convenience, or retaliation by staff. The term "restraint" includes either a physical restraint or a drug that is being used as a restraint. A physical restraint is any manual method or physical or mechanical device, material, or equipment attached or adjacent to the patient's body that he or she cannot easily remove that restricts freedom of movement or normal access to one's body. A drug used as a restraint is a medication used to control behavior or to restrict the patient's freedom of movement and is not a standard treatment for the patient's medical or psychiatric condition. Seclusion is the involuntary confinement of a person in a room or an area where the person is physically prevented from leaving.

(2) Seclusion or a restraint can only be used in emergency situations if needed to ensure that patient's physical safety and less restrictive interventions have been determined to be ineffective.

(3) The use of a restraint or seclusion must be—

(i) Selected only when less restrictive measures have been found to be ineffective to protect the patient or others from harm;

(ii) In accordance with the order of a physician or other licensed independent practitioner permitted by the State and hospital to order seclusion or restraint. The following requirements will be superceded by existing State laws that are more restrictive:

(A) Orders for the use of seclusion or a restraint must never be written as a standing order or on an as needed basis (that is, PRN).

(B) The treating physician must be consulted as soon as possible, if the restraint or seclusion is not ordered by the patient's treating physician.

(C) A physician or other licensed independent practitioner must see and evaluate the need for restraint or seclusion within 1 hour after the initiation of this intervention.

(D) Each written order for a physical restraint or seclusion is limited to 4 hours for adults; 2 hours for children and adolescents ages 9 to 17; or 1 hour for patients under 9. The original order may only be renewed in accordance with these limits for up to a total of 24 hours. After the original order expires, a physician or licensed independent practitioner (if allowed under State law) must see and assess the patient before issuing a new order.

(iii) In accordance with a written modification to the patient's plan of care;

(iv) Implemented in the least restrictive manner possible;

(v) In accordance with safe appropriate restraining techniques; and

(vi) Ended at the earliest possible time.

(4) A restraint and seclusion may not be used simultaneously unless the patient is—

(i) Continually monitored face-to-face by an assigned staff member; or

(ii) Continually monitored by staff using both video and audio equipment. This monitoring must be in close proximity to the patient.

(5) The condition of the patient who is in a restraint or in seclusion must continually be assessed, monitored, and reevaluated.

(6) All staff who have direct patient contact must have ongoing education and training in the proper and safe use of seclusion and

restraint application and techniques and alternative methods for handling behavior, symptoms, and situations that traditionally have been treated through the use of restraints or seclusion.

(7) The hospital must report to HCFA any death that occurs while a patient is restrained or in seclusion, or where it is reasonable to assume that a patient's death is a result of restraint or seclusion.

HCFA on May 22, 2000 issued Interpretive Guidelines for the hospital CoPs for Patients' Rights. These Guidelines give surveyors guidance on how to assess whether hospitals are complying with the CoPs in this sphere. These guidelines are available at www.hcfa.gov/ quality/4b2.htm.

Discussion Questions

1. Why do patients' rights need to be so extensively regulated? Do these regulations amount to too much government intrusion or micromanagement in a hospital's internal affairs? Do they create an adversarial relationship between patients/families on one side and caregivers on the other?

2. Note the provision in § 482.13(b)(2) that "This right [to make informed medical decisions] must not be construed as a mechanism to demand the provision of treatment or services deemed medically unnecessary or inappropriate." Why was this provision included? See the discussion of Medical Futility in Chapter 7.

3. Extensive new requirements regarding the use of physical and chemical restraints in hospitals are contained in § 482.13(e) and (f). Why are these requirements included in the regulations? Are these requirements reasonable and realistic? What are the practical alternatives to the use of restraints?

See Marshall B. Kapp, *Physical Restraint Use in Acute Care Hospitals: Legal Liability Issues,* 1 Elder's Advisor: The Journal of Elder Law and Post-Retirement Planning 1–10 (1999):

In addition [to the CoPs], the federal Food and Drug Administration (FDA) now has turned its attention to the status of physical restraints as medical devices. On November 16, 1991, the FDA issued a medical bulletin entitled "Potential Hazards with Protective Restraint Devices," which was reissued on July 15, 1992 as an FDA Safety Alert to hospital administrators, nursing directors, and directors of emergency room services. On August 28, 1995, the FDA issued a Safety Alert (to, among other intended audiences, hospital administrators and risk managers) entitled "Entrapment Hazards with Hospital Bed Side Rails."

Since 1992, restraints must be labeled as "prescription-only" devices. On March 4, 1996, the FDA published a final rule (21 C.F.R. §880.6760) that ended restraint manufacturers' previous exemption from the requirement (21 C.F.R. Part 807, Subpart E) to notify the FDA of the intent to market most restraint devices; effective September 3, 1996, these devices needed FDA prior-approval for marketing and sale.

Perhaps most importantly, the FDA actively maintains complaint files concerning restraining devices. The information contained in those files is accessible from the FDA by members of the public, including plaintiffs' attorneys, on request under the federal Freedom of Information Act (5 U.S.C. §552). Under the Safe Medical Devices Act (SMDA), passed in 1990 (21 U.S.C.§360) and effective November 28, 1991, and its implementing regulations (21 C.F.R. Part 803), hospitals (as well as nursing homes, ambulatory surgical facilities, and outpatient treatment facilities) are obligated to report certain incidents to the FDA on Form 3500A within ten working days. A medical device report must be submitted whenever the "user facility" receives or otherwise becomes aware of information, from any source, that reasonably suggests that a device may have caused or contributed to either (a) the death of a patient or employee of the facility or (b) serious injury to a patient or facility employee.

"Caused or contributed" includes problems that arise because of device failure, malfunction, improper or inadequate design, manufacture defects, mislabeling, or (particularly relevant in the restraint context) user (i.e., hospital) error. "Serious injury" means an illness or injury that (a) is life-threatening, (b) results in permanent impairment of a body function or permanent damage to a body structure, or (c) necessitates medical or surgical intervention to preclude permanent impairment of a body function or permanent damage to a body structure.

Hospitals are covered by a slew of other federal laws. Most significant are the mandates of the Americans With Disabilities Act (ADA), 42 U.S.C. §§ 12101-12213, Rehabilitation Act, 29 U.S.C. § 794, Occupational Safety and Health Act (OSHA) and its regulations, 29 C.F.R. § 1910.20, and the Fair Labor Standards Act (FLSA), 29 U.S.C. § 201 *et. seq.*

State Regulation

The primary way in which states regulate hospitals is to require them to be licensed to treat patients. State licensure of hospitals is based on the state's inherent *police power* to protect and promote the general health, safety, and welfare of the community.

Alaska Statutes § 18.20.020:

> A person or government unit, except the federal government, acting severally or jointly with another person or governmental unit may not establish, conduct, or maintain a hospital in the state without a license.

As noted earlier, a number of states recognize JCAHO accreditation of a hospital as sufficient for licensure purposes. Alaska Statutes § 18.20.080 provides:

> The department [of health] shall make annual inspections and investigations of hospital facilities. The department may accept accreditation by the Joint Commission on the Accreditation of Hospitals in lieu of an annual inspection by the department for the year in which the accreditation was granted if the accreditation standards of the commission are substantially similar to the inspection standards of the department.

Discussion Questions

Is it appropriate for the state to delegate its police powers regarding hospital licensure to a private entity like the JCAHO? What are the arguments for and against this approach to licensure?

States also require the licensure of individual professionals (including physicians, nurses, pharmacists, social workers, and therapists) who treat patients in hospitals. A hospital is responsible for assuring that its professional staff members have appropriate legal authorization to practice.

Local Regulation

Hospitals also are subject to local zoning, land use, building, fire, and safety ordinances.

NURSING FACILITIES REGULATION

Federal Regulation

Marshall B. Kapp, *Quality of Care and Quality of Life in Nursing Facilities: What's Regulation Got to Do With It?* 31 McGeorge Law Review 707–731 (2000):

The most significant influence on provider behavior . . . is exerted by mandatory conditions set forth by the federal Department of Health and Human Services (DHHS) through the Health Care Financing Administration (HCFA). The DHHS oversees all NFs that wish to be certified to participate in the Medicare and Medicaid programs. Enforcement of mandatory standards occurs through regular survey and certification by a state administrative agency (usually the state health department) that has been designated by contract between the specific state and the federal government. HCFA provides the state survey agency with interpretive guidelines, compiled in the *Medicaid State Operations Manual* (authorized by 42 U.S.C.§§1395:-3(g)(2)(C)(I), 1396r(g)(2)(C)(I) and available at www.hcfa.gov/medicaid/LTCS/LTCSHMPG), and a form for use during NF surveys. Frequently, state surveys examine NFs for compliance with both the federal certification standards and state licensure requirements. Violation of federal standards may lead to decertification of the NF from participation in Medicare or Medicaid financing. Moreover, HCFA is empowered under the "look behind" statute to conduct its own validation surveys of NFs and to terminate a NF's participation in the Medicaid program despite findings of compliance by the state survey agency . . .

As part of the Omnibus Budget Reconciliation Act of 1987 (OBRA 87) (Public Law No. 100-203)), Congress enacted the Nursing Home Quality Reform Act (codified at 42 U.S.C. §§1395:-3(a)-(h) and 1396r (a) (h)). This Act is modeled on many of the recommendations made in a 1986 Institute of Medicine report that Congress had directed HCFA to commission. Passage of the 1987 legislation demonstrated the impatience of Congress and the courts with what they and the public perceived as HCFA's ineffectual regulation of NFs. OBRA 87 amended Titles 18 (Medicare) and 19 (Medicaid) of the Social Security Act to require substantial upgrading in NF quality and enforcement in a number of areas.

To implement this legislation, HCFA published final regulations on February 2, 1989, becoming effective on October 1, 1990 (54 Fed. Reg. 5316). Additional final regulations were published on

September 26, 1991 (56 Fed. Reg. 48826). Among the most important requirements imposed by these regulations (codified at 42 C.F.R. §§483.10, 483.13) are those relating to: ensuring resident privacy and decisional rights regarding accommodations, medical treatment, personal care, visits, written and telephone communications, and meetings with others, maintaining confidentiality of personal and clinical records, guaranteeing facility access and visitation rights to persons of the resident's choosing, requiring issuance of notice of rights at the time of admission, ensuring proper use of physical restraints and psychoactive drugs, protecting resident funds being managed in the facility, ensuring transfer and discharge rights, and issuing related notices; requiring minimum staffing levels regarding nursing and social work coverage, requiring comprehensive resident assessments and individualized care plans drawn in accordance with those assessments; and requiring state prescreening of all prospective NF admittees, and prohibiting admission of individuals with mental illness or mental retardation unless those individuals are found specifically to need nursing services.

In 1994, HCFA published a final rule governing survey, certification and enforcement of Requirements of Participation for Medicare SNFs and Medicaid NFs (59 Fed. Reg. 56116). This rule, which became effective July 1, 1995, made significant changes to the survey and certification process and describes the intermediate sanctions that states and the federal government have available to respond to facilities that do not meet federal standards. On Mary 28, 1999, HCFA published a final rule (with a comment period) that gives states and HCFA new authority to impose civil money penalties in the event of noncompliance.

. . . the federal appetite for new NF regulations continues unsatiated. For example, on March 25, 1999, President Clinton signed into law the Nursing Home Resident Protection Amendments, which, among other items, protect NF residents from eviction when an NF voluntarily withdraws from participation in the Medicaid program. (Citations omitted)

Discussion Questions

1. Why is the nursing home industry so heavily regulated in the United States? Are the negative perceptions of the public, legislators, and regulators deserved?

2. Does regulation exert a positive influence on nursing home residents' quality of care and quality of life? What are the negative ramifications of regulation, if any? For additional reading, see James

E. Allen, Nursing Home Federal Requirements and Guidelines to Surveyors, 4th ed., New York: Springer Publishing Company (2000).

An aspect of nursing facility care addressed with exceptional specificity by the federal regulations concerns the use of physical and chemical restraints. See Marshall B. Kapp, *id.*:

> Perhaps the most important change intended by supporters of OBRA 87 and its implementing regulations concerned the permissible use of physical and chemical restraints on residents in NFs. Unlike the *status quo ante,* today a resident has the right to be free from any physical restraints imposed for the purpose of discipline or staff convenience, rather than imposed under a physician's order to treat the resident's medical problems after less restrictive or intrusive interventions have been considered and attempted unsuccessfully. The same statutory and regulatory restriction applies to psychotropic drugs, which have (in the not very distant past) commonly been administered to NF residents as chemical restraints rather than as a thoughtful, unavoidable piece of the particular resident's therapeutic plan. (Citations omitted)

Discussion Questions

1. Are the regulatory restrictions on the use of physical and chemical restraints reasonable and realistic? Why were regulations needed to change provider behavior in this arena? What were the barriers to restraint minimization? To what extent do these barriers persist? Is elimination of restraint use possible?

2. How can both regulators and providers target specific residents for review of inappropriate restraint use? See Nicholas G. Castle, *Deficiency Citations for Physical Restraint Use in Nursing Homes,* 55B Journal of Gerontology: Social Sciences S33–S40 (2000).

3. What are the practical alternatives to restraint use?

Another subject receiving particular attention in the federal regulations is that of involuntary transfer or discharge of a resident from or within a nursing facility. Federal regulations limit legitimate grounds for transfer or discharge to the following situations:

- the resident agrees to the transfer or discharge
- medical necessity
- failure of the resident to pay for services provided or to cooperate in obtaining payment from a third party such as Medicaid
- the "resident's welfare or that of other patients"

The resident must be given advance notice of any proposed transfer or discharge, except in emergency situations. See Kathleen Knepper, *Involuntary Transfers and Discharges of Nursing Home Residents under Federal and State Law,* 17 Journal of Legal Medicine 215–275 (1996).

The "medical necessity" exception to the general legal prohibition against forced relocations would include, for example, situations in which the resident requires acute care that can be provided properly only in a hospital environment. It also would encompass situations in which the government mandated utilization review (UR) process determines that, for a resident whose care is being financed by Medicare, Medicaid, or another third party, nursing facility level care is no longer medically necessary or appropriate.

Discussion Questions:

1. Why has government imposed strict limitations on forced relocations from or within a nursing facility? Do you believe that residents can really suffer from "transfer trauma"? See *O'Bannon v. Town Court,* 447 U.S. 773 (1980). How can nursing facilities minimize any effects of transfer trauma?

2. What are other situations that would justify use of the "medical necessity" exception?

3. Doesn't forced relocation of a resident who depends on government financing for care, based on a UR finding and without any opportunity to challenge that finding in court, violate that resident's right to Due Process of law under the 14th Amendment of the U.S. Constitution? See *Blum v. Yaretsky,* 457 U.S. 991 (1982).

A regulation allowing HCFA to confer "deemed status" on a private accrediting organization (i.e., to treat that organization's approval of a nursing facility as sufficient to satisfy Medicare/Medicaid certification standards) was published on November 23, 1993, 58 Fed. Reg. 61837. To date, no private accrediting organization has applied for deemed status for nursing facilities.

Discussion Question

What are the arguments for and against granting private entities deemed status for nursing facilities? Would granting deemed status to private entities be more or less appropriate for nursing facilities than for hospitals?

Although no voluntary, private entity has yet been granted deemed status in this context, an increasing number of nursing facilities are seeking voluntary accreditation, mainly from the JCAHO, anyway. Besides conferring a general stamp of approval that is useful in marketing efforts to attract both residents and staff, JCAHO accreditation is required by many managed care plans as a precondition of a nursing facility's being available as an option to a plan's enrollees.

Nursing facilities, like hospitals, are covered by a host of other federal laws, including the ADA, Rehabilitation Act, OSHA, and FLSA. Under the ADA, for example, a nursing facility's denial of admission to a prospective resident solely because the applicant has acquired immune deficiency syndrome (AIDS) or a positive HIV test would be highly suspect. Federal antifraud and abuse laws attempting to maintain the financial integrity of the Medicare and Medicaid programs pertain to nursing facilities, and the DHHS OIG has issued a Compliance Program Guidance for Nursing Facilities concentrating on this area, available at *www.hhs.gov/oig* and 65 Fed. Reg. 14289 (March 16, 2000).

State and Local Regulation

In addition to federal requirements tied to Medicare and Medicaid, regulation of nursing facilities by individual states under their respective licensure authority is extensive, with specific requirements frequently exceeding those set on the federal level, especially regarding residents' rights, restraints, and involuntary transfers and discharges. Nursing facilities are also heavily regulated under state and local fire and building codes and similar business-related safety provisions. In their role as employer, nursing facilities fall within state, federal, and local labor law requirements.

Besides requiring that nursing facilities themselves be licensed, states also license the individual professionals who work within the facilities. Alaska Statutes § 08.70.080:

> Only a licensed nursing home administrator may manage, supervise, or be generally in charge of a nursing home. The care provided by a nursing home or a licensed hospital providing nursing home care through the use of skilled nursing beds or intermediate care beds shall be supervised by a licensed nursing home administrator . . .

Discussion Question

Nursing home administrators are the only type of health care administrators for whom licensure is required by the state. What is the rationale for this distinction?

Most state licensure laws impose detailed minimum staffing levels for registered nurses, licensed practical nurses, and nursing assistants in nursing facilities. See National Citizens Coalition for Nursing Home Reform, Federal & State Minimum Staffing Requirements for Nursing Homes (December 1999), *www.nccnhr.org.*

Discussion Questions

1. Is it appropriate for a state legislature or administrative agency to delineate precise minimum staffing levels for nursing facilities? See Charlene Harrington, Christine Kovner, Mathy Mczey, et al., *Experts Recommend Minimum Nurse Staffing Standards for Nursing Facilities in the United States,* 40 Gerontologist 5–16 (2000).

2. If the state requires certain minimum staffing levels, should the state be required to assure adequate funding for nursing facilities to meet those levels?

3. Should there be any enforcement leeway when a nursing facility falls below state imposed minimum staffing levels despite diligent good faith efforts to comply?

Aside from federal CoPs requiring a physician's order, the process of admitting an individual to a nursing facility is a matter of state law. In many cases, though, the legal status of that process and the resulting admission is ambiguous. Marshall B. Kapp, *"A Place Like That": Advance Directives and Nursing Home Admissions,* 4 Psychology, Public Policy, and Law 805–828 (1998):

> In theory, the nursing home admissions process is clearly and crisply defined:
> a. No one can sign a person into a nursing home against that person's will.
> b. If a person is incapacitated, a legally authorized surrogate may authorize the person's admission into a nursing home. Incapacity must be established through guardianship proceedings in a court of law, or through other procedures provided under state law.
> The law presumes that every admission to a nursing home (like every other health care decision) is based not only on a physician's

order, but also on the informed, competent, and voluntary agreement either of the new resident personally or of the legally authorized surrogate decision maker. Unlike the state's police and *parens patriae* powers to involuntarily commit mentally ill, dangerous persons to public mental institutions, which are codified in state statutes, legal authority does not exist to involuntarily commit anyone to a nursing home.

In reality, nursing home admissions practice is not always quite as legally neat as the theory supposes. Many individuals have been "voluntarily" admitted to (or more accurately, "placed in") a nursing home even though (a) they personally lacked sufficient mental capacity to engage in a rational decisionmaking process about the matter but had not been formally declared incompetent by the local court of appropriate jurisdiction; and (b) either no interested, competent family members were available at the time of admission, or interested, competent family members were available but had not been formally authorized to act as surrogate decision makers through a guardianship or conservatorship order or a previously executed durable power of attorney instrument. In these situations, as a matter of practicality, nursing homes ordinarily have accepted *de facto* decisionally incapacitated new residents despite the legal ambiguity surrounding their admission, and negative legal consequences to the nursing home and its personnel (or to anyone else) for proceeding in this extralegal manner have not materialized.

However, widespread anecdotal reports, primarily deriving from hospital discharge planners and geriatric care managers, indicate an increasing reluctance and in some cases outright unwillingness on the part of many nursing facility admission directors to engage in these kinds of admissions on a routine basis any longer. Current federal (mainly the Nursing Home Quality Reform Act included in the Omnibus Budget Reconciliation Act of 1987 and implementing regulations and the Patient Self-Determination Act, or PSDA, of 1990) and state laws and the government surveyors who enforce those laws place strong emphasis on resident autonomy (exercised either directly or through a surrogate) in decision making within nursing homes. Intense, widely publicized ethical commentary emerging during the past decade has underscored the autonomy precept. This emphasis creates apprehension within facilities about possible regulatory sanctions or civil liability for violating residents' rights. Many nursing home admissions directors appear to be balking at accepting new residents on a "voluntary" admission status unless either the present decisional capacity of the resident or explicit legal authority on the part of the putative surrogate is clearly established and documented.

Greatest difficulty in effectuating nursing home (or other long-term care) placement usually occurs in the case of mentally ill individuals with significant behavioral problems and no visible surrogates, because facilities are concerned about their legal authority to (if necessary) physically restrain or treat such individuals with psychotropic drugs that carry substantial risks. Nursing homes are prohibited by both Title III of the Americans With Disabilities Act (ADA) and the Rehabilitation Act of 1973 from discriminating in admissions on the basis of an applicant's handicap, but they can lawfully deny admission to persons exhibiting dangerously aggressive behavior that the particular facility is not equipped to handle and care for properly. Payment source still often affects one's likelihood of being admitted to the nursing home of his or her choice, as discrimination against Medicaid-eligible individuals still persists to a degree despite its current illegality in most states. Nursing homes are under great pressure not to make mistakes in admitting individuals who will pose significant management problems, because it is extremely difficult legally to transfer or discharge a resident over objection once admission has taken place.

In light of nursing home hesitance to admit certain types of individuals, some discharge planners and care managers complain that a number of persons who should be transferred to nursing homes from hospitals (who are not allowed to abandon these persons) or unsafe home environments are having those transfers delayed or disrupted until the legal question of who may voluntarily consent to the nursing home admission is clarified. Such delays often work to the physical and emotional detriment of the eventual resident as well as the financial detriment of the hospital, and the resulting "solution" is frequently the initiation and imposition of a guardianship on the individual.

Personal autonomy, in the context of medical treatment and daily living decisions that need to be made by or on behalf of individuals once they have become nursing home residents, is a subject that has already received substantial attention. The informed consent status of nursing home admissions in the first place (i.e., how one becomes a resident), on the other hand, has thus far been all but ignored by legal practitioners, lawmakers, and scholars. Current literature consists of a very few tangential allusions to the issue dealing mainly with ethical rather than legal considerations . . .

. . . I must take note of one additional potential complicating factor. In *Zinermon v. Burch* (494 U.S. 113 (1990)) the U.S. Supreme Court ruled that the state of Florida could be sued civilly for permitting an adult person (who was later held to be mentally incompetent) to "voluntarily" admit himself to a public mental institution without first explicitly ascertaining and documenting that the patient possessed sufficient cognitive and emotional capacity to make an autonomous decision about his admission.

Although the *Zinermon* reasoning has not yet been applied to the nursing home context either in any litigated cases or the legal literature, the potential for such an application and its probable consequences cannot be summarily dismissed. Admission practices of public facilities clearly implicate the "state action" that is necessary to trigger constitutional protections for the resident, and the extensive regulatory and financing (i.e., Medicare and Medicaid) entanglements between privately owned nursing homes and the government may be sufficient to satisfy the "state action" criterion for them as well. (Citations omitted)

See also Marshall B. Kapp, *The "Voluntary" Status of Nursing Facility Admissions: Legal, Practical, and Public Policy Implications,* 24 New England Journal on Criminal and Civil Confinement 1–35 (1998).

Discussion Question

Should some type of formal due process hearing be required before an individual is admitted to a nursing facility? In this respect, should a nursing facility be analogized to a private acute care hospital or a prison? What would you recommend to a nursing facility as a proper admissions procedure?

HOME CARE REGULATION

A broad range of different services fall within the general rubric of home care. Health-related services entail medical, skilled nursing, home health aide, physical therapy, occupational therapy, respiratory therapy, and similar activities taking place within the patient's home. These services usually are delivered through the auspices of a home health agency (HHA) and by private physicians working in collaboration with HHA staff. Many older persons require, either instead of home health services or in addition to them, personal care (e.g., bathing and dressing), homemaker services (e.g., cooking and cleaning), or case management; these services may be provided through HHAs or by individual independent providers hired by the patient.

Home Health Agencies

Federal Regulation

Current federal quality standards for Medicare-participating HHAs are found in OBRA 1987, Public Law 100-203, Title IV, subpart B, as implemented in 42 C.F.R. Part 484, and Surveyor *Home Health Certification Process and Interpretive Guidelines* released by DHHS on March 21, 1991. Slightly revised final regulations were published on July 18, 1991, at 56 Fed. Reg. 32967. Present regulations include an extensive enumeration of consumer rights, strict criteria for staff training, and requirements that the HHA operate and provide services in compliance with all applicable federal, state, and local laws and with accepted standards and principles that pertain to professionals providing items and services in such an HHA.

The surveyor guidelines place emphasis on surveyor home visits as a basis for evaluating the quality of services, as opposed to the former almost exclusive reliance on review of documentation. Other important sources of information about federal regulation are HCFA's *State Operations Manual* and *Medicare Home Health Agency Coverage Manual* (HCFA Pub. No. 11), available at *www.hcfa.gov/pubforms*. Whether an HHA is in compliance with federal requirements is determined through inspections conducted by the state-designated Medicare survey agency, usually the state health department, and by the local federally contracted Peer Review Organization (PRO).

Discussion Question

What are the advantages and disadvantages of surveyor home visits to evaluate the quality of services, as compared with a review of documentation?

HCFA published a proposed rule to revise the home health Medicare CoP on March 10, 1997, at 62 Fed. Reg. 11005. The proposed requirements focus on the care delivered to patients by HHAs and the outcomes of that care, reflect an interdisciplinary view of patient care, allow HHAs greater flexibility in meeting quality standards, and eliminate some procedural mandates.

Besides prescriptive CoPs aimed at setting and enforcing patient care standards, other federal laws regulate the business aspects of home health care delivery. These include the Medicare-Medicaid Antifraud and Abuse Amendments of 1977 and the Medicare and Medicaid Patient and Program Protection Act of 1987, Public Law 100-93.

42 U.S.C. § 1320a-7b (b):

(1) whoever knowingly and willfully solicits or receives any remuneration (including any kickback, bribe, or rebate) directly or indirectly, overtly or covertly, in cash or in kind—

(A) in return for referring an individual to a person for the furnishing or arranging for the furnishing of any item or service for which payment may be made in whole or in part under Medicare or Medicaid shall be guilty of a felony . . .

(2) whoever knowingly and willfully offers or pays any remuneration (including any kickback, bribe, or rebate) directly or indirectly, overtly or covertly, in cash or in kind to any person to induce such person—

(A) to refer an individual to a person for the furnishing or arranging for the furnishing of any item or service for which payment may be made in whole or in part under Medicare or Medicaid, . . . shall be guilty of a felony . . .

Discussion Questions

1. What is the rationale for these regulatory provisions?

2. If the ABC Home Health Agency gives a hospital discharge planner a box of candy as a holiday gift, has the agency violated this law? Has the discharge planner violated the law by accepting the candy? See DHHS OIG, *Compliance Program Guidance for Home Health Agencies, www.hhs.oig.*

The Sherman Antitrust Act, 15 U.S.C. § 1 *et. seq.* and the Robinson-Patman Price Discrimination Act, 15 U.S.C. § 13, regulate methods of economic competition among home care providers. Individual states also have enacted procompetitive requirements, such as Connecticut Statute § 19a-504d:

(a) If a hospital recommends home health care to a patient, the hospital discharge plan shall include two or more available options of home health care agencies.

(b) A hospital which (1) has an ownership or investment interest in a home health care agency, or (2) receives compensation or remuneration for referral of patients to a home health care agency shall disclose such interest to any patient prior to including such agency as an option in a hospital discharge plan. Such information shall be verbally disclosed to each patient or shall be posted in a conspicuous place visible to patients.

Discussion Questions

1. Is unlimited competition among home care providers in a particular locality always in the best interests of patients? Is it in the best interests of payers?

2. Is the information disclosure mandated by the Connecticut statute really useful to patients? How?

Since 1993, HCFA has considered JCAHO's standards and survey process, found in its Accreditation Manual for Home Care, to be consistent with Medicare and Medicaid requirements for HHAs. This means that HHAs can be "deemed" Medicare certified by achieving JCAHO accreditation, 58 Fed. Reg. 35007. The Community Health Accreditation Program (CHAP) of the National League of Nursing has been given deemed status regarding the skilled nursing services component of home health care, 57 Fed. Reg. 22773.

Discussion Question

What are the arguments for and against the government granting deemed status to a private entity in the home health care arena?

State Regulation

The vast majority of states do not permit HHAs to operate unless they are licensed by the state. Connecticut General Statutes Annotated § 19a-491:

> (a) No person acting individually or jointly with any other person shall establish, conduct, operate or maintain an institution in this state without a license as required by this chapter.
>
> (c) For purposes of this chapter, an institution shall include any person or public or private agency which either advertises, arranges for or provides a homemaker health aide or homemaker-home health aide services in a patient's home or a substantially equivalent environment.

Most state licensure statutes follow the federal Medicare CoP regulations for HHAs, although several states have enacted more stringent provisions. Many state statutory schemes delineate a Bill of Rights for home care clients that is more demanding than the federal regulations found at 42 C.F.R. § 440.10.

Discussion Questions

1. Are HHA licensure Acts a legitimate exercise of a state's police power to protect the general health, safety, and welfare of the community? Are they a necessary and advisable exercise of this power?

2. As a practical matter, are protections found in state Bills of Rights for HHA patients enforceable, or do they just express our aspirations? Do the regulatory provisions actually alter anyone's behavior? See Charles P. Sabatino, *Client Rights Regulations and the Autonomy of Home-Care Consumers,* 14 Generations 21–24 (Supplement, 1990).

The state has the power to force a HHA to cease activity altogether (i.e., to permanently revoke or temporarily suspend a license) in instances of serious violation of important licensure standards, especially when patient safety is compromised. Many states also have the authority under their licensure acts to impose intermediate sanctions, such as civil money fines, injunctions, criminal penalties, conditional licensure, a ban on new patients, or receivership.

Discussion Question

What are the advantages and disadvantages of allowing a state to impose a range of sanctions on HHAs for violations of regulatory standards?

In addition, every state has statutes licensing individual health care professionals who help deliver home health services. The HHA is responsible for assuring compliance by licensed professionals whom it employs or with whom it has a contractual relationship to provide services.

A number of states, for example, Ohio Revised Code § 3701.881, now require HHAs to obtain criminal records checks on prospective employees. These statutes disqualify from HHA employment persons who have been convicted of particular types of offenses.

Discussion Question

Is a requirement of criminal background checks likely to be effective in safeguarding patient welfare? Do the likely benefits clearly outweigh the costs, both financial and in terms of making it more difficult for HHAs to hire staff? Who ought to bear the costs? Should criminal background checks be required in other service settings, such as nursing homes? See H.R. 4293 (106th Congress).

Independent Providers

The hiring of independent (i.e., not employed directly by an HHA) providers for personal assistance and homemaker services creates special sets of relationships. It raises complex legal concerns about the respective rights and responsibilities of the parties to those relationships regarding quality assurance, consumers' rights, and workers' interests.

In the area of quality assurance, in Independent Provider (IP) models of home care

> [We] shift to the consumer instead of the regulator the responsibility to determine the credentials (if any) and personal characteristics in a provider that the particular consumer values as important to quality of care and satisfaction. Similarly, . . . consumers are free to set and enforce their own notions of quality by establishing the process parameters of their care (e.g., how often, at what times, and with what agenda the personal assistant will arrive), within available financial resource limits. The marketplace acting through consumer purchasing decisions is accountable for safeguarding the consumer; service providers need to compete for the business of economically empowered consumers, and those who do not provide satisfactory (as judged by consumers) quality will eventually go out of business in the new LTC marketplace.
>
> Of course, a robust consumer choice, marketplace environment depending on consumers to assure quality services for themselves assumes the sufficient availability of accurate information about competing providers and the services they offer. Thus, a strengthening of federal, 15 U.S.C.§ 45, and state consumer protection laws demanding honesty in provider representations to consumers may, paradoxically, have the effect of reducing command and control style regulation by improving the operation of a competitive marketplace.
>
> Questions may be raised regarding the continued availability and vitality of tort law as a purported quality assurance tool under consumer choice models. How, for instance, would we delineate and prove an applicable legal standard of care against which to hold independent providers coming from infinitely diverse backgrounds and implementing unique service plans individually designed by particular consumers? Who would quality as expert witnesses in such litigation? Since agencies would not be available as defendants, what about plaintiffs' practical problems in trying to collect from independent providers without professional liability insurance on judgments even if they prevailed in their malpractice suits?

Marshall B. Kapp, *Consumer Direction in Long Term Care: A Taxonomy of Legal Issues,* 24 Generations 16–21 (Fall 2000).

Regarding consumers' rights, in IP models

[C]onsumers who purchase services from providers other than Medicare certified HHAs effectively forego the protection of . . . regulatory requirements. In their stead, consumers are entitled to services delivered in accordance with the conditions for which they negotiate and contract—expressly or impliedly—with the providers they hire. Consumers are not forced to depend on the vagaries of a system of government surveys of providers for regulatory compliance and the imposition of sanctions for noncompliance, accompanied by the delay and unpredictability introduced when providers exercise their entitlements to due process. Rather, enforcement of rights in [IP] models becomes a matter of consumer responsibility exercised through the power to fire a worker whose performance fails to satisfy the consumer's personal expectations.

This approach proceeds from a conception of the consumer *qua autonomous,* self-determining adult. This worldview stands in contrast to the traditional regulatory tendency to envision consumers as essentially dependent, vulnerable, and in continual need of external supervision and protection. Reliance on consumers to autonomously effectuate their own rights involves several legal implications.

First, the meaningful exercise of autonomy in directing one's own LTC cannot occur in a vacuum. An essential foundation is an assurance that the consumer's choices are predicated on the receipt of adequate information about the viable service options and their reasonably foreseeable benefits and risks, i.e., on the doctrine of informed consent. Thus, legal questions will likely need to be fleshed out concerning who has the duty to make that information available to the consumer, minimum standards and effective methods of disclosure, the obligations of the consumer to ask the proper questions and demand adequate responses, and liability imposition and remedies for insufficient information sharing.

Second, consumers' right to autonomously control the details of their own LTC necessarily encompasses their prerogative to assume the consequences, including certain risks of harm associated with specific choices. For instance, an agency managing a publicly funded LTC program may propose that a nurse visit the consumer five days a week to dispense medications, but the consumer would rather rely on a neighbor for this purpose and have his limited allocation of dollars used for other purposes more important to him. The agency, apprehensive about its potential liability exposure, explains the foreseeable risks of this choice to the consumer and negotiates a formal agreement wherein the consumer voluntarily consents to assume legal responsibility for those risks. Although this sort of negotiated risk agreement has become increasingly prevalent in the LTC sphere, the extent and limits of such agreements' enforceability have yet to be tested and delineated in the cauldron of litigation.

Third, "A lurking question with all consumer direction . . . is how to handle the question of agency for people of any age who are incapable of directing their own care." On one hand, there is a danger that persons with certain clinical diagnoses that, rightly or wrongly, raise questions about decisional capacity will be discriminated against in the sense of LTC providers or insurers refusing to market or sell their products and services directly to them out of fear that purchase contracts may later be invalidated if challenged. Such categorical discrimination could deprive many people of the potential benefits of home and community-based LTC opportunities now available to others. It also may violate Title III of the Americans With Disabilities Act (ADA), which protects individuals against discrimination in the provision of public accommodations on the basis of actual or perceived disability. On the other hand, nihilism and neglect of those who really lack the capacity to fend for themselves must be avoided in a compassionate society that takes seriously its *parens patriae* obligation to safeguard the helpless.

How, if at all, can a marketplace paradigm of LTC for older and disabled persons be adapted to protect successfully from harm individuals who presently lack sufficient capacity to function autonomously in the consumer role? (Citations omitted)

Marshall B. Kapp, *op. cit.*

A number of the legal ramifications raised by the movement toward . . . [IP models of] home and community-based LTC concern the employment status and protected interests of the individuals who provide services under various arrangements. In the majority of existing LTC models, unless workers are clearly hired, fired, paid, directed, and supervised by a governmental or private agency, their employment status is ambiguous. Workers . . . frequently receive, beyond their basic hourly wage, no fringe benefits of employment such as health or life insurance, employer pension contributions, disability insurance, paid vacation or sick time, or workers' compensation. Responsibility, if any, for paying the employers' portion of Federal Insurance Contributions Act (FICA) (i.e., Social Security and Medicare) taxes, withholding and reporting federal and state income taxes, and verifying the worker's citizenship or legal alien status is often undefined. Additionally, a worker's status under the Fair Labor Standards Act, entailing such issues as minimum wage, maximum hours, and child labor requirements, may be cloudy. Moreover, whether the Occupational Safety and Health Administration (OSHA) has authority to regulate the conditions in the consumer's home under which the home care or personal assistance worker works is at present untested.

These and other uncertainties about various aspects of the employment situation are considerable disincentives for persons to be recruited and retained within this workforce, particularly in IP arrangements. By the same token, apprehension about undertaking possible financial liabilities as an employer may inhibit eligible LTC consumers from selecting the IP service model where it is available. If we are to create and maintain an adequate supply of qualified front-line workers to meet the demand for LTC services under consumer directed models, the legal employment status of those workers needs to be clarified. (Citations omitted)

Marshall B. Kapp, *op. cit.*

Discussion Question

The preceding excerpts raise a number of specific questions regarding the operation of the IP model in practice. Discuss these questions, keeping in mind that the value of consumer autonomy, society's need to protect consumers from harm, and the interests of home care workers may sometimes exist in a state of tension if not outright opposition.

ASSISTED LIVING REGULATION

Assisted living is the fastest growing type of senior housing in the United States. While definitions vary across states, an assisted living facility generally is defined as a residential setting that provides or coordinates personal care services, 24-hour supervision, scheduled and unscheduled assistance, social activities, meals, housekeeping, and some health-related services (e.g., assistance with medications). Assisted living facilities usually are not designed for persons requiring around the clock nursing care or continuous medical monitoring. The objective of assisted living is to maintain or enhance the capabilities of frail older persons and persons with disabilities so that they can remain as independent as possible in a homelike environment.

The states have the primary responsibility for licensing and overseeing care furnished to assisted living residents. Since neither Medicare not Medicaid dollars (except for dollars available under specific state Medicaid waiver programs) pay for assisted living services, few federal standards or guidelines are applicable to assisted living facilities. Regarding the limited, very tangential impact of federal programs on assisted living, see U.S. General Accounting Office, Long-Term Care: Consumer Protection and Quality-of-Care Issues in Assisted Living, GAO/HEHS-97-93 (1997), available at *www.gao.gov.*

Individual states address their regulatory role regarding assisted living through a variety of approaches. In terms of specific content, state laws differ significantly in their (a) standards concerning admission and discharge criteria, staffing ratios, and training requirements; (b) inspection procedures that detail frequency, notification requirements, and inspector training; and (c) the range of enforcement mechanisms that are available to be used.

Robert L. Mollica, State Assisted Living Policy: 1998, U.S. DHHS, Assistant Secretary for Planning and Evaluation (1998), available at *www.aspe.hhs/daltcp.gov:*

> [S]tate approaches to licensing, unit requirements, and the service level [of assisted living facilities include]:
>
> * Board-and-care/institutional,
> * New housing and services model,
> * Service model, and
> * Umbrella model.
>
> **Institutional models** are based on older board-and-care regulations. They allow shared bedrooms without attached baths and either do not allow nursing home eligible residents to be admitted or do not allow facilities to provide nursing services. Two states, Alabama and Rhode Island, adopted "assisted living" as the name for their board-and care licensing category. South Dakota and Wyoming renamed an existing category as assisted living and allowed a higher level of service to be provided without changing the unit requirements. Arkansas and Illinois are two states that do not allow anyone requiring nursing home services to be served in a board-and-care

facility. Some states allow skilled nursing services to be provided for limited periods by a certified home health agency. The upgraded board-and-care approach recognizes that residents are aging-in-place and need more care to prevent a move to a nursing home. State policies have allowed these facilities to admit and retain people who need assistance with activities of daily living (ADLs) and some nursing services. Mutually exclusive level of care criteria have been revised to allow people who would qualify for admission to a nursing home to be retained. The model retains the minimum requirements for the building and units (usually multiple occupancy bedroom with shared bathrooms and tub/shower areas).

The **new housing and service model** licenses or certifies facilities providing assisted living services which are defined by law or regulation. These models require apartment settings and allow facilities to admit and retain nursing home eligible tenants. Depending on the state, rules may allow some or all of the needs met in a nursing home to also be met in assisted living. Policies in states with this approach included a statement of philosophy that emphasizes resident autonomy and creates a prominent role for residents in developing and delivering services. By licensing the setting and services, states distinguish these facilities from board-and-care and have attempted to develop more flexible regulations. Examples of this approach to licensing can be found in Hawaii, Kansas, Oregon, and Vermont and Medicaid waiver standards in Arizona, North Dakota and Washington.

The **service model** focuses on the provider of service, whether it is the residence itself or an outside agency, and allows existing building codes and requirements-rather than new licensing standards-to address the housing structure. This model simplifies the regulatory environment by focusing on the services delivered rather than the architecture. Unfortunately, newer residential models serving frailer residents may not be as familiar to local building inspectors and code enforcement officials who may want to apply more institutional requirements than are needed. Service regulation approaches may include requirements that define which buildings (apartment units, minimum living space) may qualify as assisted living, but the licensing agency's staff do not otherwise apply their standards to the building's setting (Texas Medicaid waiver program).

States using an **umbrella model** issue regulations for assisted living that cover two or more types of housing and services: residential care facilities, congregate housing, multi-unit or conventional elderly housing, adult family care, and assisted living. States representing this approach include Florida, Maine, Maryland, Louisiana, New Jersey, Maryland, New York, North Carolina, and Utah.

Discussion Question

Discuss the pros and cons of the different approaches to assisted living licensure described by Mollica. Should assisted living be regulated as a service(s) or a physical setting?

In addition to state regulation via licensure laws, the LTC ombudsmen agency in each state and the Adult Protective Services (APS) agency in most states investigate complaints or allegations of problems involving residents of assisted living facilities. Also, state consumer protection agencies are involved in regulating the accuracy of materials produced by assisted living facilities to market their services to the public. For further reading, see James E. Allen, Assisted Living Administration: The Knowledge Base, Springer Publishing Company: New York (1999); U.S. General Accounting Office, Assisted Living: Quality-of-Care and Consumer Protection Issues in Four States, GAO/HEHS-99-27 (1999), available at *www.gao.gov.*

Discussion Questions

1. Should the states regulate assisted living facilities? Under which of the approaches outlined above? What particular aspects of assisted living should be targeted in regulations? When assisted living facilities are cited for deficiencies currently, what would you suppose are the most common problem areas? In this context, are regulations likely to be protective or counterproductive? See Kitty Buckwalter, Cynthia Liebrock, and Pamela E. Klein, *Residential Care for Persons With Dementia: Are Codes and Regulations Protective or Counter-Productive?* Journal of Gerontological Nursing 43–47 (June 1996).

2. How can potential consumers be assisted to evaluate the marketing claims of assisted living providers?

Since mid-2000, CARF—The Rehabilitation Accreditation Commission—operates a voluntary accreditation program for assisted living facilities. Among other things, CARF surveyors check for conformance with standards pertaining to: assisted living's core values and mission; input from residents, families, and other stakeholders; disclosure of information; outcomes management; individual-centered planning, design, and delivery of services; residents' rights; and quality and appropriateness of services.

Discussion Questions

1. Is voluntary accreditation of assisted living facilities likely to be an effective quality assurance tool? Should CARF or some other private, non-profit entity be granted deemed status?

2. What kinds of expertise should be represented in a survey team that is accrediting assisted living facilities?

For additional reading, see William F. Lasky, *Growth and Development of the Assisted Living Industry,* 2 Elder's Advisor: Journal of Elder Law and Post-Retirement Planning 50–61 (Summer 2000).

REGULATION OF CONTINUING CARE RETIREMENT COMMUNITIES/LIFE CARE COMMUNITIES

One attempt to address the LTC needs of an aging population has been the development of Continuing Care Retirement Communities (CCRCs). The conventional CCRC is a physical plant (whose parts may run the gamut from high rise apartments to garden apartments to cottages to nursing facilities) that provides shelter and certain supportive, personal, and health services for as long as one remains in the CCRC, in return for a sizable entry fee plus monthly fees. The comprehensiveness of the bundle of services included in the pre-paid package varies among CCRCs; the most comprehensive plans, which include long-term skilled nursing care for no additional fees, are often termed *Life Care Communities.*

Discussion Questions

1. Why does the CCRC concept appeal to many older persons?

2. Besides the issue of affordability, what are some of the other potential concerns about which older persons should be counseled before committing to enter a CCRC? See H. Terri Brower, *Policy Implications for Life Care Environments,* 20 Journal of Gerontological Nursing 17–22 (1994).

3. In helping a person to review a CCRC admission contract before signing it, on what specific issues should one focus? What items would be included on the review checklist, regarding (among other things) services provided and financial responsibility for those services?

State regulation of CCRCs generally deals with three areas: consumer protection, the CCRC's financial stability, and quality of care provided by particular licensed units (e.g., skilled nursing facility care). CCRCs may seek voluntary accreditation from the Continuing Care Accreditation Commission (CCAC).

Discussion Question

What is the state's interest in regulating a CCRC's financial stability? When a consumer enters a CCRC, what is that consumer actually "buying"?

HOSPICE REGULATION

For a growing number and variety of terminally ill patients, care is being provided through hospices. Hospice care focuses on providing palliative and supportive services to the patient and family rather than aggressive medical intervention at the end of life. Hospice emphasis is placed on symptom control and preparation and support before and after death, with full-scope health services being provided by an organized interdisciplinary team on a full-time basis regardless of the patient's physical location.

The hospice movement entails several legal implications. First, individual health care professionals who provide hospice care are licensed directly by the state regardless of the specific setting in which they are working. In addition, hospice organizations themselves encounter many of the same types of legal issues that concern other institutional and agency health care providers. States require that hospices be licensed. See Ohio Rev. Code § 3712.

Hospices that wish to participate in the Medicare program must meet federal requirements. HCFA has published the *Medicare Hospice Manual*, Pub. No. 21, available at *www.hcfa.gov/ pubforms*. The DHHS OIG issued in 1999 a Compliance Guidance Program for Hospices regarding the development of voluntary compliance programs to avert fraud, abuse, and inefficiency in terms of the services for which the hospice bills the government, 64 Fed. Reg. 54031, available at *www.hhs.gov/progorg/oig/modcomp/hospic99*. The OIG identified a number of risk areas of specific concern to hospices:

- failure to obtain informed consent to elect the Medicare Hospice Benefit
- discriminatory admission practices
- improper arrangements with another health care provider that a hospice knows is submitting claims for services already covered by the Medicare Hospice Benefit
- underutilization
- falsifying medical records or plans of care
- untimely or forged physician certifications on plans of care
- inadequate or incomplete services rendered by the hospice's interdisciplinary group
- insufficient oversight of patients receiving more than 6 consecutive months of hospice
- hospice incentives to actual or potential referral sources that may violate antikickback or other fraud and abuse laws
- overlap in the services that a nursing home provides, resulting in insufficient care provided by a hospice to a nursing home resident
- improper relinquishment of core services and professional management responsibilities to nursing homes, volunteers, or privately paid professionals
- providing hospice services in a nursing home before a written agreement was finalized, if required
- billing for a higher level of services than is necessary
- knowingly billing for inadequate or substandard care
- inadequate justification in the medical record when a patient revokes the Medicare Hospice Benefit
- billing for hospice care provided by unqualified or unlicensed personnel
- falsely dating amendments to medical records
- high pressure marketing of hospice care to ineligible beneficiaries
- improper patient solicitation activities
- inadequate management of subcontracted services, which results in improper billing
- sales commissions based on a patient's length of stay in the hospice
- deficient coordination of volunteers
- improper indication in Medicare claim forms of the location where hospice services were delivered
- failure to comply with applicable requirements for verbal orders for hospice services

- nonresponse to late hospice referrals by physicians
- deliberate misuse of provider certification numbers
- failure to adhere to hospice licensing requirements and Medicare CoPs
- knowing failure to return overpayments made by federal health care programs

Discussion Questions

1. Why are the areas noted in the OIG Guidance particularly risky for hospices?

2. What strategies can hospices use to minimize these legal dangers?

3. Are laws attempting to prevent fraud and abuse really attempts to "legislate morality"? Can this be done effectively? Is this a proper role for the law? Aren't all laws in a sense attempts to legislate morality?

In addition to the formal legal requirements that a hospice must satisfy, it may apply for voluntary accreditation by the JCAHO under its hospice accreditation program. The American Board of Hospice and Palliative Medicine operates a Certification Program in Hospice and Palliative Medicine for physicians. The National Hospice and Palliative Care Organization, *www.nho.org,* has promulgated voluntary standards for hospice programs and the Hospice Association of America has developed and disseminated a Code of Ethics and a Hospice Patient's Bill of Rights for its members.

Discussion Question

Should any private organization be given deemed status for Medicare regarding hospice? Why or why not? Absent deemed status, what is the incentive for any hospice to comply with voluntary standards?

ADULT DAY CARE REGULATION

Adult day care refers to a variety of services and levels of care that are provided to older or disabled persons in a congregate setting for less than twenty-four hours per day. Licensure of adult day care programs is a matter of state option, e.g., Ohio Rev. Code § 3722.16. State laws vary regarding the specific services that a program may provide and the manner in which those services may be provided.

One especially controversial area is the administration of medication. Ohio Rev. Code § 3722.011:

> All medication taken by residents of an adult care facility shall be self-administered, except that medication may be administered to a resident by a home health agency, hospice care program, nursing home staff, mental health agency, or board of alcohol, drug addiction, and mental health services . . . Members of the staff of an adult care facility shall not administer medication to residents. No person shall be admitted to or retained by an adult care facility unless the person is capable of taking the person's own medication and biologicals, as determined in writing by the person's personal physician, except that a person may be admitted to or retained by such a facility if the person's medication is administered by a home health agency, hospice care program, nursing home staff, mental health agency, or board of alcohol, drug addiction, and mental health services . . . Members of the staff of an adult care facility may do any of the following:
>
> (A) Remind a resident when to take medication and watch to ensure that the resident follows the directions on the container;
>
> (B) Assist a resident in the self-administration of medication by taking the medication from the locked area where it is stored, . . . and handing it to the resident. If the resident is physically unable to open the container, a staff member may open the container for the resident.
>
> (C) Assist a physically impaired but mentally alert resident, such as a resident with arthritis, cerebral palsy, or Parkinson's disease, in removing oral or topical medication from containers and in consuming or applying the medication, upon request by or with the consent of the resident. If a resident is physically unable to place a dose of medicine to the resident's mouth without spilling it, a staff member may place the dose in a container and place the container to the mouth of the resident.

Discussion Question

Are these sorts of legal limitations on medication administration necessary and sensible, or do they just make the job of the adult day care program more difficult without really protecting the client? Do such legal restrictions unduly exclude from adult day care some older persons who might benefit from that service?

Adult Day Care programs may seek voluntary accreditation from CARF, the Rehabilitation Accreditation Commission, *www.carf.org*.

Discussion Questions:

1. What are the incentives and disincentives for adult day care programs to seek CARF accreditation?

2. On what aspects of Adult Day Care should regulators and private accrediting bodies place the most emphasis?

5

Confidentiality: Rights, Responsibilities, and Limits

THE DUTY OF CONFIDENTIALITY

As a general legal and ethical precept, health care and human service professionals have a duty to hold in confidence all personal patient/client information entrusted to them. The patient/client has a right to expect the fulfillment of that duty.

The American Medical Association's Principles of Medical Ethics provide:

> A physician shall respect the rights of patients, of colleagues, and of other health professionals, and shall safeguard patient confidences within the constraints of the law . . . The patient has the right to confidentiality. The physician should not reveal confidential communications or information without the consent of the patient, unless provided for by law or by the need to protect the welfare of the individual or the public interest.

The American Nurses Association's Code for Nurses With Interpretive Statements provides:

> The right to privacy is an inalienable human right. The client trusts the nurse to hold all information in confidence. This trust could be destroyed and the client's welfare jeopardized by injudicious disclosure of information provided in confidence. The duty of confidentiality, however, is not absolute when innocent parties are in direct jeopardy.

The National Association of Social Workers' Code of Ethics provides:

> Social workers should respect clients' right to privacy. Social workers should not solicit private information from clients unless it is essential to providing services or conducting social work evaluation or research. Once private information is shared, standards of confidentiality apply.

The American Psychological Association's Ethical Principles of Psychologists and Code of Conduct provide:

> Psychologists have a primary obligation and take reasonable precautions to respect the confidentiality rights of those with whom they work or consult, recognizing that confidentiality may be established by law, institutional rules, or professional or scientific relationships.

Discussion Questions

1. What are the rationales for the professional's confidentiality duty toward patients/clients? Are these rationales valid, both in theory and practice?

2. Do these rationales apply more or less forcefully when older individuals are involved? Why?

3. Why do we impose more demanding confidentiality duties on health and human service professionals than we do on others (e.g., hairdressers, electricians, grocers)?

Most state professional practice acts impose a duty of confidentiality. For example, the Illinois Medical Practice Act, IL. ST. CH. 225 s60/22, provides:

> (A) The [state] may revoke, suspend, place on probationary status, or take any other disciplinary action as [it] may deem proper with regard to the license . . . of any person issued under this Act to practice medicine . . . upon any of the following grounds: (30) Wilfully or negligently violating the confidentiality between physician and patient except as required by law.

Additionally, courts have allowed patients/clients to impose civil liability on health and human service professionals for violating their duty of confidentiality. As summarized in *McCormick v. England*, 328 S.C. 627, 494 S.E.2d 431 (1998):

The modern trend recognizes that the confidentiality of the physician-patient relationship is an interest worth protecting. A majority of the jurisdictions faced with the issue have recognized a cause of action against a physician for the unauthorized disclosure of confidential information unless the disclosure is compelled by law or is in the patient's interest or the public interest . . . In the absence of express legislation, courts have found the basis for a right of action for wrongful disclosure in four main sources: (1) state physician licensing statutes, (2) evidentiary rules and privileged communication statutes which prohibit a physician from testifying in judicial proceedings, (3) common law principles of trust, and (4) the Hippocratic Oath and principles of medical ethics which proscribe the revelation of patient confidences . . . The jurisdictions that recognize the duty of confidentiality have relied on various theories for the cause of action, including invasion of privacy, breach of implied contract, medical malpractice, and breach of a fiduciary duty or a duty of confidentiality. (Citations omitted)

Discussion Question

Do you agree that, unless there is an applicable exception, violation of confidentiality should be the basis for professional discipline? Should it be the basis for civil liability in lawsuits brought by patients/clients? Should the plaintiff have to demonstrate tangible damage or injury?

Some courts have held that the professional's obligation to maintain confidences is legally enforceable against employees of that professional, under the legal principle of *respondeat superior* (literally, "let the master answer"). According to *Hobbs v. Lopez*, 96 Ohio App.3d 670, 645 N.E.2d 1261 (1994):

The purpose of any privileged communication, whether between doctor and patient or attorney and client, is to ensure that the patient or client may reveal necessary information about his health or care without fear of such information reaching the wrong people . . . [O]ne would conclude that the privilege applied as well to a nurse acting as an agent for a doctor . . . [The nurse] was bound by the same obligation as [the employing physician] to keep [the patient's condition] in confidence. (citations omitted)

An important fact in *Hobbs* was that the nurse revealed the confidential information in a telephone call that the employer physician had instructed her to make. By contrast, some courts have refused to hold an employer liable for employees' improper disclosure of a patient's confidential information on the grounds that the employees were acting on their own. *Jones v. Baisch,* 40 F.3d 252 (8 Cir. 1994):

> We also reject [plaintiff's] argument that, in these circumstances, [we should] extend liability to [employer] defendants on the basis of respondeat superior for failure to maintain the confidentiality of [plaintiff's] medical records . . . [T]o recover under the doctrine of respondeat superior, a plaintiff must demonstrate that, at the time of the alleged tort, a master and servant relationship existed and that the servant was acting within the scope of his employment . . . The uncontroverted evidence shows that the [employees] were not acting within the scope of their employment when they disclosed [the plaintiff's] diagnosis. In their depositions, the [employees] testified that they were not authorized to reveal patients' medical records and that disclosure of Jones' condition did not occur substantially within the authorized work time and space limits. In fact, the employee handbook specifically forbade disclosures of patients' medical records, and, after learning of the disclosures, [the employer] reprimanded [the employees] and warned them against further disclosures. Moreover, it is clear that the unauthorized disclosures made by the [employees] were not actuated in any way by a purpose to serve their employer. (citations omitted)

Discussion Question

Are both *Hobbs* and *Jones* fair approaches to the confidentiality responsibility question? In *Hobbs,* is the employer being treated unfairly by being held liable for the acts of an employee? In *Jones,* is the plaintiff being unfairly deprived of the chance to sue a defendant (the employer) with deep enough financial pockets to rectify the injury suffered by the plaintiff?

NATIONAL CONFIDENTIALITY INITIATIVES

The whole area of medical privacy, especially regarding the information contained in medical records, is in a state of flux. On September 11, 1997, the U.S. Department of Health and Human Services (DHHS) submitted to Congress an 81-page report entitled *Confidentiality of Individually Identifiable Health Information,* calling for a national set of standards to replace—or at least supplement—the current patchwork (see *www.healthprivacy.org*) of state and federal statutes, regulations, and judicial rulings in this area:

We recommend that the traditional control on use and disclosure of information, the patient's written authorization, be replaced by comprehensive statutory controls on all who get health information for health care and payment purposes.

Discussion Question

What are the advantages and dangers of replacing the requirement of patient authorization with a set of national standards for release of health information? See Paul S. Appelbaum, *A Health Information Infrastructure and the Threat to Confidentiality of Health Records,* 49 Psychiatric Services 27–33 (1998).

On December 28, 2000, DHHS issued a Rule, 65 Fed. Reg. 82462-01, governing protection of individually identifiable health information, as required under the Administrative Simplification section of the Health Insurance Portability and Accountability Act, Public Law No. 104-191 (HIPAA). This rule attempted to provide for sharing of treatment and payment data, while limiting disclosure of the individual patient's information. This rule was withdrawn for further study when the Bush administration took office in January, 2001.

Discussion Question

Why does such a balance need to be struck? Who needs to have treatment and payment information about patients, and why? See Bernard Lo & Ann Alpers, *Uses and Abuses of Prescription Drug Information in Pharmacy Benefits Management Programs,* 283 Journal of the American Medical Association 801–806 (2000); U.S. General Accounting Office, Medicare: Improvements Needed to Enhance Protection of Confidential Health Information, GAO/HEHS-99-140 (1999).

As a general matter, the federal privacy rule would preempt state law that is contrary to the privacy rule.

Discussion Question

Is confidentiality regarding health and human services for older patients/clients a matter that ought to be dealt with under a uniform national law or by the individual states?

Voluntary, private national accrediting bodies impose standards on accredited service providers regarding the protection of patient/client privacy. See Joint Commission on Accreditation of Healthcare Organizations (JCAHO) and National Committee for Quality Assurance (NCQA), Protecting Personal Health Information: A Framework for Meeting the Challenges in a Managed Care Environment (1999), *www.jcaho.org* or *www.ncqa.org*.

EXCEPTIONS TO THE CONFIDENTIALITY DUTY

The duty of the health care or human service professional to maintain confidentiality of the patient/client's disclosure and records is not absolute. There are a variety of circumstances in which the professional is permitted, or even required, to reveal what would otherwise be confidential information.

Waiver

First, since it is the patient/client who owns the right of confidentiality, he or she may waive, or give up, that right as long as this is done in a voluntary, competent, and informed manner. A daily example of this is a patient/client giving authorization to release personal information to third-party payers or auditors, such as HCFA or a Medicare fiscal intermediary.

Discussion Questions

1. When patients/clients authorize release of personal information to third-party payers or auditors, how often is that waiver of confidentiality really informed and voluntary? Do most patients/clients actually know the content of their records that they are authorizing being released? What can health and human service professionals do to help assure that waivers of confidentiality are more informed and voluntary on the part of patients/clients?

2. Can a professional refuse to release information about a patient/client, even when the patient/client authorizes and requests the release of that information? On what grounds? For example, can a professional refuse a patient/client's request to release information to another professional until all outstanding balances for services rendered have been paid?

3. Should health and human service professionals assume that older patients/clients implicitly approve the sharing of information about them with involved family members? Should professionals require that such approval be explicit? If so, how should that explicit waiver of confidentiality be obtained and documented?

Mandatory or Permissive Reporting
Under Statute or Regulation

The expectation of confidentiality must yield when the health or human service professional is mandated or permitted by state law to report to specified public health authorities the existence of certain enumerated conditions known or reasonably suspected in their patients. Such provisions may be based on the state's inherent police power to protect and promote the health, safety and welfare of society as a whole. This rationale would support, for example, reporting requirements concerning infectious diseases or vital statistics (such as death) (regarding death reporting requirements, see chapter 7). Minnesota Stat. Ann. § 144.4808, for example, provides:

Subdivision 1. Mandatory reporting. A licensed health professional must report to the [health] commissioner or a disease prevention officer within 24 hours of obtaining knowledge of a reportable person as specified in subdivision 3, unless the licensed health professional is aware that the facts causing the person to be a reportable person have previously been reported . . .

Subdivision 2. Voluntary reporting. A person other than a licensed health professional may report to the commissioner or a disease prevention officer if the person has knowledge of a reportable person as specified in subdivision 3, or has probable cause to believe that a person should be reported under subdivision 3.

Subdivision 3. Reportable person. A licensed health professional must report to the commissioner or a disease prevention officer if the licensed health professional has knowledge of:

(1) a person who has been diagnosed with active tuberculosis;

(2) a person who is clinically suspected of having active tuberculosis;

(3) a person who refuses or fails to submit to a diagnostic tuberculosis examination when the person is clinically suspected of having tuberculosis;

(4) a carrier who has refused or failed to initiate or complete treatment for tuberculosis, including refusal or failure to take medication for tuberculosis to keep appointments for directly observed therapy or other treatment of tuberculosis; or

(5) a person who refuses or fails to follow contagion precautions for tuberculosis after being instructed on the precautions by a licensed health care professional or by the commissioner.

Subdivision 5. Immunity for reporting. A licensed health professional who is required to report under subdivision 1 or a person who voluntarily reports in good faith under subdivision 2 is immune from liability in a civil, administrative, disciplinary, or criminal action for reporting under this section.

Discussion Questions

1. How does a mandatory reporting statute such as this promote the state's police power interests?

2. Why are certain persons (i.e., health professionals) required to report, while other persons are only permitted—but not required—to report?

3. What arguments might be raised against such mandatory reporting requirements?

Alternatively to the police power, reporting of certain conditions may be mandated or allowed under the state's *parens patriae* power to beneficently protect those individuals who are unable and unwilling to care for their own needs. Mandatory and permissible reporting of elder abuse and neglect (see chapter 6) and other forms of suspected violence are justified on this ground.

Protecting Innocent Third Parties

Even absent a specific statute or regulation on point, courts may impose a common law requirement or recognize a common law right for a health or human service professional to violate a patient/client's confidentiality to protect innocent third parties from harm. In most jurisdictions, for instance, a professional is expected to report to the potential victim and to law enforcement officials an express threat made by a dangerously psychotic patient. See *Tarasoff v. Regents of the University of California,* 131 Cal. Rptr. 14, 551 P.2d 334 (1976).

Dangerous Driving

A number of states, either by statute or regulation or as a matter of common law, have spoken to the reporting obligations of a physician when a patient's driving abilities have become impaired by age-related neurodegenerative illness or sensory impairment. Some states expressly mandate physicians to report to drivers' licensing authorities a medical condition that might be hazardous to driving. California Health and Safety Code § 103900(a):

> Every physician and surgeon shall report immediately to the local health officer in writing, the name, date of birth, and address of every patient at least 14 years of age or older whom the physician and surgeon has diagnosed as having a case of a disorder characterized by lapses in consciousness. However, if a physician and surgeon reasonably and in good faith believes that the reporting of a patient will serve the public interest, he or she may report a patient's condition even if it may not be required under the department's definition of disorders characterized by lapses of consciousness . . .

Violation of a mandatory reporting requirement may lead to professional discipline. In some cases, it may also give rise to liability being imposed on the physician or other covered professional for injuries to third parties caused by the dangerous driver. However, a physician's failure to obey a mandatory reporting statute will not always make that physician civilly legally responsible for injuries suffered by a third party when the reporting statute is silent on this point. See *Estate of Witthoeft v. Kiskaddon,* 557 Pa. 340, 733 A.2d 623 (1999). California is the only state that specifically requires physicians to report all cases of diagnosed Alzheimer's disease and related disorders, Cal. Health & Safety Code § 103900(d).

Even in the absence of a mandatory reporting statute, some physicians have been held civilly liable under a common law negligence theory when they should have foreseen a patient's dangerous driving but did nothing effective to prevent it and the patient then harmed an innocent third party in a motor vehicle accident. Other cases, however, have declined to impose civil liability in such circumstances. See *Praesel v. Johnson,* 967 S.W.2d 391, 398 (Tex. 1998) ("The responsibility for safe operation of a vehicle should remain primarily with the driver who is capable of ascertaining whether it is lawful to continue to drive once a disorder such as epilepsy has been diagnosed and seizures have occurred.").

Discussion Questions

1. Should states impose a mandatory reporting obligation on physicians regarding dangerous drivers? What are the arguments for and against mandatory reporting laws in this area? Should the requirement to report be imposed on others besides physicians? On whom?

2. Do mandatory reporting laws in the driving ability arena discriminate unfairly against older persons?

3. Do you agree with California's approach of using the diagnosis of Alzheimer's disease as the trigger for mandatory reporting, without allowing or expecting the physician to consider whether the Alzheimer's disease impairs that particular patient's present driving ability? Why did the legislature single out Alzheimer's in this manner? See David B. Reuben & Peggy St. George, *Driving and Dementia: California's Approach to a Medical and Policy Dilemma,* 164 Western Journal of Medicine 111–121 (1996). Is this sort of approach likely to be effective in achieving its legitimate goals? See Richard A. Marottoli, *New Laws or Better Information and Communication?* 48 Journal of the American Geriatrics Society 100–102 (2000).

4. If a professional violates a mandatory reporting law and the patient/client then injures a third party in a motor vehicle accident, should the professional be civilly liable to the third party? Why or why not?

5. What proactive alternative or complementary strategies—legal, social, and technological—ought to be pursued to keep the roads safe while safeguarding the rights and interests of older persons with transportation needs?

American Medical Association, Code of Medical Ethics §2.24: Impaired Drivers and Their Physicians

The purpose of this report is to articulate physicians' responsibility to recognize impairments in patients' driving ability that pose a strong threat to public safety and which ultimately may need to be reported to the Department of Motor Vehicles. It does not address the reporting of medical information for the purpose of punishment or criminal prosecution.

1. Physicians should assess patients' physical or mental impairments that might adversely affect driving abilities. Each case must be evaluated individually since not all impairments may give rise to an obligation on the part of the physician. Nor may all physicians be in a

position to evaluate the extent or the effect of an impairment (e.g., physicians who treat patients on a short-term basis). In making evaluations, physicians should consider the following factors:

   a) the physician must be able to identify and document physical or mental impairments that clearly relate to the ability to drive;

   b) the driver must pose a clear risk to public safety.

   2. Before reporting, there are a number of initial steps physicians should take. A tactful but candid discussion with the patient and family about the risks of driving is of primary importance. Depending on the patient's medical condition, the physician may suggest to the patient that he or she seek further treatment, such as substance abuse treatment or occupational therapy. Physicians also may encourage the patient and the family to decide on a restricted driving schedule. Efforts made by physicians to inform patients and their families, advise them of their options, and negotiate a workable plan may render reporting unnecessary.

   3. Physicians should use their best judgment when determining when to report impairments that could limit a patient's ability to drive safely. In situations where clear evidence of substantial driving impairment implies a strong threat to patient and public safety, and where the physician's advice to discontinue driving privileges is ignored, it is desirable and ethical to notify the Department of Motor Vehicles.

   4. The physician's role is to report medical conditions that would impair safe driving as dictated by his or her state's mandatory reporting laws and standards of medical practice. The determination of the inability to drive safely should be made by the state's Department of Motor Vehicles.

   5. Physicians should disclose and explain to their patients this responsibility to report.

   6. Physicians should protect patient confidentiality by ensuring that only the minimal amount of information is reported and that reasonable security measures are used in handling that information.

   7. Physicians should work with their state medical societies to create statutes that uphold the best interests of patients and community, and that safeguard physicians from liability when reporting in good faith.

Information Compelled by Legal Process

When information is requested about a patient/client in the context of litigation, ordinarily the health care or human service professional is precluded from providing that information. A variety of specific state statutes create testimonial privileges between a patient/client and professionals with whom they have a relationship.

Ohio Revised Code § 2317.02

> The following persons shall not testify in certain respects:
> (A) An attorney, concerning a communication made to the attorney by a client in that relation or the attorney's advice to a client . . .
> (B) A physician or a dentist concerning a communication made to the physician or dentist by a patient in that relation or the physician's or dentist's advice to a patient . . .
> (C) A member of the clergy, rabbi, priest, or regularly ordained, accredited, or licensed minister of an established and legally cognizable church, denomination, or sect . . . concerning a confession made, or any information confidentially communicated, to the member of the clergy, rabbi, priest, or minister for a religious counseling purpose in the member of the clergy's, rabbi's, priest's, or minister's professional character . . .

Discussion Questions

1. Why would a legislature create testimonial privileges like these? What are the underlying policy justifications? Are these justifications valid?

2. Different legislatures have created statutory privileges pertaining to different categories of professionals. Which professionals ought to be covered by a testimonial privilege statute?

Health care and human service professionals may be allowed, or even compelled, to reveal otherwise privileged information when the patient/client consents to or requests such release. Revelation also may be required by the force of legal process, that is, by a judge's order requiring such information release. This may occur when the patient/client has placed issues pertaining to her health or care in issue in the litigation, when the communication to the professional was done in the presence of a third party (and therefore done without a reasonable expectation of privacy), or the public welfare need for the information outweighs the individual's right to confidentiality in the particular case.

Discussion Question

Give examples of cases in which a health or human services professional might be compelled by the court to reveal information about an older patient/client despite the existence of a testimonial privilege statute.

In understanding legal process, it is crucial to distinguish between a subpoena and a court order. A subpoena is a directive from the clerk of a court, issued at the request of an attorney in the case, for an individual to appear at a specific time and place for the purpose of giving sworn testimony. A subpoena *duces tecum* directs one to bring certain identified tangible items, such as medical records, at the time of testimony. A subpoena may not be ignored, but it may be challenged legally; the court may quash the subpoena if it runs afoul of an applicable testimonial privilege statute. It is only if the judge rejects the challenge to the subpoena and orders disclosure over the objection of the patient/client (or the patient/client has been notified about the subpoena and declines to challenge it) that the professional is obligated to comply. Noncompliance with a judge's order constitutes contempt of court and is criminally and civilly punishable.

Allen v. Smith, 179 W.Va. 360, 368 S.E.2d 924 (1988):

> Dr. Smith argues here that his release of Mrs. Allen's medical records were pursuant to a valid court order [because he was responding to a subpoena *duces tecum*]. Nothing, however, could be farther from the truth. A subpoena is issued automatically by a clerk of court upon the ex parte [i.e., without the involvement of the other side] application of one party litigant. Although a subpoena is enforceable through the court's power of contempt until it has been quashed by regular, in-court proceedings, a bare subpoena is not the type of binding court order contemplated by [the testimonial privilege statute].

Discussion Question

If you are served with a subpoena to testify and/or produce your records in a lawsuit about a patient/client, how should you respond?

Rost v. Board of Psychology, 659 A.2d 626, 629 (Pa. 1995):

> In the present case, [the psychologist defendant] did not even attempt to obtain the consent of her client before releasing confidential information [in response to a subpoena]. Although [the client] was eventually found to have waived the psychologist-client privilege, this does not absolve [the psychologist] from her ethical duty of confidentiality. [The psychologist] had a duty to either obtain written permission to release the records from [the client] or challenge the propriety of the subpoena before a judge.
>
> [This psychologist] did neither. Instead, she unilaterally gave [the client's] records to [the requesting party] without consulting with [the client] or her attorney.

6

Family Law Issues and Older Persons

GRANDPARENTS' RIGHTS

Grandparents' Visitation Rights

All fifty states have statutes that provide for grandparent visitation of minor grandchildren in some form. See Ala. Code §30-3-4.1 (1989); Alaska Stat. Ann. §25.20.065 (1998); Ariz. Rev. Stat. Ann. §25-409 (1994); Ark. Code Ann. §9-13-103 (1998); Cal. Fam. Code Ann. §3104 (West 1994); Colo. Rev. Stat. §19-1-117 (1999); Conn. Gen. Stat. §46b-59 (1995); Del. Code Ann., Tit. 10, §1031(7) (1999); Fla. Stat. §752.01 (1997); Ga. Code Ann. §19-7-3 (1991); Haw. Rev. Stat. §571-46.3 (1999); Idaho Code §32-719 (1999); Ill. Comp. Stat., ch. 750, §5/607 (1998); Ind. Code §31-17-5-1 (1999); Iowa Code §598.35 (1999); Kan. Stat. Ann. §38-129 (1993); Ky. Rev. Stat. Ann. §405.021 (Baldwin 1990); La. Rev. Stat. Ann. §9:344 (West Supp. 2000); La. Civ. Code Ann., Art. 136 (West Supp. 2000); Me. Rev. Stat. Ann., Tit. 19A §1803 (1998); Md. Fam. Law Code Ann. §9-102 (1999); Mass. Gen. Laws §119:39D (1996); Mich. Comp. Laws Ann. §722.27b (Supp. 1999); Minn. Stat. §257.022 (1998); Miss. Code Ann. §93-16-3 (1994); Mo. Rev. Stat. §452.402 (Supp. 1999); Mont. Code Ann. §40-9-102 (1997); Neb. Rev. Stat. §43-1802 (1998); Nev. Rev. Stat. §125C.050 (Supp. 1999); N.H. Rev. Stat. Ann. §458:17-d (1992); N.J. Stat. Ann. §9:2-7.1 (West Supp. 1999-2000); N.M. Stat. Ann. §40-9-2 (1999); N.Y. Dom. Rel. Law §72 (McKinney 1999); N.C. Gen. Stat. §§50-13.2, 50-13.2A (1999); N.D. Cent. Code §14-09-

05.1 (1997); Ohio Rev. Code Ann. §§3109.051, 3109.11 (Supp. 1999); Okla. Stat., Tit. 10, §5 (Supp. 1999); Ore. Rev. Stat. §109.121 (1997); 23 Pa. Cons. Stat. §§5311-5313 (1991); R.I. Gen. Laws §§15-5-24 to 15-5-24.3 (Supp. 1999); S.C. Code Ann. §20-7-420(33) (Supp. 1999); S.D. Codified Laws §25-4-52 (1999); Tenn. Code Ann. §§36-6-306, 36-6-307 (Supp. 1999); Tex. Fam. Code Ann. §153.433 (Supp. 2000) ; Utah Code Ann. §30-5-2 (1998); Vt. Stat. Ann., Tit. 15, §§1011-1013 (1989); Va. Code Ann. §20-124.2 (1995); W. Va. Code §§48-2B-1 to 48-2B-7 (1999); Wis. Stat. §§767.245, 880.155 (1993-1994); Wyo. Stat. Ann. §20-7-101 (1999).

The state legislatures' authority to enact these statutes is included within the *parens patriae* power of the states, in appropriate circumstances, to regulate "the family itself . . . in the public interest." *Prince v. Massachusetts,* 321 U.S. 158, 166 (1944).

Discussion Questions

Even if states have the legal authority to intervene in the area of grandparents' visitation rights, why should a state legislature exercise that power? What are the policy justifications for a state to legislatively intervene in this arena? See Bernadette W. Hartfield, *Legal Recognition of the Value of Intergenerational Nurturance: Grandparent Visitation Statutes in the Nineties,* XX Generations 53–56 (Spring 1996).

The states' authority in this arena is not unlimited. In *Troxel v. Granville,* 120 S. Ct. 2054 (2000), the U.S. Supreme Court dealt with the validity of Washington's grandparent visitation statute in the context of a dispute between the paternal grandparents and the minor children's mother.

> The Fourteenth Amendment provides that no State shall "deprive any person of life, liberty, or property, without due process of law." . . .
> The liberty interest at issue in this case—the interest of parents in the care, custody, and control of their children—is perhaps the oldest of the fundamental liberty interests recognized by this Court.
> ***
> Section 26.10.160(3) [of Washington Statutes], as applied to Granville and her family in this case, unconstitutionally infringes on that fundamental parental right. The Washington nonparental visitation statute is breathtakingly broad. According to the statute's text, "*[a]ny person* may petition the court for visitation rights at *any time,*" and the court may grant such visitation rights whenever "visitation may serve *the best interest of the child.*" §26.10.160(3) (emphases added).
> ***

As we have explained, the Due Process Clause does not permit a State to infringe on the fundamental right of parents to make child-rearing decisions simply because a state judge believes a "better" decision could be made. Neither the Washington nonparental visitation statute generally—which places no limits on either the persons who may petition for visitation or the circumstances in which such a petition may be granted—nor the Superior Court in this specific case required anything more. Accordingly, we hold that §26.10.160(3), as applied in this case, is unconstitutional.

Because we rest our decision on the sweeping breadth of §26.10.160(3) and the application of that broad, unlimited power in this case, we do not consider the primary constitutional question passed on by the Washington Supreme Court—whether the Due Process Clause requires all nonparental visitation statutes to include a showing of harm or potential harm to the child as a condition precedent to granting visitation. We do not, and need not, define today the precise scope of the parental due process right in the visitation context. In this respect, we agree . . . that the constitutionality of any standard for awarding visitation turns on the specific manner in which that standard is applied and that the constitutional protections in this area are best elaborated with care.

Discussion Questions

1. Do you agree that a parent's right to control who has visits with her child ought to be treated as a "fundamental liberty interest" under the Constitution? Where, specifically, is this right enumerated in the Constitution? See dissenting opinions of Justices Thomas and Scalia in *Troxel*.

2. The majority opinion in *Troxel* found fault with the broadness of the Washington statute. Examine your own state's statute on grandparents' visitation rights and analyze whether it, too, is written in overly broad language that could not now pass constitutional muster. Could your state's statute be interpreted more narrowly, such that it might be constitutionally acceptable?

Medical Authority

The demographic changes of the past century make it difficult to speak of an average American family. The composition of families varies greatly from household to household. While many children may have two married parents and grandparents who visit regularly, many other children are raised in single-parent households. In 1996, children living with only one parent accounted for 28 percent of all children under age 18 in the United States . . . Understandably, in these single-parent households, persons outside the nuclear family are called upon with increasing frequency to assist in the everyday tasks of child rearing. In many cases, grandparents play an important role. (Citations omitted)

Troxel v. Granville, 120 S. Ct. 2054 (2000). One aspect of assisting in the everyday tasks of child rearing is making decisions about the child's medical care. Several states explicitly give grandparents the authority, under certain circumstances, to make medical decisions on behalf of their minor grandchildren even when the grandparents have not been appointed their grandchildren's guardian. California Family Code § 6550:

> (a) A caregiver's authorization affidavit that meets the requirements of this part authorizes a caregiver 18 years of age or older who completes items 1–4 of the affidavit provided in Section 6552 and signs the affidavit to enroll a minor in school and consent to school-related medical care on behalf of the minor. A caregiver who is a relative and who completes items 1–8 of the affidavit provided in Section 6552 and signs the affidavit shall have the same rights to authorize medical care and dental care for the minor that are given to guardians under Section 2353 of the Probate Code. The medical care authorized by this caregiver who is a relative may include mental health treatment . . .

Florida Statutes § 743.0645:

> (2) Any of the following persons, in order of priority listed, may consent to the medical care or treatment of a minor . . . when, after a reasonable attempt, a person who has the power to consent as otherwise provided by law cannot be contacted by the treatment provider and actual notice to the contrary has not been given to the provider by that person:
>
> ***
>
> (c) The grandparent of the minor.

Discussion Questions

1. Are statutes empowering grandparents to make medical decisions for their grandchildren advisable? What are some of the

dangers raised by such laws? How can those dangers be averted or minimized?

2. Some statutes empowering grandparents as medical decision makers for their grandchildren, such as D.C. Code § 16-4901, depend on the parent signing a form giving the grandparents that decision making authority; in other statutes, such as the California and Florida statutes quoted above, parental consent is not required. Which approach is better, and why?

FAMILY ROLES VIS-À-VIS THE OLDER PERSON

The Family as Decisionmaker

Marshall B. Kapp, *Ethical, Legal, and Financial Issues in Family Caregiving,* in Family Caregiving—Agenda for the Future (Marjorie H. Cantor, ed.), San Francisco: American Society on Aging (1994), pp. 137–144:

> Numerous . . . decisions arise in the (often extended) course of homecare for a disabled person. Family caregivers may be involved in the . . . decision-making process in several ways.
>
> For an older person who retains adequate cognitive capacity to function as an autonomous decision-maker, the caregiver may provide essential emotional or logistical support and empowerment, enabling or assisting the client's consent to or refusal of . . . intervention. Family "support," though, can easily turn into subtle or sometimes overt coercion, with . . . providers tending to go along with the family's wishes even where the client's own authentic choice is unclear. Thus, the family's ethical commitment to their relative's right of self-determination is central, particularly since the law really has neither a solid theoretical foundation nor practical instruments for dealing with the phenomenon of shared . . . decision-making.
>
> For cognitively incapacitated persons, there exists a longstanding ethical and legal presumption in favor of the family as the most appropriate surrogate decision-maker. Family members qua . . . proxies may make many different kinds of . . . decisions, including those about when it is necessary to move the client and his or her care into formal environments. While routine court involvement in prospectively affirming or retrospectively reviewing family decision-making ought to be soundly disfavored as a matter of public policy, the judiciary does need to remain available for the unusual instance where such involvement is indicated. (Citations omitted)

Marshall B. Kapp, *Health Care Decision Making by the Elderly: I Get by with a Little Help from My Family*, 31 Gerontologist 619–623 (1991):

. . . Where the older person is decisionally incapacitated, either in law (de jure) or in fact (de facto), a great deal of energy has been devoted to the topic of surrogate decision making on the patient's behalf . . . Legal doctrines and mechanisms of surrogate decision making have been developed to implement the ethical principles of autonomy and beneficence; these include advance planning devices, principally living wills and durable powers of attorney, family consent statutes, substituted judgment, and the best interests standard.

We need to devote much more attention, though, both theoretical and practical, to the ethical and legal issues that are implicated not when decisional power transfers from the mentally incapacitated patient to a proxy, but rather when mentally capable older persons work together with their families (taking the term in a very broad sense) at shared health care decision making. Decisional capacity refers to a minimal level of current functional ability and many older persons who meet the minimal criteria, and therefore are not candidates for surrogate decision makers, nonetheless want and can benefit from some family assistance in making difficult health care choices.

Indeed, a substantial body of empirical data clearly establishes that, in the real world, older mentally capable patients do not behave as lone, isolated, atomistic agents, but rather rely heavily on family members, particularly daughters and daughters-in-law, for assistance in medical decision making. The process of health care decision making for many older people is an excellent paradigm of the interdependence between generations.

As we think about this paradigm and its application to the health care decision-making process, we ought to consider that the autonomy model of a lone individual defending his or her choices against adversarial intervenors armed with high technology medical weapons stems chiefly from experience in acute care settings from which the patient can walk or be carried away. Different models of autonomy that are more balanced and empirically predicated, such as the concept of 'negotiated consent,' have begun to emerge recently from long-term care experience. These newer models for accommodating to indeterminately ongoing situations may contribute to our understanding of shared decision making regardless of specific care environment.

***

There are several problems associated with expecting law and the legal system to be really useful in dealing with the ethical issues implicated by the concept of shared health care decision making between older persons and their families.

Chief among the law's shortcomings in this regard is its bluntness as an instrument that tends to dissect the world in terms of adversarial disputes with zero-sum, either/or, winner/loser resolutions. This property of the legal system is the very reason that parties bring their problems to the courts-not because litigants want wisdom but because they desire definitive answers to their disagreements. Health care providers caring for older patients have a legitimate thirst for reasonable legal certainty concerning questions such as who has the legal authority to make valid health care decisions permitting specific interventions and assuming foreseeable risks, to receive medical information about the patient, to claim or waive the right of confidentiality regarding the patient's medical information, and to commit himself or herself to responsibility for paying the bill for services provided. The legal risks entailed in treating older patients in the absence of total clarity on these points about decisional authority are probably greatly exaggerated, since treatment occurs regularly within legal "gray zones," but a desire for some certainty of rights and obligations on the part of health professionals is understandable.

These legal issues and the legal system that we have to address them do not lend themselves easily to the psychosocial, interpersonal dynamics of shared decision making between older patients and their families, with its many delicate nuances and subtleties. As Joel Handler has noted perceptively, the law generally deals poorly with continuing relationships or processes; it ordinarily gets involved either in discrete, contained transactions between parties to a relationship or in repairing the damage when a relationship has broken down. While the law pretends there is a neat, precise distinction between self and others, Jecker instead finds in the real world a pattern of intimate moral relationships that enables autonomy to flourish.

The American legal system needs to accommodate better the reality of shared decision making by developing for medical decision-making purposes some workable analogue to joint banking accounts, joint tenancy, tenancy in common, and other legal devices that have been in use for hundreds of years in matters pertaining to real and personal property. Perhaps some kind of "joint medical consent account" could be established between patient, designated family member, and health care provider. Under this arrangement, the participants could agree in advance that future health care decisions affecting the patient may be made in a binding manner, while the patient retains mental capacity, only upon joint consent of the patient and the designated family member. Conversely, future decisions could be made upon the permission of either the patient or the designated family member. Our treatment of individual rights lags conceptually and operationally far behind our treatment of property rights in this regard.

Additionally, the expectations and guidelines for each patient/family/professional relationship should be discussed explicitly, defined clearly, and documented in the patient's record by the health care professional at the outset of the relationship, in terms of authority for decision making and information sharing. Patient preferences concerning family involvement should not be taken for granted, in one direction or the other. The patient and family should be consulted about their assumptions and desires. Health care providers must resist the tendency to defer too readily to the family's expressed wishes because of an overblown, free-floating apprehension about the family as a potential plaintiff who will be around to initiate any future legal action against the provider.

This clarifying discussion can be analogous to, or a part of the same process as, the discussion that should be occurring between patient, family, and provider about advance health care planning to prepare for the patient's eventual incapacity and the need for a surrogate decision maker. As with advance planning, provider dialogue with the patient and family about shared decision making should not be a single event, but instead should be an ongoing, dynamic process, especially as the patient becomes more dependent but not yet decisionally incapacitated. As in other areas, the health care provider's best legal-risk management strategy is thorough discussion with all appropriate players and timely, complete, accurate documentation of both the process and outcome of the discussion.

***

Ideally, and most of the time in practice, older individuals are not islands when it comes to making important health care decisions. The majority of older persons get by in this context not solely by themselves, but with a little help from their families. Nothing in this analysis should be read to undercut the primacy of individual autonomy; instead, the considerations enumerated are intended to help facilitate and effectuate the older patient's self-determination by supporting and buttressing it. Ethical principles that strongly support a process of shared or assisted decision making for older patients have not been artfully articulated, and certain ethical caveats await deeper exploration. New legal concepts need to be developed to accommodate the nuances and subtleties implicated when decisional autonomy concerning personal matters is shared rather than exercised exclusively or delegated completely to an agent. (Citations omitted)

Discussion Questions

1. Do you agree with the description presented above of the family's role in decision making? Should the family's role and authority be more formalized than it normally is? What role, if any, should the law play in the process of empowering and/or monitoring shared or informally delegated decision making? What are the presumptions that we should make about family behavior in the decision making context?

2. How can families be supported in their decision making role, without unduly infringing on the older person's autonomy? How can we enhance positive family involvement and keep it from becoming coercive or paternalistic? See Marshall B. Kapp, *Who's the Parent Here? The Family's Impact on the Autonomy of Older Persons,* 41 Emory Law Journal 773–803 (1992).

Family Caregiving

An individual who serves as the primary caregiver for a disabled family member in the home is protected against discrimination under the Americans With Disabilities Act (ADA), 28 C.F.R. § 36.205:

> A public accommodation shall not exclude or otherwise deny equal goods, services, facilities, privileges, advantages, accommodations, or other opportunities to an individual or entity because of the known disability of an individual with whom the individual or entity is known to have a relationship or association.

Discussion Questions

1. Can an employer fire an employee who is caring for an aged relative at home in order to try to relieve the employee of job stress? Could the employer fire or discipline that employee for absenteeism associated with the employee's caregiving responsibilities? For diminished job performance associated with the employee's caregiving responsibilities?

2. Is an employer legally required under the ADA to accommodate family caregivers with requested time off? On a paid or unpaid basis? See the federal Family and Medical Leave Act, 28 U.S.C. § 2601 *et. seq.,* allowing twelve weeks of unpaid leave at employers with fifty or more employees. Does the ADA require employers to accommodate requests from family caregivers for schedule changes?

Family care giving in the home environment raises a host of additional medical-legal and public policy ramifications. See Marshall B. Kapp, *Family Care Giving for Older Persons in the Home: Medical-Legal Implications,* 16 Journal of Legal Medicine 1–31 (1995); Marshall B. Kapp, *Legal and Ethical Issues in Family Care Giving and the Role of Public Policy,* 12 Home Health Care Services Quarterly 5–28 (1991).

Discussion Question

From a legal liability perspective, what aspects of family care giving are most worrisome to formal service providers who are involved in the older person's care plan? Why are these aspects worrisome? What actions should formal providers take in a positive risk management mode to address these concerns?

Family Financial Responsibility

Approximately thirty states have current family or filial responsibility statutes imposing a duty on adult children to provide financial assistance to indigent parents. Massachusetts Code chapter 273, § 20:

> Any person, over eighteen, who, being possessed of sufficient means, unreasonably neglects or refuses to provide for the support and maintenance of his parent, whether father or mother, residing in the commonwealth, when such parent through misfortune and without fault of his own is destitute of means of sustenance and unable by reason of old age, infirmity or illness to support and maintain himself, shall be punished by a fine of not more than two hundred dollars or by imprisonment for not more than one year, or both. No such neglect or refusal shall be deemed unreasonable as to a child who shall not during his minority have been reasonably supported by such parent, if such parent was charged with the duty so to do, nor as to a child who, being one of two or more children, has made proper and reasonable contribution toward the support of such parent.

Kentucky Revised Statutes § 530.050 (4):

> Any person who is eighteen (18) years of age or over, residing in this state and having in this state a parent who is destitute of means of subsistence and unable because of old age, infirmity, or illness to support himself or herself, has a duty to provide support for such parent and, for purposes of this section, is presumed to know of that duty.

Discussion Question

The quoted Massachusetts statute only imposes a financial duty on children who were themselves reasonably supported as minors by their parents; in other words, their duty is to reciprocate for what their parents earlier did for them. The Kentucky statute makes the duty of the adult children to support their parents unconditional, rather than reciprocal. Which approach represents better public policy?

Some of these family responsibility statutes have been challenged on the grounds (among others) that they violate the federal Constitution's 14th Amendment mandate of Equal Protection of the law and the Constitution's prohibition against government "taking" property from individuals without just compensation. The courts have upheld the validity of these statutes against constitutional attacks. *Americana Health Care Center v. Randall,* 513 N.W.2d 566, 572-573 (S.D. 1994):

> The fact that an indigent parent has supported and cared for a child during that child's minority provides an adequate basis for imposing a [legal] duty on the child to support that parent . . . [I]t logically follows that the adult child should bear the burden of reciprocating on that benefit in the event a parent needs support in their later years.

Discussion Question

1. What are the ethical and public policy arguments in favor of state family responsibility statutes? What are the arguments against such statutes?

2. Practically speaking, family responsibility statutes tend not to be enforced very vigorously or effectively. What are the practical barriers to vigorous, effective enforcement of these statutes? Can, and should, these barriers be overcome?

3. What would be the likely social implications of more vigorous enforcement of family responsibility statutes, including effects on family dynamics? For insight into another country's experience, see Peter Waldman, *In Singapore, Mother of All Lawsuits is Often Filed by Mom: Act to Protect Aging Parents from Neglect Spurs Rash of Intrafamily Litigation,* Wall Street Journal A1 (September 17, 1996).

4. What different policy strategies might be pursued to address the problems posed by indigent older persons in the U.S.?

See Robin M. Jacobson, *Americana Healthcare Center v. Randall: The Renaissance of Filial Responsibility,* 40 South Dakota Law Review 518–545 (1995).

ELDER ABUSE AND NEGLECT

Definitions

According to a position paper on elder mistreatment published by the American Medical Association:

> Abuse shall mean an act or omission which results in harm or threatened harm to the health or welfare of an elderly person. Abuse includes intentional infliction of physical or mental injury; sexual abuse; or withholding of necessary food, clothing, and medical care to meet the physical and mental needs of an elderly person by one having the care, custody or responsibility of an elderly person.

AMA Council on Scientific Affairs, *Elder Abuse and Neglect,* 257 Journal of the American Medical Association 966–971 (1987).

Under the federal Older Americans Act (OAA)

> Abuse is the willful infliction of injury, unreasonable confinement, intimidation, or cruel punishment with resulting physical harm, pain, or mental anguish; or deprivation by . . . a care giver of goods or services . . . necessary to avoid physical harm, mental anguish, or mental illness. 42 U.S.C. § 3002(13)(A-B)
>
> Neglect is the failure to provide for oneself goods or services necessary to avoid physical harm, mental anguish, or mental illness . . . [or the] failure of a caretaker to provide such goods or services. 42 U.S.C. § 3002(37)(A-B)
>
> Exploitation means the illegal or improper act or process of an individual, including a care giver, using the resources of an older individual for monetary or personal benefit, profit, or gain. 42 U.S.C. § 3002(26).

Every state has enacted a statute that includes relevant definitions. North Dakota Code 50-25.2-01 (1):

> Abuse means any willful act or omission of a care giver . . . which results in . . . mental anguish.

Nevada Revised Statutes 41.1395(4)(a)(1):

Abuse means willful and unjustified infliction of pain, injury, or mental anguish . . .

Mississippi Code Annotated 43-47-5(i):

Exploitation shall mean the illegal or improper use of a vulnerable adult or his resources for another's profit or advantage.

Discussion Questions

1. Which of these definitions are most useful in sorting out conduct which is abusive, neglectful, or exploitative from that which is not? Are some definitions too broad and all-inclusive? Are some too narrow?

2. What are the various forms that abuse, neglect, and exploitation may take?

3. The majority of states include self-neglect as a category of elder mistreatment. Is this appropriate, or does it amount to unwanted paternalism on the part of government? See Carmel Dyer & Angela M. Goins, *The Role of the Interdisciplinary Geriatric Assessment in Addressing Self-Neglect of the Elderly*, XXIV Generations 23–27 (Summer 2000).

4. Which, if any, of the following examples constitute abuse or neglect under the legal definitions cited above:

a. A family asks a physician to administer, for the purpose of controlling (i.e., restraining) the undesirable behavior (e.g., constant physical moving around, shouting outbursts, and fighting with family members) of an agitated, demented elder being cared for in the home.

b. A physician prescribes, and a home care nurse or nurse's aide applies and monitors, a Posey vest for a home care client in order to make the client more physically manageable for the professionals and family members providing care and, at least purportedly, to protect the client from injurious falls and other movement-associated accidents.

c. The family, feeling physically and psychologically stretched to the endurance limit by the constant stress of informal care giving, purchases on its own (with a physician's prescription) from a supplier mechanical restraining devices such as a Posey vest, leg and arm straps, or soft ties, and applies those restraints to the older person being cared for in the home.

d. All the members of the care giving family work during the day, and to prevent the demented individual from wandering away or harming himself while they are gone, they lock him in one room when no one else is present in the home.

Marshall B. Kapp, *Restraining Impaired Elders in the Home Environment*, 4 Journal of Case Management 54–59 (1995).

Criminalizing Elder Abuse

Almost every state has enacted a statute explicitly imposing criminal liability for willful acts or omissions amounting to elder mistreatment. Some states make elder mistreatment a misdemeanor, e.g., Utah Code § 76-5-111, while others classify this conduct more seriously as a felony, e.g., Nevada Revised Statutes § 200.5099. A few state statutes do not specifically deal with the question of punishment for violation, e.g., Alaska Statutes § 47.24.010-47.24.900. The criminal statutes typically apply to the older person's "care giver" and others. Alaska Statutes § 47.24.900(3)(A):

> Care giver means a person who is providing care to a vulnerable adult as a result of a family relationship, or who has assumed responsibility for the care of a vulnerable adult voluntarily, by contract, or by court order.

Mistreatment of older persons also violates generic assault and battery criminal statutes in every jurisdiction.

Discussion Questions

1. Do you agree with the definition of "caregiver" in the quoted statute? Are there other people you would add to this definition?

2. Is exposing the care giver to criminal liability the best way to assure proper treatment for vulnerable adults? What does this approach actually accomplish? What alternative strategies exist? See Lori A. Stiegel, *The Changing Role of the Courts in Elder-Abuse Cases*, XXIV Generations 59–64 (Summer 2000). Courts have the authority to issue civil protective or restraining orders or injunctions ordering the wrongdoer to discontinue the mistreatment; are such orders likely to be effective? Of how much practical value is the victim's right to sue the perpetrator civilly for monetary damages likely to be

in most cases? How sophisticated are most judges regarding the subject of elder mistreatment, and what can be done to educate them? See Lori A. Stiegel, Elder Abuse in the State Courts—Three Curricula for Judges and Court Staff, Washington, DC: American Bar Association (1997).

3. What is the potential impact of criminal liability statutes on family dynamics? Are criminal liability statutes likely to exert the unintended consequence of discouraging family members from taking on the care giver role?

4. Should the older adult's acquiescence to the way he or she is (mis)treated carry weight as a defense to a charge of elder mistreatment? Can one "consent" to be the victim of elder mistreatment? Why do many older persons not cooperate in the reporting and investigation of abuse and neglect? If legal intervention is undertaken over the alleged victim's objection, is such intervention unduly paternalistic?

State statutes differ in their specification of who qualifies for protection under mistreatment statutes. In some states, all "vulnerable," "disabled," or "incapacitated" adults are protected, regardless of age. Elsewhere, only persons over a designated age—usually 60 or 65—are covered.

Discussion Question

Which of these approaches do you support, and why? Is it in the best interests of older persons to be singled out for special protection?

Reporting Requirements

The vast majority of states have enacted statutes mandating a wide variety of professionals to report known or suspected cases of elder mistreatment to designated public bodies, ordinarily local Adult Protective Services (APS) agencies, Elizabeth Capezuti, Barbara L. Brush, & William T. Lawson, *Reporting Elder Mistreatment*, 23 Journal of Gerontological Nursing 24–32 (July 1997), or law enforcement agencies, for further investigation. Alabama Code § 38-9-8(a):

> All physicians and other practitioners of the healing arts having reasonable cause to believe that any adult protected under the provisions of this chapter has been subjected to physical abuse, neglect, or exploitation shall report or cause a report to be made . . .

Arkansas Code § 5-28-203(a)(1):

> Whenever any physician . . . registered nurse, hospital personnel . . .
> social worker . . . mental health professional, . . . has reasonable cause
> to suspect that an endangered adult has been subjected to . . . abuse . . .
> he shall immediately report or cause a report to be made in accor-
> dance with the provisions of this section.

Several of these statutes extend the duty to report to "any person."
These mandatory reporting statutes make non-compliance punishable as a criminal misdemeanor.

A few states make the reporting of elder mistreatment voluntary,
by keeping reporters' identities confidential and immunizing
reporters against any legal liability if they make reports, but not
punishing nonreporting. Illinois Statutes ch. 320, para. 20/4 (a):

> Any person wishing to report a case of alleged or suspected abuse or
> neglect may make such a report . . .

Discussion Questions:

1. What assumptions about the various actors underlie the enactment of state reporting statutes and form the rationale for this legislation? Do you agree with these assumptions?

2. Which legal approach is likely to be most effective in achieving
desired goals, mandatory or voluntary (and protected) reporting?
What are the pros and cons of each approach?

3. What categories of professionals and lay persons ought to be
covered by mandatory or voluntary reporting provisions? Do you
agree with mandatory or voluntary reporting statutes that apply to
"any person"?

4. The trigger activating reporting statutes is "reasonable suspicion" of elder mistreatment. Why have states made this, rather than
a more stringent standard, the trigger for reporting? From a practical, operational perspective, how much evidence must one have in
order to hold such a "reasonable suspicion"? How would you
develop a workable protocol for identifying and assessing such suspicion? See Kurt C. Kleinschmidt, *Elder Abuse: A Review,* 30 Annals
of Emergency Medicine 463–472 (1997); American Medical
Association, Diagnostic and Treatment Guidelines on Elder Abuse
and Neglect (1992).

5. Should physicians or other health care professionals be exposed to professional license discipline by the state or civil malpractice lawsuits initiated by or on behalf of mistreatment victims for failure to timely report mistreatment that was or should have been reasonably suspected? What would be the likely positive and negative consequences of enlarging such legal exposure? Seymour Moskowitz, *Saving Granny from the Wolf: Elder Abuse and Neglect—The Legal Framework,* 31 Connecticut Law Review 77–204 (1998); Seymour Moskowitz, *Private Enforcement of Criminal Mandatory Reporting Laws,* 9 Journal of Elder Abuse and Neglect 2–4 (1998).

6. To whom should reports of elder mistreatment be made, that is, Should elder mistreatment usually be handled as a police or a social service problem? Compare Candace J. Heisler, *Elder Abuse and the Criminal Justice System: New Awareness, New Responses,* XXIV Generations 52–58 (Summer 2000) and Joanne M. Otto, *The Role of Adult Protective Services,* XXIV Generations 33–38 (Summer 2000).

7. The rate of compliance by certain professionals, particularly physicians, with mandatory and voluntary elder mistreatment reporting statutes is low. How would you explain this professional behavior? How can a higher rate of reporting be encouraged? See Dorrie E. Rosenblatt, Kyung-Hwan Cho, & Paul W. Durance, *Reporting Mistreatment of Older Adults: The Role of Physicians,* 44 Journal of the American Geriatrics Society 65–70 (1996). In terms of social policy, *should* a higher rate of reporting be encouraged?

FAMILY INTERESTS AND GENETIC TESTING

The advent of possible genetic testing relating to both the prediction of Alzheimer's Disease (AD) in asymptomatic individuals and the diagnosis of AD in symptomatic individuals raises issues concerning the rights of persons who are related to the tested patient. Marshall B. Kapp, *Physicians' Legal Duties Regarding the Use of Genetic Tests to Predict and Diagnose Alzheimer Disease,* 21 Journal of Legal Medicine 445–475 (2000):

> As a general proposition, physicians owe patients a fiduciary duty of confidentiality not to reveal, without explicit patient authorization, personal information about a patient obtained by the physician as a result of the physician/patient relationship. Physicians have been

held civilly liable for violating that duty. This obligation is not absolute, though. One recognized exception to the general rule justifies, and may even require, the physician violating a patient's confidences and revealing what would otherwise be private information when doing so is indicated to prevent serious harm to innocent third parties posed by, for example, a dangerously violent mentally ill patient, a patient who may spread an infectious disease, or a patient whose unsafe driving poses a serious risk to others on the road. Breach of patient confidentiality may also be expressly mandated or encouraged (through the provision of legal immunity against liability for the breach) when a patient is the victim of child or elder abuse or another form of domestic violence.

Many have expressed particular concern about the potential perils of unauthorized release of individually identifiable genetic information in light of this information's extremely personal and powerfully symbolic nature as well as the practical consequences of its release. In practice, testing laboratories vary substantially in their attention to the details of information protection. Possible minuses of such information [arise] in the context of the physician's duty to warn the patient about the risk of test results-related discrimination by insurers and employers. A number of states have enacted statutes conveying to patients a civil right of confidentiality in their own genetic information.

However, the confidentiality of even genetic information "may be breached when doing so is necessary to protect public safety." In the APOE genotyping context, the most perplexing issue is what legal duty, if any, a physician of a patient who has been genotyped and found to possess at least one APOE ε4 allele encoded on chromosome 19 owes to make certain that the patient's blood relatives are aware of the patient's APOE status.

Ideally, the physician ought to initiate an anticipatory discussion of this question at the time that APOE testing is first being considered, as part of the initial informed consent interchange with the patient. "Prior to testing, persons need to know to whom results will be disclosed . . ." At that preliminary stage, the physician may impose a condition of cooperating with the patient in the conduct of the testing a promise by the patient to either personally inform family members of relevant test results or give permission for the physician to inform those family members. The patient may have an ethical responsibility to inform relatives about the patient's APOE status and the fact that the relatives may—or, then again, may not—be at higher risk for developing AD themselves at some unforeseeable future point; at the least, the alerted family members would then be placed on notice that they should seek out appropriate genetic counseling, both generally and regarding APOE testing in particular.

However, the real tension between the principle of confidentiality, on one hand, and the physician's duty to protect third parties from avoidable harm (in this situation, being deprived of the chance to plan ahead adequately), on the other, will materialize in one of two situations: when either (1) the physician has neglected to timely initiate an anticipatory discussion about dissemination of test results or (2) the patient has undergone testing on a walk-in, self-referral basis by an independent commercial laboratory and then places the results in the physician's lap with a plea for help. There is direct legal precedent in the AD context for resolving the tension in neither of these situations. Moreover, existing case law emanating from other arenas of genetic testing presents uncertain guidance. One physician/attorney recently has summarized the very limited pertinent precedent as follows:

1. Many jurisdictions do not recognize any duty of a physician to disclose medical information to relatives of an affected patient; in such jurisdictions a case is usually dismissed by the court.
2. The jurisdictions that have considered genetic cases—New Jersey and Florida—recognize such a duty.
3. When a duty to disclose is recognized, the duty can be discharged by informing the patient of the genetic nature of the disease [and encouraging the patient to inform the relatives].
4. The third-party relative must be "readily identifiable." This criterion is seldom a limiting factor in familial disease, but the possibility of a long-lost relative still lurks.

A zone of legal conform is created or reinforced in states that have enacted legislation that, although not requiring disclosure of genetic information to at-risk third parties, immunizes physicians from any liability if they voluntarily choose to so inform. This optional approach is consistent with the recommendation of the American Society on Human Genetics that providers performing genetic testing services for their patients be afforded a legal privilege to disclose genetic risk information directly to relatives of a patient if disclosure is necessary to mitigate a serious risk of harm.

Thoughtful commentators oppose mandating physicians to inform a patient's family members that they may be at greater risk for particular diseases, and would recognize exceptions to the privacy imperative only with the patient's explicit authorization. According to one:

> Physicians not only have a duty of confidentiality to their patients, but should also consider the likelihood a disease will actually manifest itself in a particular patient, whether there is treatment available for the genetic disease, [and] the reasons a patient might not want to disclose information . . . Courts should consider these practicalities before imposing a duty on physicians.

As summarized by another:

> [W]hile physicians should talk with their patients about genetic risks and patients, in most instances, should discuss these risks with their relatives, neither patients nor their physicians should be legally responsible for warning family members about genetic risks. That result may seem harsh, but imposing liability would represent a major expansion of the law that is unsupported by current public policies and would wreak havoc on the protection of confidentiality and on the physician's focus on the patient before her.

Any argument for imposing liability on a physician for failure to assure that family members are made aware of a relative's genetic status seems especially weak in the circumstance of an APOE ε4 allele-positive patient and suspected or anticipated AD. Under the present state of genetic knowledge (or ignorance) about AD, the analogies supporting claims that a physician is obligated to share a patient's genotyping with the patient's relatives—namely, the analogies drawing on the dangers associated with the spread of contagious diseases or the violent acts of the mental ill—are rather unpersuasive. Today, even if a relative were fully informed, he or she still would have no realistic clue regarding what preventive precautions to take; the information simply would not be useful in the same way that information about the serious, imminent danger posed by someone carrying an infectious disease or psychotically intent on harming others would be. The information about a relative's APOE status would not even be as useful as information that the relative has a genotype that clearly predicts or demonstrably shows increased susceptibility to a particular disease. Currently, the only arguable benefit of knowing a relative's APOE status would be the added incentive created by the information to engage in advance health care and financial planning activities, but that argument is defeated by the fact that the individual could and should have been doing that sort of advance planning anyway. (Citations omitted).

Discussion Question

Do you think that a physician is obligated to share a patient's APOE genotyping with the patient's relatives? Would you want to know the results of APOE genotyping that a blood relative of your own had undergone? Do you have a right to that information? If you were tested and found to be APOE ε4 allele-positive, would you tell your family? Should you have a legally enforceable duty to tell your family?

Discussion Question

7

Legal Aspects of Death and Dying

Decisions often must be made about whether to begin, continue, withhold, or withdraw life-sustaining medical treatments (LSMTs) for a critically ill patient. In the overwhelming majority of such situations, a satisfactory resolution is reached through a process of discussion and negotiation involving the patient (when still able to participate), family or significant others, physician, other members of the health care team, and perhaps some form of institutional ethics committee (IEC). Most of the time, decisions quite properly are made and carried out without any formal involvement of the legal system.

In some cases, however, the informal or extrajudicial (i.e., outside the legal system) decisionmaking process breaks down, and the parties go to court to initiate a judicial ruling. A body of case law has evolved since the famous *In re Karen Quinlan,* 70 N.J. 10, 355 A.2d 647 (1976) case was decided in New Jersey. The various courts that have confronted these issues have achieved a high, but not a total, degree of consensus on the major points. Although litigated LSMT cases are relatively small in number, these well-publicized cases exert a tremendous influence on the delivery of health care and the rights of patients and families near the end of life. Thus, it is important that the general boundaries or parameters for LSMT decision making set by the courts, as well as by legislatures, be understood by those who have to render professional services within those legal limits.

LIMITING MEDICAL TREATMENT

Competent Patients

There is virtually universal agreement that a decisionally capable adult patient has a right to make personal medical treatment decisions, including the right to accept or refuse even LSMT. This consensus is based on the ethical principle of autonomy or self-determination. See, e.g., Christine K. Cassel & Kathleen M. Foley, Principles for Care of Patients at the End of Life: An Emerging Consensus Among the Specialties of Medicine, Milbank Memorial Fund: NY (1999), stating as a Core Principle for End-of-Life Care, "Clinical policy of care at the end of life and the professional practice it guides should . . . [r]espect the right to refuse treatment." According to the American Geriatrics Society's Position Statement on *The Care of Dying Patients* (1998), "The care of the dying patient, like all medical care, should be guided by the values and preferences of the individual patient. Dignity and control are central issues for many dying patients."

Discussion Question

The contemporary American commitment to patient autonomy is not universally shared. Discuss the implications when older, critically ill patients and their families come from cultures or ethnic groups that do not believe that patients ought to have the right to make their own treatment decisions. See, e.g., Arieh Oppenheim & Charles L. Sprung, *Cross-Cultural Ethical Decision-Making in Critical Care*, 26 Critical Care Medicine 423–424 (1998); Carlton A. Hornung, G. Paul Eleazer, Harry S. Strothers, et al., *Ethnicity and Decision-Makers in a Group of Frail Older People*, 46 Journal of the American Geriatrics Society 280–286 (1998); James Hallenbeck, Mary K. Goldstein, & Eric W. Mebane, *Cultural Considerations of Death and Dying in the United States*, 12 Clinics in Geriatric Medicine 393–406 (1996).

The ethical underpinning of autonomy is firmly reflected in recognition of a competent patient's legal right to choose or refuse LSMT. This legal right is predicated both on the liberty interest contained in the 14th Amendment Due Process provision of the U.S. Constitution ("nor shall any state deprive any person of life, liberty, or property, without due process of law") and the common law right of informed consent (see chapter 2).

Anderson v. St. Francis-St. George Hospital, 77 Ohio St.3d 82, 84, 671
N.E.2d 225 (1996):

> "Because a person has a right to die, a medical professional who
> has been trained to preserve life, and who has taken an oath to
> do so, is relieved of that duty and is required by a legal duty to
> accede to a patient's express refusal of medical treatment."

Cruzan v. Director, Missouri Department of Health, 497 U.S. 261 (1990):

> "The common-law doctrine of informed consent is viewed as gen-
> erally encompassing the right of a competent individual to
> refuse medical treatment" (at 277).

> "[F]or purposes of this case, we assume that the United States
> Constitution would grant a competent person a constitutional-
> ly protected right to refuse lifesaving hydration and nutrition"
> (at 279).

> "[A] liberty interest in refusing unwanted medical treatment may
> be inferred from our prior decisions" (at 287).

Various state courts have also relied on provisions in state constitu-
tions and statutes to support a competent patient's right to choose.

Discussion Questions

1. Under any of these rationales, should the patient's right to
choose about LSMT be applied only to those who are "terminally ill?"
Can a meaningful legal distinction be drawn between "terminally ill"
(i.e., imminently dying) individuals and those who are not? How
imminent must the death be in order for the patient to be "terminally
ill"? Can we predict the time of death with that degree of certainty?

2. Under any of these rationales, can a meaningful legal distinction be drawn between withholding LSMT in the first place, on one
hand, and withdrawing it once begun, on the other?

3. How should a health care professional respond when an older,
decisionally capable patient refuses LSMT that the professional feels
is clinically indicated and in the patient's best interests? What are the
professional's continuing goals and duties in this sort of situation?

Incompetent Patients

Difficult legal dilemmas may be presented when a critically ill
patient is mentally or physically incapable of making and expressing

rational decisions regarding LSMT. For a long time, the customary practice regarding such patients has been for the health care team to confer and negotiate with, and generally to defer to, the wishes of the patient's available family members and additional significant others. The rationales for this deference are the presumptions, first, that families are most likely to know what decisions the patient would make personally if he or she were decisionally capable at present and, second, that families ordinarily act honestly in the best interests of their loved ones. The former decision standard is termed "substituted judgment," and the latter is referred to as the "best interests" test.

Discussion Question

Do you agree with these presumptions about how families ordinarily make surrogate decisions for their decisionally incapacitated loved ones? Do these presumptions justify deference to the family without any formal involvement of the legal system? See Kathleen M. Boozang, *An Intimate Passing: Restoring the Role of the Family and Religion in Dying*, 58 University of Pittsburgh Law Review 549–617 (1997) (not only answering these questions affirmatively, but arguing that families should not even be constrained by considerations of the patient's substituted judgment or best interests).

In most circumstances, an informal, extralegal process of surrogate decision making works fine. Nevertheless, contentious or anxious family members or health care professionals sometimes ask the courts to intervene in what is normally a private matter. In addition, state legislatures have ventured into this arena. From the combination of case precedent and state statutes has evolved a set of guidelines for (1) identifying proper surrogate decision makers for an incapacitated patient and (2) delineating appropriate substantive decisionmaking criteria for use by the surrogate.

The most important case involving surrogate decision making for an incapable patient in the LSMT context is the Supreme Court's *Cruzan* decision (cited above).

> Petitioner Nancy Beth Cruzan was rendered incompetent as a result of severe injuries sustained during an automobile accident. Co-petitioners Lester and Joyce Cruzan, Nancy's parents and co-guardians, sought a court order directing the withdrawal of their daughter's artificial feeding and hydration equipment after it

became apparent that she had virtually no chance of recovering her cognitive faculties.

On the night of January 11, 1983, Nancy Cruzan lost control of her car as she traveled down Elm Road in Jasper County, Missouri. The vehicle overturned, and Cruzan was discovered lying face down in a ditch without detectable respiratory or cardiac function. Paramedics were able to restore her breathing and heartbeat at the accident site, and she was transported to a hospital in an unconscious state. An attending neurosurgeon diagnosed her as having sustained probable cerebral contusions compounded by significant anoxia (lack of oxygen). . . . permanent brain damage generally results after 6 minutes in an anoxic state; it was estimated that Cruzan was deprived of oxygen from 12 to 14 minutes. She remained in a coma for approximately three weeks and then progressed to an unconscious state in which she was able to orally ingest some nutrition. In order to ease feeding and further the recovery, surgeons implanted a gastrostomy feeding and hydration tube in Cruzan with the consent of her then husband. Subsequent rehabilitative efforts proved unavailing. She now lies in a Missouri state hospital in what is commonly referred to as a persistent vegetative state: generally, a condition in which a person exhibits motor reflexes but evinces no indications of significant cognitive function. The State of Missouri is bearing the cost of her care.

After it had become apparent that Nancy Cruzan had virtually no chance of regaining her mental faculties her parents asked hospital employees to terminate the artificial nutrition and hydration procedures. All agree that such a removal would cause her death. The employees refused to honor the request without court approval.

We granted certiorari to consider the question of whether Cruzan has a right under the United States Constitution which would require the hospital to withdraw life-sustaining treatment from her under these circumstances.

***

This is the first case in which we have been squarely presented with the issue of whether the United States Constitution grants what is in common parlance referred to as a "right to die."

***

Petitioners insist that under the general holdings of our cases, the forced administration of life-sustaining medical treatment, and even of artificially-delivered food and water essential to life, would implicate a competent person's liberty interest.

***

Petitioners go on to assert that an incompetent person should possess the same right in this respect as is possessed by a competent person.***

The difficulty with petitioners' claim is that in a sense it begs the question: an incompetent person is not able to make an informed and voluntary choice to exercise a hypothetical right to refuse treatment or any other right. Such a "right" must be exercised for her, if at all, by some sort of surrogate. Here, Missouri has in effect recognized that under certain circumstances a surrogate may act for the patient in electing to have hydration and nutrition withdrawn in such a way as to cause death, but it has established a procedural safeguard to assure that the action of the surrogate conforms as best it may to the wishes expressed by the patient while competent. Missouri requires that evidence of the incompetent's wishes as to the withdrawal of treatment be proved by clear and convincing evidence. The question, then, is whether the United States Constitution forbids the establishment of this procedural requirement by the State. We hold that it does not.

***

The choice between life and death is a deeply personal decision of obvious and overwhelming finality. We believe Missouri may legitimately seek to safeguard the personal element of this choice through the imposition of heightened evidentiary requirements. It cannot be disputed that the Due Process Clause protects an interest in life as well as an interest in refusing life-sustaining medical treatment. Not all incompetent patients will have loved ones available to serve as surrogate decisionmakers.*** A State is entitled to guard against potential abuses in such situations. Similarly, a State is entitled to consider that a judicial proceeding to make a determination regarding an incompetent's wishes may very well not be an adversarial one, with the added guarantee of accurate factfinding that the adversary process brings with it. Finally, we think a State may properly decline to make judgments about the "quality" of life that a particular individual may enjoy, and simply assert an unqualified interest in the preservation of human life to be weighed against the constitutionally protected interests of the individual.

In our view, Missouri has permissibly sought to advance these interests through the adoption of a "clear and convincing" standard of proof to govern such proceedings.

***

We think it self-evident that the interests at stake in the instant proceedings are more substantial, both on an individual and societal level, than those involved in a run-of-the-mine civil dispute. But not only does the standard of proof reflect the importance of a particular adjudication, it also serves as a societal judgment about how the risk of error should be distributed between the litigants. The more stringent the burden of proof a party must bear, the more that party bears the risk of an erroneous decision. We believe that Missouri may permissibly place an increased risk of an erroneous decision on those seeking to terminate an incompetent individual's life-sustaining treatment. An erroneous decision not to terminate results is a maintenance of the status quo; the possibility of subsequent developments such as advancements in medical science, the discovery of new evidence regarding the patient's intent, changes in the law, or simply the unexpected death of the patient despite the administration of life-sustaining treatment, at least create the potential that a wrong decision will eventually be corrected or its impact mitigated. An erroneous decision to withdraw life-sustaining treatment, however, is not susceptible of correction.

***

In sum, we conclude that a State may apply a clear and convincing evidence standard in proceedings where a guardian seeks to discontinue nutrition and hydration of a person diagnosed to be in a persistent vegetative state.***

Discussion Questions

1. Do you agree with Ms. Cruzan's parents that Missouri's requirement of "clear and convincing" evidence for surrogate decisions to withdraw treatment unduly interferes with Ms. Cruzan's constitutional right to refuse LSMT? Does it set up an impossible standard of proof? Is it fair for the parents to be the ones who bear this burden of proof? What kinds of evidence might be introduced by surrogates to overcome this burden of proof?

2. Do you agree with the Court majority that the state's interests in situations like this are strong enough to empower the state to set a very stringent standard of proof, if the state chooses, for surrogate withdrawal of treatment?

3. As a matter of public policy, what standard of proof (i.e., beyond a reasonable doubt, clear and convincing, or preponderance of the evidence) would you want your own state legislature to adopt regarding surrogate decisions to withdraw or withhold LSMT from an incompetent patient? Should it make any difference whether the surrogate is a family member versus someone else?

4. Ms. Cruzan was a young woman. Should the age of the patient make any difference in delineating the powers and limits of a surrogate decision maker to withdraw or withhold LSMT?

5. Should the law distinguish between decisions like that in *Cruzan,* regarding the withdrawal of artificially delivered food and hydration, on one hand, and decisions regarding the withdrawal or withholding of other types of LSMT (e.g., resuscitation, dialysis, antibiotics, artificial ventilation), on the other? Do you agree with Justice O'Connor's concurring opinion in *Cruzan?*

> I agree that a protected liberty interest in refusing unwanted medical treatment may be inferred from our prior decisions, and that the refusal of artificially delivered food and water is encompassed within that liberty interest.
> Artificial feeding cannot readily be distinguished from other forms of medical treatment.*** Whether or not the techniques used to pass food and water into the patient's alimentary tract are termed "medical treatment," it is clear they all involve some degree of intrusion and restraint. Feeding a patient by means of a nasogastric tube requires a physician to pass a long flexible tube through the patient's nose, throat and esophagus and into the stomach. Because of the discomfort such a tube causes, "[m]any patients need to be restrained forcibly and their hands put into large mittens to prevent them from removing the tube."*** A gastrostomy tube (as was used to provide food and water to Nancy Cruzan), or jejunostomy tube must be surgically implanted into the stomach or small intestine.*** Requiring a competent adult to endure such procedures against her will burdens the patient's liberty, dignity, and freedom to determine the course of her own treatment. Accordingly, the liberty guaranteed by the Due Process Clause must protect, if it protects anything, an individual's deeply personal decision to reject medical treatment, including the artificial delivery of food and water.

The idea that a surrogate ought to base treatment decisions on what the decisionally incapable patient would have chosen if currently capable of making and expressing choices is the doctrine of "substituted judgment." This is the approach favored by most courts and legislatures.

Discussion Question

Why is substituted judgment the generally preferred mode of surrogate decision making about LSMT? What are the problems with trying to apply this approach in specific cases? How can we know what the incapable patient would have wanted? Do you agree with the cautious approach taken by the Michigan Supreme Court in *In re Michael Martin,* 450 Mich. 204, 538 N.W.2d 399 (1995):

> The substituted judgment standard has subjective and objective components. Through this standard, the surrogate attempts to ascertain, with as much specificity as possible, the decision the incompetent patient would make if he were competent to do so. The surrogate first determines whether the patient, while competent, explicitly stated his intent regarding the type of medical treatment in question. Where there is no explicit evidence of what the patient would choose, the surrogate may still decide to terminate treatment on the basis of evidence of the patient's value system.
>
> ***
>
> Courts have generally acknowledged that the substituted judgment standard entails some level of objective analysis. For this reason, commentators, as well as many judges, have forcefully assailed the substituted judgment standard as a legal fiction that in reality substitutes the surrogate's decision to withdraw treatment for that of the patient.
>
> ***
>
> We find that a purely subjective analysis is the most appropriate standard to apply under the circumstances of this case. The pure subjective standard allows the surrogate to withhold life-sustaining treatment from an incompetent patient when it is clear that the particular patient would have refused the treatment under the circumstances involved. Given the right the surrogate is seeking to effectuate is the incompetent patient's right to control his own life, the question is not what a reasonable or average person would have chosen to do under the circumstances but what the particular patient would have done if able to choose for himself. The patient's statements, made while competent, must illustrate a firm and settled commitment to the termination of life supports under the circumstances like those presented.
>
> In the cases that have applied a more objective test or suggested that an objective test would be proper, the patient generally has been comatose or in a persistent vegetative state. In this case, Michael's life and health are not threatened by infirmities of this nature. Because he was competent and able to express his wishes and desires, we decline to move along the continuum from the subjective standard.
>
> ***
>
> We agree that the clear and convincing evidence standard, the most demanding standard applied in civil cases, is the proper evidentiary standard for assessing whether a patient's statements, made while competent, indicate a desire to have treatment withheld. (Citations omitted)

See Thomas J. Marzen & Daniel Avila, *Will the Real Michael Martin Please Speak Up! Medical Decisionmaking for Questionably Competent Persons,* 72 University of Detroit Mercy Law Review 833–871 (1995).

When direct or even inferential evidence of the patient's substituted judgment is absent, the prevailing legal tack—disagreeing with the Michigan Supreme Court's approach in *In re Michael Martin*—is to defer to the surrogate's opinion about the course of care that will most likely promote the patient's "best interests." Maine Revised Statutes Annotated § 5-802 (e):

> An agent shall make a health-care decision in accordance with the principal's individual instructions, if any, and other wishes to the extent known to the agent. Otherwise, the agent shall make the decision in accordance with the agent's determination of the principal's best interest. In determining the principal's best interest, the agent shall consider the principal's personal values to the extent known to the agent.

Discussion Questions

1. From whose perspective (i.e., the patient's, a "reasonable person's," health care providers') should the patient's best interests be determined? Do you agree with the Maine statute cited above?

2. A best interests analysis is supposed to take relative benefits and burdens into account. How can one accurately weigh and compare the respective benefits and burdens of potential choices about LSMT?

3. Do you agree with the Supreme Court of Wisconsin in its analysis of best interests, and particularly with the court's distinction between patients who are in a persistent vegetative state (PVS) and those who are not, in *In the Matter of Edna M.F.,* 210 Wis.2d 557, 563 N.W.2d 485 (1997):

> Edna M.F. is a 71-year-old woman who has been diagnosed with dementia of the Alzheimer's type. She is bedridden, but her doctors have indicated that she responds to stimulation from voice and movement. She also appears alert at times, with her eyes open, and she responds to mildly noxious stimuli. According to these doctors, her condition does not meet the definition of a persistent vegetative state. In 1988, a permanent feeding tube was surgically inserted in Edna's body. Edna currently breathes without a respirator, but she continues to receive artificial nutrition and hydration. Edna's condition is not likely to improve.

Edna's sister and court-appointed guardian, Betty Spahn, seeks permission to direct the withholding of Edna's nutrition, claiming that her sister would not want to live in this condition. However, the only testimony presented at trial regarding Edna's views on the use of life-sustaining medical treatment involves a statement made in 1966 or 1967. At that time, Spahn and Edna were having a conversation about their mother, who was recovering from depression, and Spahn's mother-in-law, who was dying of cancer. Spahn testified that during this conversation, Edna said to her: "I would rather die of cancer than lose my mind." Spahn further testified that this was the only time that she and Edna discussed the subject and that Edna never said anything specifically about withholding or withdrawing life-sustaining medical treatment.

***

This court has established a bright-line rule that the guardian of an incompetent ward possesses the authority to direct withholding or withdrawal of life-sustaining medical treatment, including artificial nutrition and hydration, if it is in the best interests of the ward and the ward is in a persistent vegetative state. Spahn now asks this court to extend the scope of [our previous rulings] to include those incompetent patients who are afflicted with incurable or irreversible conditions of health. We decline to go down this slippery slope, for the consequences and the confusion may be great.

***

Even though Edna M.F. is not currently existing in a persistent vegetative state, if her guardian can demonstrate by a preponderance of the evidence a clear statement of Edna's desires in these circumstances, then it is in the best interests of Edna to honor those wishes. The reason this court requires a clear statement of the ward's desires is because of the interest of the state in preserving human life and the irreversible nature of the decision to withdraw nutrition from a person.

***

There is a presumption that continuing life is in the best interests of the ward. The only evidence in the record of Edna's desires is the general statement she made to her sister in 1966 or 1967. We understand how difficult Edna's illness has been on her loved ones, and we sympathize with their plight, but the evidence contained in the record is simply not sufficient to rebut the presumption that Edna would choose life. A perusal of the record and the insufficiency of the evidence contained therein supports the result the trial court reached, even though there was no explicit factual finding by the trial court on this issue.

In conclusion, this court declines to extend the scope of [prior law] beyond those incompetent wards who are currently in a persistent vegetative state; we will not apply [prior law] to those with incurable or irreversible conditions.

***

Consequently, we hold that a guardian may only direct the withdrawal of life-sustaining medical treatment, including nutrition and hydration, if the incompetent ward is in a persistent vegetative state and the decision to withdraw is in the best interests of the ward. We further hold that in this case, where the only indication of Edna's desires was made at least 30 years ago and under different circumstances, there is not a clear statement of intent such that Edna's guardian may authorize the withholding of her nutrition. (Citations omitted)

Do you agree with the court that "[t]here is a presumption that continuing life is in the best interests of the [incompetent patient]?" Or, do you agree with the court in *Conservatorship of Wendland*, 78 Cal.App.4th 517, 93 Cal.Rptr.2d 550, 577 (2000):

We thus conclude there should be no presumption in favor of continued existence. The state has an interest in protecting [the incompetent's] right to have appropriate medical treatment decisions made on his behalf. The problem is not to preserve life under all circumstances but to make the right decisions. A conclusive presumption in favor of continuing treatment impermissibly burdens a person's right to make the other choice. However, there should also be no presumption in favor of death, because the conservatee has a right to life. (Citation omitted)

Deference to family decisions regarding decisionally incapable relatives has been a long tradition in medical practice and judicial opinions. A majority of states have formalized this deference by enacting what have been generically termed "family consent" statutes. These statutes codify usual practice by explicitly authorizing family members (in a stated priority order) to make LSMT decisions about a decisionally incapacitated person who had not executed an advance directive (discussed below). States have placed surrogate consent provisions either in specialized surrogate consent statutes, in a comprehensive health care decisions act, in an advance directives statute, or in a general informed consent statute. Surrogate consent statutes ordinarily specify that the surrogate is to make decisions first on the basis of the incapacitated patient's substituted judgment and, secondarily, on the basis of the patient's best interests. Some state statutes limit the kinds of decisions a surrogate may make for an incompetent patient, while other statutes are more expansive.

IL. ST. CH. 755 § 40/25:

(a) When a patient lacks decisional capacity, the health care provider must make a reasonable inquiry as to the availability and authority of a health care agent under the Powers of Attorney for Health Care Law. When no health care agent is authorized and available, the health care provider must make a reasonable inquiry as to the availability of possible surrogates listed in items (1) through (4) of this subsection. The surrogate decision makers, as identified by the attending physician, are then authorized to make decisions as follows: . . . (ii) for patients who lack decisional capacity and have a qualifying condition, medical treatment decisions including whether to forgo life-sustaining treatment on behalf of the patient may be made without court order or judicial involvement in the following order of priority:

(1) the patient's guardian of the person;
(2) the patient's spouse;
(3) any adult son or daughter of the patient;
(4) either parent of the patient;
(5) any adult brother or sister of the patient;
(6) any adult grandchild of the patient;
(7) a close friend of the patient;
(8) the patient's guardian of the estate.

The health care provider shall have the right to rely on any of the above surrogates if the provider believes after reasonable inquiry that neither a health care agent under the Powers of Attorney for Health Care Law nor a surrogate of higher priority is available.

Where there are multiple surrogate decision makers at the same priority level in the hierarchy, it shall be the responsibility of those surrogates to make reasonable efforts to reach a consensus as to their decision on behalf of the patient regarding the forgoing of life-sustaining treatment. If 2 or more surrogates who are in the same category and have equal priority indicate to the attending physician that they disagree about the health care matter at issue, a majority of the available persons in that category (or the parent with custodial rights) shall control, unless the minority (or the parent without custodial rights) initiates guardianship proceedings . . . No health care provider or other person is required to seek appointment of a guardian.

***

(e) The surrogate decision maker shall have the same right as the patient to receive medical information and medical records and to consent to disclosure.

Discussion Questions

1. Do you agree with the priority order of surrogates contained in this statute? Is this the priority order that most people would want if they became decisionally incapacitated? See Deon C. Hayley, Roya Stern, Carol Stocking, & Greg A. Sachs, *The Application of Health Care Surrogate Laws to Older Populations: How Good a Match?* 44 Journal of the American Geriatrics Society 185–188 (1996). Is this the priority order of surrogates that you would want making decisions for you?

2. What limits, if any, should be imposed on the surrogate's authority? For example, should the surrogate be allowed, without any formal external oversight, to enter the incapacitated person into a nursing home? A mental institution? A research protocol? A managed care plan?

Even when there is no specific authorizing legislation, the traditional practice has been for health care professionals to rely on unofficial but honest and conscientious "next of kin" to make decisions for an incompetent patient. Assuming everyone is acting in good faith, there are no negative legal repercussions. See *In re Guardianship of McInnis,* 61 Ohio Misc.2d 790, 584 N.E.2d 1389 (1991): "It is the opinion of this court that the spouse, individually and without the intervention of the court, without the appointment of a guardian, has such authority [to discontinue LSMT for her decisionally incapable husband] under the common law."

Discussion Questions

1. The American Geriatrics Society's Position Statement on *Making Treatment Decisions for Incapacitated Elderly Without Advance Directives* (1995) says that "A nontraditional surrogate, such as a close friend, a live-in companion who is not married to the patient, a neighbor, a close member of the clergy, or others who know the patient well, may, in individual cases, be the appropriate surrogate." Do you agree?

2. Under what circumstances should health care professionals insist that a surrogate obtain formal legal authority? What are the

pros and cons of insisting on explicit clarification of legal authority before following the surrogate's treatment instructions?

3. What should a health care professional do when a surrogate, whether or not formally empowered by a surrogate consent statute, is making choices that seriously deviate from both the patient's substituted judgment and the patient's best interests?

ADVANCE HEALTH CARE PLANNING

Since the mid-1970s, a great deal of attention has been focused on advance or prospective health care planning as a way for individuals to maintain some control over their future medical treatment even if they become physically or mentally incapable of speaking for themselves when decisions actually need to be made and carried out. Advance health care planning has also been promoted as a way to avoid court involvement in LSMT decisions, conserve scarce financial resources in a manner consistent with patient autonomy, and reduce the burdens on families.

Currently, there are two main legal mechanisms available for prospective health care planning. One is the proxy directive, ordinarily in the form of a durable power of attorney (DPOA). This document names a proxy or agent who is authorized to make future medical decisions on behalf of the individual delegating the authority (the "principal" or "maker") in the event of the latter's subsequent decisional incapacity. The second legal device presently available for advance health care planning is the instruction directive, usually referred to as a living will, health care declaration, or natural death declaration.

Proxy Directives

The standard power of attorney (POA) is a written agreement authorizing a person (named an "agent" or "attorney-in-fact") to sign documents and conduct transactions on behalf of another person (the "principal" or "maker") who has delegated away that authority. The principal can delegate as much (e.g., a general delegation) or as little (e.g., specifically delineating what types of decisions the agent may or may not make) power as desired. The principal may end or revoke the arrangement at any time, as long as the principal remains competent to do so.

The POA in its traditional form is unsuitable as a method for dealing with medical (or financial) decision-making authority for older persons on a voluntary basis. The traditional POA ends automatically with the death or decisional incapacity of the person who assigned it. The underlying theory is that, because a deceased or incapacitated person no longer has the ability to revoke the POA, the law should exercise that right automatically for the principal. Thus, an older person who establishes a standard POA to help in managing medical (as well as other) affairs would be cut off from such assistance at exactly the moment when assistance is needed the most.

In an effort to overcome this deficiency, every state has enacted legislation authorizing the execution of a *durable* power of attorney (DPOA). In contrast to the traditional POA, the effect of a DPOA—when proper indication is given by a decisionally capable delegating principal—may endure beyond the principal's subsequent incapacity. Maine Revised Statutes Annotated § 5-501 (a):

> A durable power of attorney is a power of attorney by which a principal designates another as the principal's attorney-in-fact in writing and the writing contains the words "This power of attorney is not affected by subsequent disability or incapacity of the principal or lapse of time" or "This power of attorney becomes effective upon the disability or incapacity of the principal" or similar words showing the intent of the principal that the authority conferred is exercisable notwithstanding the principal's subsequent disability or incapacity, and unless it states a time of termination, notwithstanding the lapse of time since the execution of the instrument.

To remove any ambiguity about the applicability of the DPOA concept to the realm of medical decision making (including choices regarding LSMT), almost every state has enacted legislation that explicitly authorizes the use of this legal device in the medical decision-making context. Maine Revised Statutes Annotated § 5-506 (a):

> A durable health care power of attorney is a durable power of attorney by which a principal designates another as attorney-in-fact to make decisions on the principal's behalf in matters concerning the principal's medical or health treatment and care. An attorney-in-fact designated under a durable health care power of attorney may be authorized to give or withhold consents or approvals relating to any medical, health or other professional care, counsel, treatment or

service of or to the principal by a licensed or professional certified person or institution engaged in the practice of, or providing, a healing art, including life-sustaining treatment when the principal is in a terminal condition or a persistent vegetative state.

Some statutes use terminology such as "Health Care Representative," "Health Care Agent," or "Health Care Proxy." In addition, a number of states use a comprehensive advance directive statute to expressly authorize the execution of both instruction and proxy directives, while others have separate statutes for each type of advance directive. Minnesota Statutes Annotated § 145C.16 Suggested Form:

HEALTH CARE DIRECTIVE

I, _____ understand this document allows me to do ONE OR BOTH of the following:

PART I: Name another person (called the health care agent) to make health care decisions for me if I am unable to decide or speak for myself. My health care agent must make health care decisions for me based on the instructions I provide in this document (Part II), if any, the wishes I have made known to him or her, or must act in my best interest if I have not made my health care wishes known.

AND/OR

PART II: Give health care instructions to guide others making health care decisions for me. If I have named a health care agent, these instructions are to be used by the agent. These instructions may also be used by my health care providers, others assisting with my health care and my family, in the event I cannot make decisions for myself.

The authority of the proxy may be made as broad or as narrow as the principal wishes. Minnesota Statutes Annotated § 145C.16:

THIS IS WHAT I WANT MY HEALTH CARE AGENT
TO BE ABLE TO DO IF I AM UNABLE
TO DECIDE OR SPEAK FOR MYSELF

(I know I can change these choices)

My health care agent is automatically given the powers listed below in (A) through (D). My health care agent must follow my health care instructions in this document or any other instructions I have given to my agent. If I have not given health care instructions, then my agent must act in my best interest.

Whenever I am unable to decide or speak for myself, my health care agent has the power to:

(A) Make any health care decision for me. This includes the power to give, refuse, or withdraw consent to any care, treatment, service, or procedures. This includes deciding whether to stop or not start health care that is keeping me or might keep me alive, and deciding about intrusive mental health treatment.

(B) Choose my health care providers.

(C) Choose where I live and receive care and support when those choices relate to my health care needs.

(D) Review my medical records and have the same rights that I would have to give my medical records to other people.

If I DO NOT want my health care agent to have a power listed above in (A) through (D) OR if I want to LIMIT any power in (A) through (D), I MUST say that here:

_____

_____

Discussion Questions

1. What are the advantages, from a patient's perspective, of using a proxy directive in the LSMT context? From the health care provider's perspective? What are the shortcomings or limitations of this approach, from the patient's and provider's respective perspectives?

2. What can health care and human service professionals do to encourage older persons to execute proxy directives in a timely fashion? Is such encouragement something that health care and human service professionals *ought* to do?

3. Why are certain categories of persons disqualified from serving as health care proxies? Do you agree with Minnesota Statutes Annotated § 145C.03, Subd.2.

Individuals ineligible to act as health care agent (a) An individual appointed by the principal to make the determination of the principal's decision-making capacity is not eligible to act as the health care agent.

(b) The following individuals are not eligible to act as the health care agent, unless the individual appointed is related to the principal by blood, marriage, registered domestic partnership, or adoption, or unless the principal has otherwise specified in the health care directive:

(1) a health care provider attending the principal on the date of execution of the health care directive or on the date the health care agent must make decisions for the principal; or

(2) an employee of a health care provider attending the principal on the date of execution of the health care directive or on the date the health care agent must make decisions for the principal.

4. Once a health care proxy is in place, how could that proxy's effectiveness in the role be optimized? See Charles P. Sabatino, *The Legal and Functional Status of the Medical Proxy: Suggestions for Statutory Reform*, 27 Journal of Law, Medicine & Ethics 52–68 (1999).

Instruction Directives

All but a couple of states have enacted legislation regarding instruction directives. Although the specifics vary from state to state, the common theme of natural death legislation is endorsement of a patient's right, while still decisionally capable, to sign a written directive concerning the patient's wishes about the use of LSMT in the event of subsequent serious illness and decisional incapacity. Such a directive (misnamed a living will, since it has nothing to do with distribution of property and deals with dying rather than living) immunizes the health care professionals and treatment facility against potential civil or criminal liability for withholding or withdrawing treatment under the specified conditions.

Discussion Questions

1. How should health and human service professionals assess whether an individual has sufficient present cognitive and emotional capacity to execute an advance directive? See Mathy Mezey, Ethel Mitty, & Gloria Ramsey, *Assessment of Decision-Making Capacity: Nursing's Role,* 23 Journal of Gerontological Nursing 28–35 (1997); Elizabeth Bradley, Leslie Walker, Barbara Blechner, & Terrie Wetle, *Assessing Capacity to Participate in Discussions of Advance Directives in Nursing Homes: Findings from a Study of the Patient Self Determination Act,* 45 Journal of the American Geriatrics Society 79–83 (1997); Michel Silberfeld, Carol Nash, and Peter A. Singer, *Capacity to Complete an Advance Directive,* 41 Journal of the American Geriatrics Society 1141–1143 (1993). Minnesota Statutes § 145C.10 (a) provides: "The principal is presumed to have the capacity to execute a health care

directive and to revoke a health care directive, absent clear and convincing evidence to the contrary."

2. Do you agree with that presumption about capacity and with the accompanying allocation of the burden of proof?

Just as is true for the DPOA, the legal force of the instruction directive goes into effect only when the patient, after executing the document, subsequently becomes incapable of making LSMT decisions. Minnesota Statutes § 145C.06:

> A health care directive is effective for a health care decision when: (2) the principal, in the determination of the attending physician of the principal, lacks decision-making capacity to make the health care decision; or if other conditions for effectiveness otherwise specified by the principal have been met.

However, Minnesota Statutes Annotated § 145C.05, Subd.2 (c) states: "A health care directive may authorize a health care agent to make health care decisions for a principal even though the principal retains decision-making capacity."

Discussion Question

Should it be left to the individual's attending physician to determine when that person has become decisionally incapable and, therefore, the advance directive becomes effective? Should there be any safeguards on this determination? What reasonable alternatives might a person specify for handling this determination?

In some countries (e.g., England), advance directives have force as a matter of common law but lack a statutory basis.

Discussion Question

What are the advantages and disadvantages of having the details pertaining to the execution of advance directives codified in the form of a statute?

Most advance instruction directive statutes use the approach of either check-off options or extremely general boilerplate language to express wishes regarding specific forms of LSMT. District of Columbia Code § 6-2422 (c):

The declaration shall be substantially in the following form . . .

Declaration

Declaration made this _____ day of _____ month, year). I, _____, being of sound mind, willfully and voluntarily make known my desires that my dying shall not be artificially prolonged under the circumstances set forth below, do declare:

If at any time I should have an incurable injury, disease, or illness certified to be a terminal condition by two physicians who have personally examined me, one of whom shall be my attending physician, and the physicians have determined that my death will occur whether or not life-sustaining procedures are utilized and where the application of life-sustaining procedures would serve only to artificially prolong the dying process, I direct that such procedures be withheld or withdrawn, and that I be permitted to die naturally with only the administration of medication or the performance of any medical procedure deemed necessary to provide me with comfort care or to alleviate pain.

In the absence of my ability to give directions regarding the use of such life-sustaining procedures, it is my intention that this declaration shall be honored by my family and physician(s) as the final expression of my legal right to refuse medical or surgical treatment and accept the consequences from such refusal.

Discussion Questions

1. Why don't more people execute advance directive documents in a timely fashion? Why are persons from some demographic groups much less likely to execute advance directives than others? See Laura C. Hanson & Eric Rodgman, *The Use of Living Wills at the End of Life,* 156 Archives of Internal Medicine 1018–1022 (1996); Gina Vaughn, Elizabeth Kiyasu, & Wayne C. McCormick, *Advance Directive Preferences Among Subpopulations of Asian Nursing Home Residents in the Pacific Northwest,* 48 Journal of the American Geriatrics Society 554–557 (2000).

2. What can health and human service professionals do to encourage older individuals to execute advance directives? What are the barriers to such encouragement, and how can they be overcome? See Gary S. Fischer, Robert M. Arnold, & James A. Tulsky, *Talking to the Older Adult About Advance Directives,* 16 Clinics in Geriatric Medicine 239–254 (2000); Paul V. Aitken, Jr., *Incorporating*

Advance Care Planning into Family Practice, 59 American Family Physician 605–612 (1999). Would it help if we paid health and human service professionals for their time spent in counseling individuals about advance health care planning?

3. What are the inherent limitations of advance instruction directives that delineate specific LSMTs to be withheld or withdrawn? See Mark R. Tonelli, *Pulling the Plug on Living Wills: A Critical Analysis of Living Wills,* 110 Chest 816–822 (1996); Allan S. Brett, *Limitations of Listing Specific Medical Interventions in Advance Directives,* 266 Journal of the American Medical Association 825–828 (1991). Can these limitations be overcome? See Norman L. Cantor, *Making Advance Directives Meaningful,* 4 Psychology, Public Policy and Law 629–652 (1998).

4. Although we usually think of advance instruction directives as instruments for *limiting* LSMT in the future, should an individual also be permitted to specify in such a directive that he or she *requests* particular medical interventions under certain enumerated circumstances? For example, South Carolina Code § 62-5-504 allows an individual to initial a provision in his or her advance directive stating: "DIRECTIVE FOR MAXIMUM TREATMENT. I want my life to be prolonged to the greatest extent possible, within the standards of accepted medical practice, without regard to my condition, the chances I have for recovery, or the cost of the procedures." What are the problems with this type of instruction?

5. Besides, or instead of, encouraging them to execute advance directives, what should health and human service professionals advise individuals to do in order to maximize their future autonomy regarding LSMT? See Henry S. Perkins, *Time to Move Advance Care Planning Beyond Advance Directives,* 117 Chest 1228–1231 (2000).

At least a few states have taken the legislative approach of providing an open-ended format for giving health care instructions, creating an opportunity for individuals to express their values, beliefs, and preferences in their own words by responding to prompts.

Minnesota Statutes § 145C.16, Part II provides the following form to be filled out:

These are instructions for my health care when I am unable to decide or speak for myself. These instructions must be followed (so long as they address my needs).

THESE ARE MY BELIEFS AND VALUES
ABOUT MY HEALTH CARE

(I know I can change these choices or leave any of them blank)

I want you to know these things about me to help you make decisions about my health care:
My goals for my health care:

_____

_____

My fears about my health care:

_____

_____

My spiritual or religious beliefs and traditions:

_____

_____

My beliefs about when life would be no longer worth living:

_____

_____

My thoughts about how my medical condition might affect my family:

_____

_____

THIS IS WHAT I WANT AND DO NOT WANT
FOR MY HEALTH CARE

(I know I can change these choices or leave any of them blank)

Many medical treatments may be used to try to improve my medical condition or to prolong my life. Examples include artificial breathing by a machine connected to a tube in the lungs, artificial feeding or fluids through tubes, attempts to start a stopped heart, surgeries, dialysis, antibiotics, and blood transfusions. Most medical treatments can be tried for a while and then stopped if they do not help.

I have these views about my health care in these situations:
(Note: You can discuss general feelings, specific treatments, or leave any of them blank)

If I had a reasonable chance of recovery, and were temporarily unable to decide or speak for myself, I would want:

_____

_____

If I were dying and unable to decide or speak for myself, I would want:

_____

_____

If I were permanently unconscious and unable to decide or speak for myself, I would want:

_____

_____

If I were completely dependent on others for my care and unable to decide or speak for myself, I would want:

_____

_____

In all circumstances, my doctors will try to keep me comfortable and reduce my pain. This is how I feel about pain relief if it would affect my alertness or if it could shorten my life:

_____

_____

There are other things that I want or do not want for my health care, if possible:
Who I would like to be my doctor:

_____

_____

Where I would like to live to receive health care:

_____

_____

Where I would like to die and other wishes I have about dying:

_____

_____

My wishes about donating parts of my body when I die:

_____

_____

My wishes about what happens to my body when I die (cremation, burial):

_____

_____

Any other things:

_____

_____

Discussion Question

What are the advantages and disadvantages of advance instructions that convey the patient's values and beliefs about end-of-life care, instead of enumerating specific forms of LSMTs to be provided or withheld in particular clinical scenarios? Should advance instruction directives allow the individual to incorporate personal religious considerations? See Michael A. Groden, *Religious Advance Directives: The Convergence of Law, Religion, Medicine, and Public Health,* 83 American Journal of Public Health 899–903 (1993).

Prehospital Medical Care Directives

Some states have enacted legislation authorizing competent adults to execute a prehospital medical care directive. Arizona Revised Statutes § 36-3251:

> A. Notwithstanding any law or a health care directive to the contrary, a person may execute a prehospital medical care directive that, in the event of cardiac or respiratory arrest, directs the withholding of cardiopulmonary resuscitation by emergency medical system and hospital emergency department personnel. For the purposes of this article, "cardiopulmonary resuscitation" shall include cardiac compression, endotracheal intubation and other advanced airway management, artificial ventilation, defibrillation, administration of advanced cardiac life support drugs and related emergency medical procedures. Authorization for the withholding of cardiopulmonary resuscitation does not include the withholding of other medical

interventions, such as intravenous fluids, oxygen or other therapies deemed necessary to provide comfort care or to alleviate pain.

B. A prehospital medical care directive shall be printed on an orange background and may be used in either letter or wallet size. The directive shall be in the following form:

Prehospital Medical Care Directive
(side one)

In the event of cardiac or respiratory arrest, I refuse any resuscitation measures including cardiac compression, endotracheal intubation and other advanced airway management, artificial ventilation, defibrillation, administration of advanced cardiac life support drugs and related emergency medical procedures.

***

D. If the person has designated an agent to make health care decisions . . . or has been appointed a guardian for health care decisions, . . . that agent or guardian shall sign if the person is no longer competent to do so.

E. A prehospital medical care directive is effective until it is revoked or superseded by a new document.

Other states have enacted statutes that deal specifically with out-of-hospital Do Not Resuscitate (DNR) orders, discussed below.

Restrictive Advance Directive Statutes

In their advance directive statutes, many states legislatures have attempted to draw distinctions between artificial sustenance, on one hand, and other forms of LSMT, on the other. Many statutes also distinguish between patients who are terminally ill and/or persistently vegetative and those who are not. South Carolina Statutes § 44-77-50:

INSTRUCTIONS CONCERNING ARTIFICIAL
NUTRITION AND HYDRATION

INITIAL ONE OF THE FOLLOWING STATEMENTS

If my condition is terminal and could result in death within a reasonably short time,

_____ I direct that nutrition and hydration BE PROVIDED through any medically indicated means, including medically or surgically implanted tubes.

_____ I direct that nutrition and hydration NOT BE PROVID-ED through any medically indicated means, including medically or surgically implanted tubes.

INITIAL ONE OF THE FOLLOWING STATEMENTS

If I am in a persistent vegetative state or other condition of permanent unconsciousness,

_____ I direct that nutrition and hydration BE PROVIDED through any medically indicated means, including medically or surgically implanted tubes.

_____ I direct that nutrition and hydration NOT BE PROVID-ED through any medically indicated means, including medically or surgically implanted tubes.

These distinctions that such statutory provisions attempt to make, by imposing a degree of specificity not required for other LSMTs and restricting certain medical choices to persons who are terminally ill and persistently vegetative, run counter to the weight of judicial authority and are probably unconstitutional. See Marshall B. Kapp, *State Statutes Limiting Advance Directives: Death Warrants or Life Sentences?* 40 Journal of the American Geriatrics Society 722–726 (1992).

Discussion Question

Why have states enacted these sorts of restrictive provisions as part of their advance directives statutes? Do such provisions serve a valid purpose or need? What are their drawbacks in both theory and application?

The courts and legislatures have made it clear that state advance directive statutes are not intended to be the exclusive means by which patients may exercise their right to make LSMT decisions. *In re Tavel,* 661 A.2d 1061 (Del. 1995):

This Act provides the authority for a person to make a living will . . . . This Act would permit an adult to explicitly state his or her desires regarding medical treatment, through the execution of a legal document, in the event he or she is diagnosed as having a terminal condition. It establishes a simple and easily-administered process which serves to protect the patient's right to medical self-determination by allowing the patient to reject unwanted medical treatment that only prolongs dying, and causes needless suffering. . . .

The document only becomes operative if the person has been diagnosed as having a terminal condition by two physicians, and there is a clear need for a treatment decision regarding maintenance medical treatment. Both the terms "terminal condition" and "maintenance medical treatment" are defined within the Act. . . .

It is not the intent of this legislation to force all persons to be involved with a "living will." Under this Act a person who wishes to prepare for the possible situation where he might not wish to continue with procedures or medications which may be painful or expensive, may do so. The only persons affected by this Act are those who voluntarily and affirmatively take advantage of its provisions; and even then the Act is effective only as directed in such person's Declaration. . . . the Act was not intended to affect the rights of persons who do not choose to take advantage of its provisions.

ENFORCEMENT OF PATIENTS' WISHES

Presumably, most competent patients express their wishes regarding LSMT, either at the time that decisions need to be made or prospectively, because they want and expect those wishes to be respected and implemented. There is a substantial body of data, however, indicating that very often the contemporaneous or prospectively stated wishes of patients regarding LSMT are not respected and implemented. In actuality, critically ill patients frequently receive more aggressive LSMT than they say they want. See SUPPORT Principal Investigators, *A Controlled Trial to Improve Care for Seriously Ill Hospitalized Patients: The Study to Understand the Prognoses and Preferences for Outcomes and Risks of Treatments,* 274 Journal of the American Medical Association 1591–1598 (1995).

Discussion Questions

1. Do you agree with the above presumption that most patients really want their stated wishes regarding LSMT to be implemented by their health care providers? Don't some patients really want their health care providers to exercise independent judgment at the time a LSMT decision actually needs to be made?

2. Why would health care providers fail to implement patient wishes regarding LSMT? Are these reasons valid ethical justifications? Should these explanations be recognized as justifications by the law?

State advance directive statutes invariably excuse a health care provider who chooses not to implement a patient's (or surrogate's) express preferences concerning LSMT. Minnesota Statutes Annotated § 145C.11 Subd.2:

> (c) A health care provider who administers health care necessary to keep the principal alive, despite a health care decision of the health care agent to withhold or withdraw that treatment, is not subject to criminal prosecution, civil liability, or professional disciplinary action if that health care provider promptly took all reasonable steps to:
>   (1) notify the health care agent of the health care provider's unwillingness to comply;
>   (2) document the notification in the principal's medical record; and
>   (3) permit the health care agent to arrange to transfer care of the principal to another health care provider willing to comply with the decision of the health care agent.

In the same vein, courts have refused to hold health care providers legally liable for failing to follow a patient's or surrogate's instructions to withdraw or withhold particular forms of LSMT, on the grounds that providing life-prolonging intervention cannot be the cause of legally compensable injuries. See *Anderson v. St. Francis-St. George Hospital,* 77 Ohio St.3d 82, 671 N.E.2d 225 (1996).

Discussion Questions

1. Do you agree with the statutes and judicial decisions providing immunity against liability for health care providers who refuse to follow a patient's or surrogate's wishes regarding LSMT? What is the rationale for providing immunity?

2. Conversely, do we need to create a new tort to allow a patient or family to hold a noncomplying health care provider liable? See Adam A. Milani, *Better Off Dead than Disabled?: Should Courts Recognize a Wrongful Living Cause of Action When Doctors Fail to Honor Patients' Advance Directives?* 54 Washington & Lee Law Review 149–228 (1997); Tricia J. Hackleman, *Violation of an Individual's Right to Die: The Need for a Wrongful Living Cause of Action,* 64 University of Cincinnati Law Review 1355–1381 (1996).

3. Practically speaking, what can a patient do to enhance the likelihood that his or her preferences regarding LSMT will be implemented?

4. If a patient (or surrogate) has not consented—and perhaps has even objected—to the provision of LSMT, but it is provided nonetheless, does the health care provider have a right to be paid for that treatment? See *First Healthcare Corporation v. Rettinger*, 118 N.C.App. 600, 456 S.E.2d 347 (1995); Marshall B. Kapp, *Enforcing Patient Preferences: Linking Payment for Medical Care to Informed Consent*, 261 Journal of the American Medical Association 1935–1938 (1989).

INSTITUTIONAL POLICIES AND PROCEDURES

Congress enacted the Patient Self-Determination Act (PSDA) in 1990, codified at 42 United States Code §§ 1395cc(a)(1) and 1396a(a):

[The Medicare and Medicaid laws are] amended— . . .

(Q) in the case of hospitals, skilled nursing facilities, home health agencies, and hospice programs, to comply with the requirement of subsection (f) (relating to maintaining written policies and procedures respecting advance directives) . . .

(f)(1) . . . the requirement of this subsection is that a provider of services or prepaid or eligible organization (as the case may be) maintain written policies and procedures with respect to all adult individuals receiving medical care by or through the provider or organization—

(A) to provide written information to each such individual concerning—

(i) an individual's rights under State law (whether statutory or as recognized by the courts of the State) to make decisions concerning such medical care, including the right to accept or refuse medical or surgical treatment and the right to formulate advance directives (as defined in paragraph (3)), and

(ii) the written policies of the provider or organization respecting the implementation of such rights;

(B) to document in the individual's medical record whether or not the individual has executed an advance directive;

(C) not to condition the provision of care or otherwise discriminate against an individual based on whether or not the individual has executed an advance directive;

(D) to ensure compliance with requirements of State law (whether statutory or as recognized by the courts of the State) respecting advance directives at facilities of the provider or organization; and

(E) to provide (individually or with others) for education for staff and the community on issues concerning advance directives. Subparagraph (C) shall not be construed as requiring the provision of care which conflicts with an advance directive.

(2) The written information described in paragraph (1)(A) shall be provided to an adult individual—

(A) in the case of a hospital, at the time of the individual's admission as an inpatient,

(B) in the case of a skilled nursing facility, at the time of the individual's admission as a resident,

(C) in the case of a home health agency, in advance of the individual coming under the care of the agency,

(D) in the case of a hospice program, at the time of initial receipt of hospice care by the individual from the program, and

(E) in the case of an eligible organization . . . at the time of enrollment of the individual with the organization.

(3) In this subsection, the term 'advance directive' means a written instruction, such as a living will or durable power of attorney for health care, recognized under State law (whether statutory or as recognized by the courts of the State) and relating to the provision of such care when the individual is incapacitated.

Discussion Questions

1. In enacting the PSDA, what assumptions did Congress make about the behavior of patients and health care providers, and about how the law might influence that behavior? Are these assumptions realistic?

2. Although applying to a variety of different health care providers, the PSDA does not apply to physicians in their private office settings. Should the PSDA requirements apply to physicians in their private office settings? What are the problems and costs associated with such an extension?

3. What are the operational and resource allocation implications for health care providers who must implement the PSDA in practice?

4. Draft a sample institutional protocol under the PSDA. What process should be used to draft such protocols? What content should they contain?

5. What can be done to make it more likely that health care providers will implement the requirements of the PSDA in spirit (i.e., to achieve Congress' goals in enacting the PSDA), as well as complying with the strict letter of the law?

"DO NOT" ORDERS

Many acute and long-term care providers have developed and implemented written protocols regarding prospective physician orders to withhold the beginning of particular kinds of LSMTs under specified circumstances. Such "do not" orders are a variety of advance directive and ordinarily are entered by the physician with the consultation and consent of the competent patient or the proxy of an incompetent patient. Although most attention has focused on Do Not Resuscitate (DNR) orders to withhold cardiopulmonary resuscitation (CPR) in the event of cardiac or respiratory arrest, other forms of prospective instructions to limit LSMT, such as Do Not Hospitalize or Do Not Intubate orders, also may be entered. The PSDA requires covered health care providers and prepaid plans to adopt DNR policies, as does the JCAHO for accredited facilities.

Discussion Questions

1. In the absence of an applicable "Do Not" order (or advance directive), should we presume that the patient has at least implicitly consented to a particular type of LSMT?

2. What are some of the possible impediments to physicians writing "Do Not" orders? How can those impediments be overcome? See Arn H. Eliasson, Joseph M. Parker, Andrew F. Shorr, et al., *Impediments to Writing Do-Not-Resuscitate Orders*, 159 Archives of Internal Medicine 2213–2218 (1999).

3. Should surrogates be allowed to consent to DNR orders on behalf of incompetent persons? To other forms of "Do Not" orders? What restrictions, if any, should be imposed on the surrogate's authority in this regard? See Christina M. Puchalski, Zhenshao Zhong, Michelle M. Jacobs, et al., *Patients Who Want their Family and Physician to Make Resuscitation Decisions for Them: Observations from SUPPORT and HELP,* 48 Journal of the American Geriatrics Society S84–S90 (2000).

4. Some hospitals still unofficially permit "[s]low codes, also known as partial, show, light blue, or Hollywood codes, [which] are cardiopulmonary resuscitative attempts that involve a deliberate decision not to attempt aggressively to bring a patient back to life. Either because the full armamentarium of pharmacologic and mechanical interventions is not used, or because the length of the

effort is shortened, a full attempt at resuscitation is not made." Gail Gazelle, *The Slow Code-Should Anyone Rush to Its Defense?* 338 New England Journal of Medicine 467–469 (1998). Why would a hospital staff engage in a "slow code?" What are the legal risk management implications of this practice, as compared with either engaging in a full code (i.e., attempting aggressively to resuscitate the patient) or withholding all resuscitative attempts in compliance with a true DNR order?

5. Should a physician be allowed legally to enter a unilateral DNR order, that is, without the approval of the patient or proxy? In *Wendland v. Sparks,* 574 N.W.2d 327 (Iowa 1998), the court held a physician liable for unilaterally deciding to withhold attempted CPR from a patient with a 10% chance of survival. Do you agree with the court? How would you compute the financial damages to be awarded in this case? See the discussion below regarding futility.

Policies and procedures for withholding LSMT in the home have also been developed. See Marshall B. Kapp, *Problems and Protocols for Dying at Home in a High-Tech Environment,* in Bringing the Hospital Home: Ethical and Social Implications of High-Tech Home Care (John D. Arras, ed.), Baltimore: Johns Hopkins University Press (1995), pp. 180–196. Over half the states have passed statutes explicitly authorizing DNR or "No Code" orders to be applied in situations of cardiac or respiratory arrest taking place outside of a health care institution. See Charles P. Sabatino, *Survey of State EMS-DNR Laws and Protocols,* 27 Journal of Law, Medicine & Ethics 297–315 (1999). Texas Health and Safety Code § 166.081:

> (6) "Out-of-hospital DNR order":
> (A) means a legally binding out-of-hospital do-not-resuscitate order, in the [prescribed] form . . . prepared and signed by the attending physician of a person, that documents the instructions of a person or the person's legally authorized representative and directs health care professionals acting in an out-of-hospital setting not to initiate or continue the following life-sustaining treatment:
> (i) cardiopulmonary resuscitation;
> (ii) advanced airway management;
> (iii) artificial ventilation;
> (iv) defibrillation;
> (v) transcutaneous cardiac pacing; and
> (vi) other life-sustaining treatment specified by the board [of health] . . . ; and

(B) does not include authorization to withhold medical interventions or therapies considered necessary to provide comfort care or to alleviate pain or to provide water or nutrition.

(7) "Out-of-hospital setting" means a location in which health care professionals are called for assistance, including long-term care facilities, in-patient hospice facilities, private homes, hospital outpatient or emergency departments, physician's offices, and vehicles during transport.

Discussion Questions

1. Some states impose medical prerequisites (e.g., diagnosis of terminal illness, permanent vegetative state, resuscitation would be medically futile) in order for an out-of-institution DNR to be effective. Do you agree with these prerequisites? Which particular ones would you include in legislation? Do such prerequisites violate the 14th Amendment Equal Protection rights of other persons?

2. Do you agree with the requirement that there be a physician's order before emergency personnel may withhold LSMT outside the hospital, or should a competent patient be able to execute a binding out-of-hospital DNR directive without a physician's order?

3. Many states use some form of specially designed identification (e.g., a bracelet) to be kept on or near the patient as part of the out-of-institution DNR process. Is this requirement necessary and helpful?

Many state out-of-institution DNR statutes have provisions similar to Michigan Code § 333.1062, Sec. 12: "A person or organization is not subject to civil or criminal liability for withholding resuscitative procedures from a declarant . . ."

Discussion Questions

1. What is the rationale for this sort of immunity provision? Is such a provision necessary? Is it likely to influence emergency health care providers' behavior?

2. Under what circumstances should an emergency health care provider be permitted to attempt resuscitation despite the existence of a DNR order?

LEGAL LIABILITY AND LSMT

There persists a deep-seated and pervasive anxiety on the part of many health care providers about suffering potential criminal liability or professional sanctions connected with caring for dying persons. This apprehension may influence provider behavior in two contradictory and unfortunate directions; it may inspire both overtreatment, in terms of inappropriate provision of LSMT, and undertreatment, in terms of inadequate and ineffective palliative care.

Fear of Liability for Undertreatment

According to one survey, "In actual practice, when prosecutors closely examine a case, they are very unlikely to prosecute, as evidenced by the fact that there is only one prosecution of physicians for forgoing life-sustaining treatment reported in official legal case reports, and at that time (1981–1983) the particular practice—termination of tube-feeding from a patient in a persistent vegetative state—was not nearly as well-accepted in law or medical practice as today. This is consistent with our finding that only 12% of [responding district attorneys] had ever been involved in any way in an end-of-life case." Alan Meisel, Jan C. Jernigan, & Stuart J. Youngner, *Prosecutors and End-of-Life Decision Making,* 159 Archives of Internal Medicine 1089, 1093–1094 (1999).

Discussion Question

Is the fact that legal entanglements, and especially criminal prosecutions, connected to the withholding or withdrawal of LSMT are exceedingly rare likely to alleviate health care providers' anxiety? What level of assurance would health care providers need to be psychologically comfortable?

Fear of Liability and Palliative Care

Anxiety about criminal liability or professional discipline (e.g., loss of license) has been blamed for widespread lapses in proper pain control and palliative care for dying patients. Although usually very exaggerated, this anxiety has not been without some foundation. See Ann Alpers, *Criminal Act or Palliative Care? Prosecutions Involving the Care of the Dying,* 26 Journal of Law, Medicine & Ethics 308–331 (1998). Since the mid-1990s, there have been attempts on several fronts to address this situation.

The American Geriatrics Society Position Statement on *The Care of Dying Patients* (1998) states:

> Position 5—Administrative, regulatory, and reimbursement struc-tures often serve as barriers to palliative care and should be reshaped . . . Many laws and regulations made for other purposes end up mak-ing good palliative care difficult . . . Laws intended to make it more difficult to divert narcotics into abuse can also make it very difficult to ensure adequate supplies for persons who need pain relief. Laws and regulations like these should be rewritten or revised.

Recent state legislative efforts have focused primarily on access to effective pain management. A majority of states have enacted statutes that explicitly allow physicians to prescribe controlled sub-stances to alleviate severe or intractable pain.

Nebraska Revised Statutes § 71-2419:

> A physician licensed under the Uniform Licensing Law who pre-scribes, dispenses, or administers or a nurse licensed under the Nurse Practice Act or pharmacist licensed under the Uniform Licensing Law who administers or dispenses a controlled substance in excess of the recommended dosage for the treatment of pain shall not be sub-ject to discipline or criminal prosecution when: (1) In the judgment of the physician, appropriate pain management warrants such dosage; (2) the controlled substance is not administered for the pur-pose of causing, or the purpose of assisting in causing, death for any reason; and (3) the administration of the controlled substance con-forms to policies and guidelines for the treatment of pain adopted by the Board of Examiners in Medicine and Surgery.

New Mexico Statutes § 24-2D-3:

> No health care provider who prescribes, dispenses or administers medical treatment for the purpose of relieving intractable pain and who can demonstrate by reference to an accepted guideline that his practice substantially complies with that guideline and with the stan-dards of practice identified in Section 4 of the Pain Relief Act shall be subject to disciplinary action or criminal prosecution, unless the showing of substantial compliance with an accepted guideline is rebutted by clinical expert testimony . . . .

B. In the event that a disciplinary action or criminal prosecution is pursued, the board or prosecutor shall produce clinical expert testimony supporting the finding or charge of violation of disciplinary standards or other legal requirements on the part of the health care provider. A showing of substantial compliance with an accepted guideline can only be rebutted by clinical expert testimony.

C. The provisions of this section shall apply to health care providers in the treatment of all patients for intractable pain, regardless of the patients' prior or current chemical dependency or addiction.

Criminal prosecutions of physicians for prescribing controlled substances as part of palliative care in end-of-life scenarios are not only increasingly rare, they also are being successfully defended and the physicians exonerated. See *State of Kansas v. Naramore,* 25 Kan.App.2d 302, 965 P.2d 211 (1998).

State medical boards have altered their policies and practices regarding the prescribing of controlled substances to encourage physicians to treat severe or intractable pain in dying patients more effectively. See Ann M. Martino, *In Search of a New Ethic for Treating Patients With Chronic Pain: What Can Medical Boards Do?* 26 Journal of Law, Medicine & Ethics 332–349 (1998). Model guidelines have been developed by the Federation of State Medical Boards. Moreover, in 1999 the Oregon Board of Medical Examiners disciplined a physician who grossly undertreated pain in six patients. Additionally, several families of deceased patients have brought civil malpractice lawsuits against physicians for inadequately treating the pain experienced by their dying relatives.

Discussion Questions

1. Why have states and the federal government generally been so restrictive about the prescribing of controlled substances? Do these concerns apply to situations involving dying individuals experiencing pain?

2. Besides anxiety about criminal prosecution and/or professional disciplinary action, what other factors work as barriers to effective pain management and palliative care for dying patients? What strategies might be used to overcome these barriers?

3. Are changes in statutes and regulations likely to be effective in influencing physicians to treat pain and otherwise palliate dying patients more effectively? What protections should statutes and

regulations contain to discourage the misuse of controlled substances? What are the problems with limiting permission to prescribe controlled substances to dying patients in "intractable" pain, which the American Society of Law and Medicine's model Pain Relief Act defines as "a state of pain, even if temporary, in which reasonable efforts to remove or remedy the cause of the pain have failed or have proven inadequate"?

4. What are the advantages and disadvantages of a strategy of permitting, or even encouraging, malpractice lawsuits and/or disciplinary actions against physicians for undertreating pain in dying patients? How is such a strategy likely to influence physician behavior?

5. What additional or alternative legal or nonlegal strategies might be pursued to bring about improved palliative treatment of dying patients?

Some have suggested that patients have a constitutional right to receive adequate pain control. See Robert A. Burt, *The Supreme Court Speaks: Not Assisted Suicide But a Constitutional Right to Palliative Care,* 337 New England Journal of Medicine 1234–1236 (1997).

Discussion Question

Is there a legal right to adequate pain control for dying patients? On what basis? If not, should there be such a right? Against whom should such a right be enforceable, that is, who has the duty to provide the pain control?

ASSISTED DEATH

Health care professionals' anxieties about potential criminal prosecution and/or professional disciplinary sanctions are well-founded in situations involving the provider engaging in some active intervention for the purpose, and with the result, of hastening a patient's death. Current U.S. law unambiguously, in homicide statutes, criminally condemns health care providers engaging in active (voluntary, positive) euthanasia (i.e., affirmatively and intentionally doing something, such as administering a lethal injection, to hasten the death of a patient without that patient's permission). For example,

Arkansas Statutes § 5-10-102 provides: "(a) A person commits murder in the first degree if: (2) with a purpose of causing the death of another person, he causes the death of another person."

Discussion Question

Do you agree with the legal distinction made between active euthanasia, which constitutes murder, and passive euthanasia (i.e., withholding or withdrawing LSMT with death resulting), which is not illegal? See Norman L. Cantor & George C. Thomas III, *The Legal Bounds of Physician Conduct Hastening Death,* 48 Buffalo Law Review 83–173 (2000); David Orentlicher, *The Alleged Distinction Between Euthanasia and the Withdrawal of Life-Sustaining Treatment: Conceptually Incoherent and Impossible to Maintain,* 1998 University of Illinois Law Review 837–859 (1998).

In addition, almost all states criminalize physician-assisted suicide (PAS), either through judicial interpretations of their general homicide statutes or enactment of a specific statute on the subject. Arkansas Statutes § 5-10-106:

(a)(1) For purposes of this section, "physician-assisted suicide" means a physician or health care provider participating in a medical procedure or willfully prescribing any drug, compound, or substance for the express purpose of assisting a patient to intentionally end his or her life.

***

(b) It shall be unlawful for any physician or health care provider to commit the offense of physician-assisted suicide by:

(1) Prescribing any drug, compound, or substance to a patient with the express purpose of assisting the patient to intentionally end his or her life; or

(2) Assisting in any medical procedure for the express purpose of assisting a patient to intentionally end his or her life.

(d) Nothing in this section shall prohibit physicians or health care providers from carrying out advanced directives or living wills, nor shall this section prohibit physicians from prescribing any drug, compound, or substance for the specific purpose of pain relief.

In 1997, the U.S. Supreme Court unanimously upheld the validity of state laws making it criminal for physicians or other health care professionals to assist a patient to commit suicide. In these decisions, the Court rejected the notion of any constitutional right to PAS.

Washington v. Glucksberg, 117 S.Ct. 2302 (1997):

The history of the law's treatment of assisted suicide in this country has been and continues to be one of the rejection of nearly all efforts to permit it. That being the case, our decisions lead us to conclude that the asserted "right" to assistance in committing suicide is not a fundamental liberty interest protected by the Due Process Clause. The Constitution also requires, however, that Washington's assisted-suicide ban be rationally related to legitimate government interests. This requirement is unquestionably met here. . . . Washington's assisted-suicide ban implicates a number of state interests.

First, Washington has an "unqualified interest in the preservation of human life." The State's prohibition on assisted suicide, like all homicide laws, both reflects and advances its commitment to this interest. . . .

Relatedly, all admit that suicide is a serious public-health problem, especially among persons in otherwise vulnerable groups. . . . The State has an interest in preventing suicide, and in studying, identifying, and treating its causes.

Those who attempt suicide—terminally ill or not—often suffer from depression or other mental disorders. . . . Thus, legal physician-assisted suicide could make it more difficult for the State to protect depressed or mentally ill persons, or those who are suffering from untreated pain, from suicidal impulses.

The State also has an interest in protecting the integrity and ethics of the medical profession. . . . [T]he American Medical Association, like many other medical and physicians' groups, has concluded that "[p]hysician-assisted suicide is fundamentally incompatible with the physician's role as healer." . . . Any physician-assisted suicide could, it is argued, undermine the trust that is essential to the doctor-patient relationship by blurring the time-honored line between healing and harming.

Next, the State has an interest in protecting vulnerable groups—including the poor, the elderly, and disabled persons-from abuse, neglect, and mistakes. . . . We have recognized . . . the real risk of subtle coercion and undue influence in end-of-life situations. . . . If physician-assisted suicide were permitted, many might resort to it to spare their families the substantial financial burden of end-of-life health-care costs.

The State's interest here goes beyond protecting the vulnerable from coercion; it extends to protecting disabled and terminally ill people from prejudice, negative and inaccurate stereotypes, and "societal indifference." The State's assisted suicide ban reflects and reinforces its policy that the lives of terminally ill, disabled, and elderly people must be no less valued than the lives of the young and healthy, and that a seriously disabled person's suicidal impulses should be interpreted and treated the same way as anyone else's. . . .

Finally, the State may fear that permitting assisted suicide will start it down the path to voluntary and perhaps even involuntary euthanasia. . . .

We need not weigh exactingly the relative strengths of these various interests. They are unquestionably important and legitimate, and Washington's ban on assisted suicide is at least reasonably related to their promotion and protection. We therefore hold that Wash. Rev. Code §9A.36.060(1) (1994) does not violate the Fourteenth Amendment, either on its face or as applied to competent, terminally ill adults who wish to hasten their deaths by obtaining medication prescribed by their doctors. (Citations omitted)

Vacco v. Quill, 117 S.Ct. 2293 (1997):

New York's statutes outlawing assisting suicide affect and address matters of profound significance to all New Yorkers alike. They neither infringe fundamental rights nor involve suspect classifications.

. . . On their faces, neither New York's ban on assisting suicide nor its statutes permitting patients to refuse medical treatment treat anyone differently than anyone else or draw any distinctions between persons. *Everyone,* regardless of physical condition, is entitled, if competent, to refuse unwanted lifesaving medical treatment; *no one* is permitted to assist a suicide. Generally speaking, laws that apply evenhandedly to all unquestionably comply with the Equal Protection Clause.

. . . [W]e think the distinction between assisting suicide and withdrawing life-sustaining treatment, a distinction widely recognized and endorsed in the medical profession and in our legal traditions, is both important and logical; it is certainly rational. . . .

The distinction comports with fundamental legal principles of causation and intent. First, when a patient refuses life-sustaining medical treatment, he dies from an underlying fatal disease or pathology; but if a patient ingests lethal medication prescribed by a physician, he is killed by that medication. . . .

Furthermore, a physician who withdraws, or honors a patient's refusal to begin, life-sustaining medical treatment purposefully intends, or may so intend, only to respect his patient's wishes and to cease doing useless and futile or degrading things to the patient when [the patient] no longer stands to benefit from them. . . . The same is true when a doctor provides aggressive palliative care; in some cases, painkilling drugs may hasten a patient's death, but the physician's purpose and intent is, or may be, only to ease his patient's pain. A doctor who assists a suicide, however, must, necessarily and indubitably, intend primarily that the patient be made dead. Similarly, a patient who commits suicide with a doctor's aid necessarily has the specific intent to end his or her own life, while a patient who refuses or discontinues treatment might not. . . .

The law has long used actors' intent or purpose to distinguish between two acts that may have the same result. . . .

Given these general principles, it is not surprising that many courts have carefully distinguished refusing life-sustaining treatment from suicide. . . .

Similarly, the overwhelming majority of state legislatures have drawn a clear line between assisting suicide and withdrawing or permitting the refusal of unwanted lifesaving medical treatment by prohibiting the former and permitting the latter. . . .

This Court has also recognized, at least implicitly, the distinction between letting a patient die and making that patient die. . . .

For all of these reasons, we disagree with respondents' claim that the distinction between refusing lifesaving medical treatment and assisted suicide is "arbitrary" and "irrational." Granted, in some cases, the line between the two may not be clear, but certainty is not required, even were it possible. Logic and contemporary practice support New York's judgment that the two acts are different, and New York may therefore, consistent with the constitution, treat them differently. By permitting everyone to refuse unwanted medical treatment while prohibiting anyone from assisting a suicide, New York law follows a longstanding and rational distinction. (Citations omitted) (Emphasis in original)

Although the Constitution does not require it, the door is open legally for particular states to choose, as a matter of their own respective public policies, to decriminalize PAS or even active euthanasia. As the Supreme Court said in *Glucksberg*, "Throughout the Nation, Americans are engaged in an earnest and profound debate about the morality, legality, and practicality of physician-assisted suicide. Our holding permits this debate to continue, as it should in a democratic society." Oregon is the only state thus far that has shifted PAS from a criminal to a regulated activity. Oregon Statutes § 127.805.§ 2.01:

(1) An adult who is capable, is a resident of Oregon, and has been determined by the attending physician and consulting physician to

be suffering from a terminal disease, and who has voluntarily expressed his or her wish to die, may make a written request for medication for the purpose of ending his or her life in a humane and dignified manner . . .

Oregon Statutes § 127.885.§ 4.01

(1) No person shall be subject to civil or criminal liability or professional disciplinary action for participating in good faith compliance with ORS 127.800 to 127.897. This includes being present when a qualified patient takes the prescribed medication to end his or her life in a humane and dignified manner.

(2) No professional organization or association, or health care provider, may subject a person to censure, discipline, suspension, loss of license, loss of privileges, loss of membership or other penalty for participating or refusing to participate in good faith compliance with ORS 127.800 to 127.897.

(3) No request by a patient for or provision by an attending physician of medication in good faith compliance with the provisions of ORS 127.800 to 127.897 shall constitute neglect for any purpose of law or provide the sole basis for the appointment of a guardian or conservator.

(4) No health care provider shall be under any duty, whether by contract, by statute or by any other legal requirement to participate in the provision to a qualified patient of medication to end his or her life in a humane and dignified manner. If a health care provider is unable or unwilling to carry out a patient's request under ORS 127.800 to 127.897, and the patient transfers his or her care to a new health care provider, the prior health care provider shall transfer, upon request, a copy of the patient's relevant medical records to the new health care provider.

Discussion Questions

1. Do you agree, as a public policy matter, with decriminalizing PAS? Should active euthanasia be decriminalized? Why or why not? Are there special issues that are implicated when elderly patients are involved? See Marshall B. Kapp, *Old Folks on the Slippery Slope: Elderly Patients and Physician-Assisted Suicide,* 35 Duquesne Law Review 443–453 (1996).

2. If PAS should be decriminalized, what requirements and limitations should be enacted to protect patients and the public? Are those procedural protections contained in the Oregon statute sufficient? Are they excessive?

Oregon Statutes § 127.815. § 3.01:

(1) The attending physician shall:

(a) make the initial determination of whether a patient has a terminal disease, is capable, and has made the request voluntarily;

(b) Request that the patient demonstrate Oregon residency;

(c) To ensure that the patient is making an informed decision, inform the patient of:

(A) His or her medical diagnosis;

(B) His or her prognosis;

(C) The potential risks associated with taking the medication to be prescribed;

(D) The probable result of taking the medication to be prescribed; and

(E) The feasible alternatives, including, but not limited to, comfort care, hospice care and pain control;

(d) Refer the patient to a consulting physician for medical confirmation of the diagnosis, and for a determination that the patient is capable and acting voluntarily;

(e) Refer the patient for counseling if appropriate;

(f) Recommend that the patient notify next of kin;

(g) Counsel the patient about the importance of having another person present when the patient takes the medication prescribed and of not taking the medication in a public place;

(h) Inform the patient that he or she has an opportunity to rescind the request at any time and in any manner, and offer the patient an opportunity to rescind at the end of the 15-day waiting period;

(i) Verify, immediately prior to writing the prescription for medication that the patient is making an informed decision;

(j) Fulfill the medical record documentation requirements;

(k) Ensure that all appropriate steps are carried out in accordance with ORS 127.800 to 127.897 prior to writing a prescription for medication to enable a qualified patient to end his or her life in a humane and dignified manner; and

(l) (A) Dispense medications directly, including ancillary medications intended to facilitate the desired effect to minimize the patient's discomfort, provided the attending physician is registered as a dispensing physician with the Board of Medical Examiners, has a current Drug Enforcement Administration certificate and complies with any applicable administrative rule; or

(B) With the patient's written consent:

(i) Contact a pharmacist and inform the pharmacist of the prescription; and

(ii) Deliver the written prescription personally or by mail to the pharmacist, who will dispense the medications to either the patient, the attending physician or an expressly identified agent of the patient.

Oregon Statutes § 127.820. § 3.02:

Before a patient is qualified under ORS 127.800 to 127.897, a consulting physician shall examine the patient and his or her relevant medical records and confirm, in writing, the attending physician's diagnosis that the patient is suffering from a terminal disease, and verify that the patient is capable, is acting voluntarily and has made an informed decision.

Oregon Statutes § 127.830. § 3.04:

No person shall receive a prescription for medication to end his or her life in a humane and dignified manner unless he or she has made an informed decision as defined in ORS 127.800 (7). Immediately prior to writing a prescription for medication under ORS 127.800 to 127.897, the attending physician shall verify that the patient is making an informed decision.

Oregon Statutes § 127.840. § 3.06:

In order to receive a prescription for medication to end his or her life in a humane and dignified manner, a qualified patient shall have made an oral request and a written request, and reiterate the oral request to his or her attending physician no less than fifteen (15) days after making the initial oral request. At the time the qualified patient makes his or her second oral request, the attending physician shall offer the patient an opportunity to rescind the request.

Oregon Statutes § 127.880. § 3.14:

Nothing in ORS 127.800 to 127.897 shall be construed to authorize a physician or any other person to end a patient's life by lethal injection, mercy killing or active euthanasia.

FUTILE MEDICAL TREATMENT

The issue of whether a health care professional has a legal obligation to effectuate a patient's or family's (or other surrogate's) demands for LSMT that the professional believes to be futile is unclear. This is despite the venerable legal maxim, *lex neminem cogit ad vana seu inutilia peragenda!*—"the law compels no one to do vain or useless things!"

Under Maryland Health General Code § 5-601(n), "medically ineffective treatment means that, to a reasonable degree of medical certainty, a medical procedure will not: (1) Prevent or reduce the deterioration of the health of an individual; or (2) Prevent the impending death of an individual." In the context of resuscitation, New York Public Health Law § 2961 defines "medically futile" to mean that "cardiopulmonary resuscitation will be unsuccessful in restoring cardiac and respiratory function or that the patient will experience repeated arrest in a short time period before death occurs."

Discussion Question

Do you agree with these definitions? Are they helpful in determining the respective rights and responsibilities of the parties to health care decision making?

The American College of Emergency Physicians' Policy Statement on *Nonbeneficial ("Futile") Emergency Medical Interventions*, 32 Annals of Emergency Medicine 126–127 (1998) states: "Physicians are under no ethical obligation to render treatments that they judge have no realistic likelihood of medical benefit to the patient."

Discussion Question

Do you agree with this position? Does this position also mean that physicians have no legal obligation to render such treatments? Do physicians have a duty to at least offer such treatments? How should the physician determine which treatments "have no realistic likelihood of medical benefit to the patient"?

According to the *Consensus Statement of the Society of Critical Care Medicine's Ethics Committee Regarding Futile and Other Possibly Inadvisable Treatments*, 25 Critical Care Medicine 887–891 (1997): "Treatments that offer no physiologic benefit to the patient are futile and should never be offered . . . Treatments in which the benefit is unlikely, uncertain, or controversial from the viewpoint of one or more of the appropriately involved decision-makers should not be labeled futile . . . Treatments that are beneficial but extremely costly should be made available in a limited fashion, governed by principles of distributive justice."

Discussion Question

Do you find this categorization of treatments valid and helpful? Are the costs of treatment a valid consideration at the level of the individual patient? Should the patient's age be taken into account in the determination of medical futility?

The American Medical Association Council on Ethical and Judicial Affairs' Report on *Medical Futility in End-of-Life Care,* 281 Journal of the American Medical Association 937–941 (1999) recommends a process-based approach to disagreements about the futility of a particular LSMT for a particular patient. This approach would be defined within "parameters set by a regulatory body of the institution or the community . . . An important advantage to having a fair process approach is that arbitration can occur in a setting that is usually more convenient, more knowledgeable in medicine, more rapidly responsive, and less expensive in financial and emotional terms than court action." Texas Health & Safety Code § 166.046 provides that an institutional ethics committee must be involved in any conflict between a patient or surrogate and the treating physician about whether treatment should be continued, with appeal to the courts as a last resort; compliance with the ethics committee's finding that a particular treatment is medically inappropriate provides a physician who refuses to obey the patient's or surrogate's demands with a degree of legal protection.

Discussion Questions

1. What process would you recommend for resolving disagreements about the futility of particular LSMTs? When, if ever, should the courts be involved in these determinations?

2. What strategies should health care providers engage in to reduce the possibility of disagreements about the futility of particular LSMTs escalating and becoming the source of litigation? Why shouldn't the health care providers always obey the patient's or surrogate's demands for particular LSMTs?

DEFINITIONS OF DEATH

For most of our history, cessation of cardiorespiratory functioning has served adequately as a definition of death for all purposes. The usefulness of this definition has been seriously impaired in more recent times, however, as advances in biomedical technology have made it possible to sustain cardiopulmonary functioning artificially in certain individuals almost indefinitely. Thus, states have had to search for a definition of death that is comprehensive (legal, ethical, and clinical) and that responds to the following questions: (1) When is a person dead, so that there is no question about withholding or withdrawing LSMT, and (2) When is a person dead, so that organs may be removed and transplanted into another living human being?

In 1981, the President's Commission for the Study of Ethical Problems in Medicine and Biomedical and Behavioral Research recommended a Uniform Determination of Death Act (UDDA) stating:

> Any individual who has sustained either (1) irreversible cessation of circulatory and respiratory functions, or (2) irreversible cessation of all functions of the entire brain, including the brain stem, is dead.

Either by statute or judicial decision, virtually all the states have adopted the UDDA, although controversies persist. See Stuart J. Youngner, Robert M. Arnold, & Renie Schapiro, eds., The Definition of Death: Contemporary Controversies, Baltimore: Johns Hopkins University Press (1999).

Discussion Questions

1. Current law requires irreversible cessation of the whole brain, including the stem, before an individual is dead. This "whole brain" definition means that someone like Nancy Cruzan, who was in a PVS, was alive as long as her brain stem functioned. Some have suggested that the states change their laws to consider dead those individuals who have suffered irreversible cessation of all upper, or cognitive, brain function even if the brain stem continues to function. See Robert D. Truog & James C. Fackler, *Rethinking Brain Death*, 20 Critical Care Medicine 1705–1713 (1992). Do you agree with the current whole brain definition of death or would you favor adopting an upper brain definition? What are the arguments for and against each approach?

2. Some people hold religious objections to the concept of brain death, believing that a person is alive as long as the heart and lungs

are working, even if artificially. Should state statutes defining death take such religious beliefs into account? See New Jersey Statutes § 26:6A-5:

> The death of an individual shall not be declared upon the basis of neurological criteria . . . when the licensed physician authorized to declare death, has reason to believe, on the basis of information in the individual's available medical records, or information provided by a member of the individual's family or any other person knowledgeable about the individual's personal religious beliefs that such a declaration would violate the personal religious beliefs of the individual. In these cases, death shall be declared, and the time of death fixed, solely upon the basis of cardio-respiratory criteria . . .

The UDDA states that "[a] determination of death must be made in accordance with accepted medical standards." All state statutes on this subject concur. The state of the art in this realm continues to evolve, along with the rest of medicine.

Once a patient meets the legal criteria, the attending physician is obligated to make a declaration of death. Once the criteria are met, there also is an obligation to respect a family's request to discontinue any LSMT.

CERTIFICATION OF DEATH AND AUTOPSIES

When a person dies, a death certificate must be filed. Colorado Revised Statutes § 25-2-110:

> (1) A certificate of death for each death which occurs in Colorado shall be filed with the state registrar or as otherwise directed by the state registrar, within five days after such death occurs and prior to final disposition . . .
>
> (3) The funeral director or person acting as such who first assumes custody of a dead body or dead fetus shall be responsible for the filing of the death certificate required by subsection (1) of this section. He shall obtain the personal data required by the certificate from the next of kin or the best qualified person or source available. He shall obtain the medical certification necessary to complete the portion of the certificate pertaining to the cause of death from the best qualified person or source available, pursuant to subsection (4) of this section.

(4) Except when [referral to the coroner] . . . is required, the physician in charge of the patient's care for the illness or condition which resulted in death shall complete, sign, and return to the funeral director or person acting as such all medical certification within forty-eight hours after a death occurs. In the absence of said physician or with his approval, the certificate may be completed and signed by his associate physician, by the chief medical officer of the institution in which the death occurred, or by the physician who performed an autopsy upon the decedent, if such individual has access to the medical history of the case, if he views the deceased at or after the time of death, and if the death is due to natural causes.

(5) When inquiry is required . . . the coroner shall determine the cause of death and shall complete and sign the medical certification within forty-eight hours after taking charge of the case.

Discussion Question

What is the public health rationale for requiring that death certificates be filed in a central location? See Grace B. Huffman, *Death Certificates: Why It Matters How Your Patient Died,* 56 American Family Physician 1287–1290 (1997).

Certain deaths must be referred to a coroner or medical examiner, depending on the particular jurisdiction. See Randy Hanzlick & Debra Combs, *Medical Examiner and Coroner Systems: History and Trends,* 279 Journal of the American Medical Association 870–874 (1998). Pennsylvania Statutes § 450.503 provides:

The local registrar or person in charge of interment or other person having knowledge of the death shall refer to the coroner the following cases: (1) where no physician or dentist who is a staff member of an approved hospital was in attendance during the last illness of the deceased, or (2) where the physician or dentist who is a staff member of an approved hospital in attendance during the last illness of the deceased is physically unable to supply the necessary data, or (3) where the circumstances suggest that the death was sudden or violent or suspicious in nature or was the result of other than natural causes, or (4) where the physician, dentist or coroner who provided or would provide the medical certification is a member of the immediate family of the deceased. In every instance of a referral under this section, the coroner shall make an immediate investigation and shall supply the necessary data, including the medical certification of the death . . .

Once a referral has been made, the coroner or medical examiner must determine what steps, including autopsy or postmortem examination, are needed to properly investigate the circumstances of the deceased's death. When a coroner or medical examiner conducts an autopsy, some states treat the results as an easily accessible public record.

Discussion Question

Should the results of an autopsy conducted by a coroner or medical examiner be accessible to the public?

There are cases in which referral to a coroner or medical examiner is not legally mandated, but the attending physician may recommend that a hospital autopsy be performed. In situations in which referral to a coroner or medical examiner is not required by statute, an autopsy may be performed only if there is valid informed consent from the individual, while alive, or a legally authorized surrogate. Pennsylvania Statutes § 1111:

An autopsy or postmortem examination may be performed upon the body of a deceased person by a physician licensed under the laws of the Commonwealth of Pennsylvania when the dead body is claimed within thirty-six hours after death for burial at the expense of the claimant and authorization for the postmortem examination has been obtained in any of the following manners:

(1) By written authorization signed by the deceased during lifetime and the written consent of his surviving spouse, if any, after death.

(2) By written authorization of any party whom the deceased during lifetime designed by written instrument to take charge of his body for burial and the written consent of decedent's surviving spouse, if any, after death.

(3) By written authorization of the decedent's surviving spouse.

(4) If the surviving spouse is incompetent, unavailable or does not claim the body for burial, or if there is no surviving spouse, by written authorization of the following in order of precedence if the claimant agrees to provide burial: (i) adult children, (ii) adult grandchildren, (iii) parents, (iv) brothers or sisters, (v) nephews or nieces, (vi) grandparents, (vii) uncles or aunts, (viii) cousins, (ix) stepchildren, (x) relatives or next of kin of previously deceased spouse.

(5) If none of the above persons are available to claim the body, by written authorization of any other relative or friend who assumes custody of the body for burial.

Discussion Questions

1. Why might an attending physician recommend that an autopsy be performed even though it is not legally required? See Kim A. Collins, Allan T. Bennett, Randy Hanzlick, and the Autopsy Committee of the College of American Pathologists, *The Autopsy and the Living*, 159 Archives of Internal Medicine 2391–2392 (1999); Teresa S. Welsh & Joseph Kaplan, *The Role of Postmortem Examination in Medical Education*, 73 Mayo Clinic Proceedings 802–805 (1998).

2. What are the potential legal uses of voluntary autopsy results regarding, for example, disputes about civil liability or probate or estate matters? What are the potential positive and negative risk management implications of autopsy findings for health care providers who had earlier been involved in the deceased's care?

8

Research With Older Human Subjects

WHAT IS RESEARCH AND WHY DO IT?

"Research" means a systematic investigation designed to develop or contribute to generalizable knowledge, 45 C.F.R. § 46.102(e).

Discussion Questions

1. How does "research" as defined in the federal regulation cited differ from usual professional practice?

2. Is "research" as defined in this federal regulation synonymous with "experimentation"? If not, what is the distinction?

3. Why should research be conducted in the field of geriatrics and gerontology? What kinds of research should be conducted?

4. When, if ever, is it appropriate to use older persons as human research subjects in biomedical and behavioral research protocols? Why would an older person agree to participate in a research protocol? See Peter V. Rabins, *Issues Raised by Research Using Persons Suffering From Dementia Who Have Impaired Decisional Capacity,* 1 Journal of Health Care & Policy 22–35, at 26 (1998):

> If the important research questions could be answered by studying individuals with intact capacity to consent, then decisionally incapacitated subjects should not be included. However, most of the important research questions about dementia require the participation of individuals who have dementia. They cannot be answered by studying cognitively intact individuals or by studying animal models.

See also American Geriatrics Society, Ethics Committee, *Informed Consent for Research on Human Subjects With Dementia,* 46 Journal of the American Geriatrics Society 1308–1310 (1998):

> Research on the causes and treatments of dementia, management of the complications of dementia, or health services research related to problems experienced by people with dementia certainly warrant conducting research on subjects with dementia. Examples of research on conditions commonly associated with dementia include studies on pressure sores and urinary incontinence. People with dementia living in long-term care settings are appropriate subjects for research and should be selected on scientific and clinical grounds.

According to leaders of the National Alliance for the Mentally Ill (NAMI):

> The existence of a hard and fast rule prohibiting research using decisionally-incapacitated individuals as subjects would have the effect of barring those who are most severely ill from participating in research which may alleviate their suffering and provide them with significant benefits. This, in our opinion, would be unjust and unnecessary. Laurie Flynn and Ronald S. Honberg, *Achieving Proper Balance in Research With Decisionally Incapacitated Subjects,* 1 Journal of Health Care Law and Policy 174–192, 181 (1998).

Do you agree with these statements? Would you go so far as to claim that older individuals have a **right** to participate in any particular research protocol?

The Regulatory Landscape

Research involving human subjects is subject to federal regulations codified at 45 C.F.R. Part 46. The key provisions concern review of research protocols by a local Institutional Review Board (IRB) and the assurance that enrollment as a human subject in a research protocol occurs only with informed consent.

> §46.107 IRB Membership
> (a) Each IRB shall have at least five members, with varying backgrounds to promote complete and adequate review of research activities commonly conducted by the institution. The IRB shall be sufficiently qualified through the experience and expertise of its

members, and the diversity of the members, including consideration of race, gender, and cultural backgrounds and sensitivity to such issues as community attitudes, to promote respect for its advice and counsel in safeguarding the rights and welfare of human subjects. In addition to possessing the professional competence necessary to review specific research activities, the IRB shall be able to ascertain the acceptability of proposed research in terms of institutional commitments and regulations, applicable law, and standards of professional conduct and practice. The IRB shall therefore include persons knowledgeable in these areas. If an IRB regularly reviews research that involves a vulnerable category of subjects, such as children, prisoners, pregnant women, or handicapped or mentally disabled persons, consideration shall be given to the inclusion of one or more individuals who are knowledgeable about and experienced in working with these subjects.

(b) Every nondiscriminatory effort will be made to ensure that no IRB consists entirely of men or entirely of women, including the institution's consideration of qualified persons of both sexes, so long as no selection is made to the IRB on the basis of gender. No IRB may consist entirely of members of one profession.

(c) Each IRB shall include at least one member whose primary concerns are in scientific areas and at least one member whose primary concerns are in nonscientific areas.

(d) Each IRB shall include at least one member who is not otherwise affiliated with the institution and who is not part of the immediate family of a person who is affiliated with the institution.

(e) No IRB may have a member participate in the IRB's initial or continuing review of any project in which the member has a conflicting interest, except to provide information requested by the IRB.

(f) An IRB may, in its discretion, invite individuals with competence in special areas to assist in the review of issues which require expertise beyond or in addition to that available on the IRB. These individuals may not vote with the IRB.

§46.109 IRB Review of Research

(a) An IRB shall review and have authority to approve, require modifications in (to secure approval), or disapprove all research activities covered by this policy.

(b) An IRB shall require that information given to subjects as part of informed consent is in accordance with §46.116. The IRB may require that information, in addition to that specifically mentioned in §46.116, be given to the subjects when in the IRB's judgment the information would meaningfully add to the protection of the rights and welfare of subjects.

(c) An IRB shall require documentation of informed consent or may waive documentation in accordance with §46.117.

(d) An IRB shall notify investigators and the institution in writing of its decision to approve or disapprove the proposed research activity, or of modifications required to secure IRB approval of the research activity. If the IRB decides to disapprove a research activity, it shall include in its written notification a statement of the reasons for its decision and give the investigator an opportunity to respond in person or in writing.

(e) An IRB shall conduct continuing review of research covered by this policy at intervals appropriate to the degree of risk, but not less than once per year, and shall have authority to observe or have a third party observe the consent process and the research.

§46.111 Criteria for IRB Approval of Research

(a) In order to approve research covered by this policy the IRB shall determine that all of the following requirements are satisfied:

(1) Risks to subjects are minimized:

(i) by using procedures which are consistent with sound research design and which do not unnecessarily expose subjects to risk, and

(ii) whenever appropriate, by using procedures already being performed on the subjects for diagnostic or treatment purposes.

(2) Risks to subjects are reasonable in relation to anticipated benefits, if any, to subjects, and the importance of the knowledge that may reasonably be expected to result. In evaluating risks and benefits, the IRB should consider only those risks and benefits that may result from the research (as distinguished from risks and benefits of therapies subjects would receive even if not participating in the research). The IRB should not consider possible long-range effects of applying knowledge gained in the research (for example, the possible effects of the research on public policy) as among those research risks that fall within the purview of its responsibility.

(3) Selection of subjects is equitable. In making this assessment the IRB should take into account the purposes of the research and the setting in which the research will be conducted and should be particularly cognizant of the special problems of research involving vulnerable populations, such as children, prisoners, pregnant women, mentally disabled persons, or economically or educationally disadvantaged persons.

(4) Informed consent will be sought from each prospective subject or the subject's legally authorized representative, in accordance with, and to the extent required by §46.116.

(5) Informed consent will be appropriately documented, in accordance with, and to the extent required by §46.117.

(6) When appropriate, the research plan makes adequate provision for monitoring the data collected to ensure the safety of subjects.

(7) When appropriate, there are adequate provisions to protect the privacy of subjects and to maintain the confidentiality of data.

(b) When some or all of the subjects are likely to be vulnerable to coercion or undue influence, such as children, prisoners, pregnant women, mentally disabled persons, or economically or educationally disadvantaged persons, additional safeguards have been included in the study to protect the rights and welfare of these subjects.

§46.113 Suspension or Termination of IRB Approval of Research

An IRB shall have authority to suspend or terminate approval of research that is not being conducted in accordance with the IRB's requirements or that has been associated with unexpected serious harm to subjects. Any suspension or termination of approval shall include a statement of the reasons for the IRB's action . . .

§46.116 General Requirements for Informed Consent

Except as provided elsewhere in this policy, no investigator may involve a human being as a subject in research covered by this policy unless the investigator has obtained the legally effective informed consent of the subject or the subject's legally authorized representative. An investigator shall seek such consent only under circumstances that provide the prospective subject or the representative sufficient opportunity to consider whether or not to participate and that minimize the possibility of coercion or undue influence. The information that is given to the subject or the representative shall be in language understandable to the subject or the representative. No informed consent, whether oral or written, may include any exculpatory language through which the subject or the representative is made to waive or appear to waive any of the subject's legal rights, or releases or appears to release the investigator, the sponsor, the institution or its agents from liability for negligence.

(a) Basic elements of informed consent. Except as provided in paragraph (c) or (d) of this section, in seeking informed consent the following information shall be provided to each subject:

(1) A statement that the study involves research, an explanation of the purposes of the research and the expected duration of the subject's participation, a description of the procedures to be followed, and identification of any procedures which are experimental;

(2) a description of any reasonably foreseeable risks or discomforts to the subject;

(3) a description of any benefits to the subject or to others which may reasonably be expected from the research;

(4) a disclosure of appropriate alternative procedures or courses of treatment, if any, that might be advantageous to the subject;

(5) a statement describing the extent, if any, to which confidentiality of records identifying the subject will be maintained;

(6) for research involving more than minimal risk, an explanation as to whether any compensation and an explanation as to whether any medical treatments are available if injury occurs and, if so, what they consist of, or where further information may be obtained;

(7) an explanation of whom to contact for answers to pertinent questions about the research and research subjects' rights, and whom to contact in the event of a research-related injury to the subject; and

(8) a statement that participation is voluntary, refusal to participate will involve no penalty or loss of benefits to which the subject is otherwise entitled, and the subject may discontinue participation at any time without penalty or loss of benefits to which the subject is otherwise entitled.

(b) additional elements of informed consent. When appropriate, one or more of the following elements of information shall also be provided to each subject:

(1) a statement that the particular treatment or procedure may involve risks to the subject (or to the embryo or fetus, if the subject is or may become pregnant) which are currently unforeseeable;

(2) anticipated circumstances under which the subject's participation may be terminated by the investigator without regard to the subject's consent;

(3) any additional costs to the subject that may result from participation in the research;

(4) the consequences of a subject's decision to withdraw from the research and procedures for orderly termination of participation in the research;

(5) a statement that significant new findings developed during the course of the research which may relate to the subject's willingness to continue participation will be provided to the subject; and

(6) the approximate number of subjects involved in the study.

(c) An IRB may approve a consent procedure which does not include, or which alters, some or all of the elements of informed consent set forth above, or waive the requirement to obtain informed consent provided the IRB finds and documents that:

(1) the research or demonstration project is to be conducted by or subject to the approval of state or local government officials and is designed to study, evaluate, or otherwise examine: (i) public benefit or service programs; (ii) procedures for obtaining benefits or services under those programs; (iii) possible changes in or alternatives to those programs or procedures; or (iv) possible changes in methods or levels of payment for benefits or services under those programs; and

(2) the research could not practically be carried out without the waiver or alteration.

(d) An IRB may approve a consent procedure which does not include, or which alters, some or all of the elements of informed consent set forth in this section, or waive the requirement to obtain informed consent provided the IRB finds and documents that:

(1) the research involves no more than minimal risk to the subjects;

(2) the waiver or alteration will not adversely affect the rights and welfare of the subjects;

(3) the research could not practically be carried out without the waiver or alteration; and

(4) whenever appropriate, the subjects will be provided with additional pertinent information after participation.

(e) The informed consent requirements in this policy are not intended to preempt any applicable Federal, State, or local laws which require additional information to be disclosed in order for informed consent to be legally effective.

§46.117 Documentation of Informed Consent

(a) Except as provided in paragraph (c) of this section, informed consent shall be documented by the use of a written consent form approved by the IRB and signed by the subject or the subject's legally authorized representative. A copy shall be given to the person signing the form.

(b) Except as provided in paragraph (c) of this section, the consent form may be either of the following:

(1) A written consent document that embodies the elements of informed consent required by §46.116. This form may be read to the subject or the subject's legally authorized representative, but in any event, the investigator shall give either the subject or the representative adequate opportunity to read it before it is signed; or

(2) A short form written consent document stating that the elements of informed consent required by §46.116 have been presented orally to the subject or the subject's legally authorized representative. When this method is used, there shall be a witness to the oral presentation. Also, the IRB shall approve a written summary of what is to be said to the subject or the representative. Only the short form itself is to be signed by the subject or the representative. However, the witness shall sign both the short form and a copy of the summary, and the person actually obtaining consent shall sign a copy of the summary. A copy of the summary shall be given to the subject or the representative, in addition to a copy of the short form.

(c) An IRB may waive the requirement for the investigator to obtain a signed consent form for some or all subjects if it finds either:

(1) That the only record linking the subject and the research would be the consent document and the principal risk would be potential harm resulting from a breach of confidentiality. Each subject will be asked whether the subject wants documentation linking the subject with the research, and the subject's wishes will govern; or

(2) That the research presents no more than minimal risk of harm to subjects and involves no procedures for which written consent is normally required outside of the research context. In cases in which the documentation requirement is waived, the IRB may require the investigator to provide subjects with a written statement regarding the research.

Local IRBs are themselves monitored by the Office of Human Research Protection (OHRP), which is in the Office of the DHHS Secretary. OPRR may award an IRB either a Single Project Assurance that allows the IRB to review a single study or a Multiple Project Assurance that allows the IRB to review any number of studies over a five year period.

Discussion Questions

1. Why should biomedical and behavioral research involving human subjects be regulated? Why should regulation take place at the federal, rather than state, level?

2. Are the regulatory provisions regarding IRB membership sufficient to overcome the conflicts of interest inherent when a local IRB reviews research protocols submitted by colleagues from the same institution or community as IRB members? Are stronger safeguards against conflicts of interest needed?

3. If an IRB regularly reviews research protocols involving older human subjects and wants to include as members "individuals who are knowledgeable about and experienced in working with these subjects," where should the IRB find such individuals? What are the specific qualifications that an IRB should seek in recruiting members for this specific role?

4. The IRB is responsible for assuring that "selection of subjects is equitable." Is it equitable to use older subjects when the research could be conducted using younger persons? When, if ever, is it equitable to use mentally impaired or institutionalized older persons as human research subjects? Regarding subject recruitment generally, see DHHS, Office of Inspector General, Recruiting Human Subjects: Sample Guidelines for Practice, OEI-01-97-00196, *www.hhs.gov./oig/oei*.

5. How do the informed consent standards for research set out in the federal regulations differ from informed consent standards applicable to usual therapeutic practice (see chapter 2)?

6. 42 C.F.R. § 46.111(b) provides that, "When some or all of the subjects are likely to be vulnerable to coercion or undue influence, such as . . . **mentally disabled persons,**" the IRB may require that "additional safeguards have been included in the study to protect the rights and welfare of these subjects." What particular **additional safeguards** might be necessary to protect the rights and welfare of disabled or institutionalized older persons who are being sought as human research subjects?

7. Do the regulations put too much emphasis on documentation of informed consent through the use of a written, signed form? What are the advantages and disadvantages of focusing on a written form to document informed consent?

The federal regulations originally applied on their face only to research involving human subjects that was conducted by the Department of Health and Human Services (DHHS) itself or funded by DHHS. However, most institutions conducting research have voluntarily agreed to apply the federal regulations to all of their research protocols, regardless of funding source for a particular study. Additionally, other federal agencies have adopted a common rule for human subjects protection in any research protocol that they sponsor, 45 C.F.R. Part 46, subpart A. See James D. Shelton, *How to Interpret the Federal Policy for the Protection of Human Subjects or 'Common Rule'* (Part A), 21 IRB: A Review of Human Subjects Research 6–9 (Nov.-Dec. 1999). Moreover, research involving the testing of investigational drugs or medical devices is concurrently regulated by the federal Food and Drug Administration (FDA), 21 C.F.R. §§ 56.101 *et. seq.* See Richard A. Merrill, *FDA Regulation of Clinical Drug Trials,* in The Handbook of Psychopharmacology Trials: An Overview of Scientific, Political, and Ethical Concerns (Marc Hertzman and Douglas E. Feltner, eds.), New York: New York University Press (1997), pp. 61–99.

Additionally, some states have adopted additional requirements pertaining to all human subjects research conducted within their respective jurisdictions. For instance, California Health and Safety Code § 24171 states:

(c) It is necessary that medical experimentation be done in such a way as to protect the rights of the human subjects involved. (d) There is, and will continue to be, a growing need for protection for citizens of the state from unauthorized, needless, hazardous, or negligently performed medical experiments on human beings. It is, therefore, the intent of the Legislature, in the enacting of this chapter, to provide minimum statutory protection for the citizens of this state with regard to human experimentation and to provide penalties for those who violate such provisions.

See also Diane Hoffmann and Jack Schwartz, *Proxy Consent to Participation of the Decisionally Impaired in Medical Research-Maryland's Policy Initiative,* 1 Journal of Health Care Law & Policy 123–153 (1998).

Also, private civil lawsuits may be brought by individual participants against researchers and protocol sponsors for negligent violation of common law tort standards of care or failure to obtain proper informed consent in the conduct of human subjects research. Further, constitutional protections based on an individual's Fourteenth Amendment rights to due process and equal protection of the laws and the Eighth Amendment's prohibition against cruel and unusual punishment may be applicable to potential subjects of research conducted or sponsored by government agencies.

CRITICISMS OF THE CURRENT REGULATORY SCHEME

Marshall B. Kapp, *Regulating Research for the Decisionally Impaired: Implications for Mental Health Professionals,* 8 Journal of Clinical Geropsychology (2002).

The effectiveness of the current regulatory scheme and the performance of IRBs in enforcing legal and ethical requirements have been harshly criticized lately from a number of directions, fueled largely by reports of abuses of subjects' rights.

On June 11, 1998, the DHHS's Office of Inspector General (OIG) issued four reports on human subjects research and IRBs. Among the concerns noted in these reports were: overburdened IRBs with insufficient time and resources to properly conduct initial and (especially) continuing reviews; ineffective monitoring of and response to adverse events happening to subjects; insufficient ethics training for researchers and IRB members; inadequate attention to evaluation of IRB effectiveness; and conflicts of interest between IRBs and the institutions of which they are a part, especially as research funds become more scarce. Also in June, 1998, the National Institutes of Health Office of Extramural Research released a contractor's report which, although considerably less critical than the OIG reports, concluded that protection of human subjects could be improved by fine-tuning IRB procedures and providing increased education and training to researchers as well as to IRB members and staff. The OIG and NIH reports were accompanied by well-publicized Congressional hearings before the Subcommittee on Human Resources of the House Committee on Government Reform and Oversight.

In 1999, the National Institute of Mental Health (NIMH) announced creation of a new review panel to screen high risk intramural and extramural studies funded by the Institute and other initiatives driven "by a desire to make sure that the science in NIMH studies is good enough to justify the use of human subjects." Typically, IRBs have essentially taken a hands-off approach to review of the scientific merits of research protocols, ignoring the logical link between the quality of the science and the justification for allowing any risk to volunteers.

Several particular types of biomedical and behavioral research studies, disproportionately utilizing mentally impaired individuals as research subjects, have been the target of specific ethical scrutiny. Regardless of the potential subjects' decisional capacity, but especially when they are unusually psychologically vulnerable, there is special concern about the necessity and safety of placebo controlled clinical trials, wherein subjects may be denied, by virtue of random assignment to the placebo control group, the chance to receive a direct benefit from a proven treatment; medication for the subject's specific medical or mental problem is taken away from the subject so that the medication's effects do not confound the results obtained by the subject receiving an experimental intervention; and symptom provocation (challenge) experiments, in which subjects are given increasingly higher doses of the study intervention until certain undesirable symptoms have been activated. (Citations omitted)

In April, 2000, the DHHS Office of Inspector General issued a report, Protecting Human Research Subjects: Status of Recommendations, OEI-01-97-00197. It found that, "overall, few of our [earlier] recommended reforms have been enacted."

Discussion Question

What are the impediments to implementing the recommendations contained in the 1998 OIG and NIH reports on protection of human research subjects?

PARTICULAR CONCERNS REGARDING THE DECISIONALLY IMPAIRED

No Specific Regulations

Marshall B. Kapp, *id*.:

The Belmont Commission recommended in 1978, that at least for individuals institutionalized as mentally disabled, the federal government should promulgate distinct regulations controlling human subjects research. Although proposed regulations were published, these were never made final (i.e., legally binding). Among the explanations for this purposeful inaction, beyond a vague admonition in the Common Rule that IRBs should be "particularly cognizant" of the needs of all vulnerable subjects and should require "additional safeguards" when such populations are included in a study, 42 C.F.R. §46.111(b), are (1) the objections of the mental health research community that specially targeted requirements would be cumbersome and stifle scientific progress and (2) acceleration of the trend toward deinstitutionalization of the mentally ill and developmentally disabled in the late 1970s and into the 1980s.

Neither has action been taken in response to subsequent calls for specific research regulations targeting the decisionally impaired. Recommendations in this vein have emanated from, among other sources, a National Institute on Aging (NIA)-sponsored study group that convened in the early 1980s to discuss the use of demented persons in research and the President's Commission for the Study of Ethical Problems in Medicine and Biomedical and Behavioral Research.

Lately, however, special protections for the decisionally impaired, both within institutions and the community, have become a renewed item of interest. The national Alzheimer's Association has called "upon state and federal authorities to clarify existing laws and regulations as they relate to people with cognitive impairments." Among the other organizations that have developed and adopted relevant research guidelines in this sphere are the American College of Physicians, the Council for International Organizations of Medical

Sciences (in collaboration with the World Health Organization), Council of Europe, and the British Medical Research Council. The American Psychiatric Association has organized a work group for the purpose of formulating ethical guidelines for psychiatric researchers dealing with the decisionally impaired. Several scholars, laboring individually and within groups, also have weighed in with comprehensive policy proposals in the area.

On December 2–3, 1997, the National Institutes of Health sponsored an Inter-Institute Conference on Research Involving Individuals With Questionable Capacity to Consent: Ethical Issues and Practical Considerations for IRBs. The latest significant foray into this arena was launched with the release of the [1998] National Bioethics Advisory Commission (NBAC) report entitled "Research Involving Persons With Mental Disorders That May Affect Decisionmaking Capacity." [available at *www.bioethics.gov/capacity*] (Citations omitted)

Discussion Question

Should there be special regulations concerning mentally impaired human research subjects? Should there be special regulations concerning the protection of elderly human research subjects? Should special regulations be restricted in applicability to persons who are institutionalized? If there should be special research regulations for the elderly subjects, what should be the unique content of those regulations?

Voluntariness of Consent

Marshall B. Kapp, *id.*:

> In order to be legally and ethically valid, a person's consent to participate as a human research subject must be given voluntarily, free from coercion. Since voluntariness in this regard may be influenced by physical setting and the potential subject's dependency on others and susceptibility to suggestion and manipulation, assuring the presence of this element of consent may be problematic in the case of the decisionally impaired. Institutionalized individuals may be especially vulnerable to subtle or direct pressure to "volunteer" their participation in a research study.
>
> Mental health professionals, functioning in their various roles, should work to minimize as much as possible those factors that might *unduly* exert influence or coercive effect on potential subjects. For instance, many individuals who are asked to participate in research

protocols agree to do so based on the misperception that the experimental intervention is likely to, and indeed is expected and intended to, provide them with direct benefit, rather than being expected and intended to generate generalizable data for future use, with any benefit to the particular subject welcome but only incidental to the research endeavor. Individuals with decisional impairments may be particularly vulnerable to the coercive influence of the therapeutic misconception, especially in light of the "sense of desperation" that many mentally disabled persons experience due to the personal disruption of their lives caused by their illnesses and the limited effectiveness of available treatments. By working to overcome misunderstandings among potential subjects about reasonably anticipated risks and benefits, and fostering the effective disclosure of accurate information, mental health professionals can improve the level of voluntariness within the actual subject cohort. (Citations omitted)

Capacity to Consent

Marshall B. Kapp, *id.*:

In order to understand such concepts as the difference between research and therapeutic interventions, a prospective human research subject must have the mental capacity to engage in a rational decision making process; individuals cannot autonomously, authentically volunteer to take part in research protocols if they are not able to comprehend material information about respective risks and benefits. This requirement of decisional capacity poses substantial ethical and legal difficulties regarding the research participation of many mental health professionals' patients. Some mentally disabled individuals lack sufficient decisional capacity to validly volunteer for research participation at the time enrollment is requested, while some who are capable of giving autonomous consent to participate at the inception of the protocol may subsequently become unable to give valid consent to continue that participation. Importantly, however, mental disability *per se* does not necessarily equal decisional incapacity, which must be assessed on a decision-specific rather than a global basis, with a focus on function rather than clinical diagnosis. Many individuals with various forms of mental disability, including early dementia and schizophrenia, are nonetheless sufficiently able to consent on their own behalf to research participation if the disability is not too severe. NBAC has recommended that capable subjects' own consent be accepted as sufficient for enrollment even in protocols entailing greater than minimal risk with no prospect of direct benefit to the subject. Ethicist Baruch Brody has suggested that better explanations of information may frequently "cure" what at first appears to be a decisional incapacity situation. Forensic psychiatrist Paul Appelbaum has chided his mental health colleagues for being too quick to discount the decisional capacity of many mental patients, urging that educational and other interventional efforts ought to be directed instead toward enhancing the decisional participation of those individuals. This position has been adopted by the American Psychiatric Association.

The identification of some degree of decision-making impairment in potential subjects need not result in their automatic exclusion from research participation. Many cognitively impaired subjects can give adequate consents when additional efforts are made to educate them about the nature and consequences of study participation. IRBs have been roundly criticized for devoting too much attention to the minute parsing of the wording of written consent forms submitted as part of the research protocols being reviewed, while spending little if any time and resources monitoring the actual process of obtaining informed consent from human subjects (or their surrogates). Of particular concern has been the virtual absence of IRB or other external oversight regarding identification of who should be assessing the present (let alone future) decisional capacity of prospective subjects and the standards and methods used to carry out the capacity assessment. Several recommendations concerning the capacity assessment process have emerged recently.

NBAC advocated the promulgation of regulation mandating that, for any human subjects research protocol involving greater than minimal risk, there be an independent assessment of each potential subject's decisional capacity. This is consistent with NAMI's position, which recognizes possible risks of error, in either direction, in the way that subjects' capacity assessment ordinarily is handled today.

[T]here may, in some instances, be incentives for researchers not to be vigilant in monitoring the capacity of vulnerable research participants or in failing to determine that certain individuals lack capacity, if such determinations will delay or interfere with the course of the research protocol. On the opposite side of the spectrum, . . . [there may be] incentives for potential subjects to be found lacking in decisional capacity, . . . [since] 'Once a patient is deemed incapable, his or her ability to have an objection of continued participation honored is severely . . . curtailed by provisions allowing for override of the objection' (quoting *T.D. v. New York State Office of Mental Health*).

The British Medical Research Council's Working Party on Research on the Mentally Incapacitated recommended that the determination of decisional capacity be made by the potential subject's physician if the physician is not involved in the research protocol; otherwise, it should be made by an independent party acceptable to the committee that reviews and approves the research protocol. Neither NBAC, NAMI, nor the British Working Party have gone so far as the New York State Court of Appeals in *T.D. v. New York State Office of Mental Health* (OMH) [650 N.Y.S. 2d173 (N.Y. App. Div. 1996)], which compelled a formal judicial assessment of incompetency for every potential research subject receiving services in a facility operated or licensed by the OMH.

NBAC also recommended that IRBs require that, in each protocol involving greater than minimal risk, the investigator explicitly describe to the IRB the process to be used to assess the decisional capacity of potential human subjects. Moreno et al., too, would command researchers to explain how capacity will be evaluated, both at the start of a protocol and as capacity changes during the course of the research. The American Psychiatric Association has issued guidelines regarding both procedures and standards for assessing decision-making capacities. While numerous commentators have endorsed development of standardized written instruments for assessing capacity to decide about research participation (as well as to decide about other matters), this author elsewhere has cautioned against placing too much weight on the quantitative results of testing with such instruments. (Citations omitted)

Discussion Questions

1. Do you agree with NBAC's recommendation that, for any human subjects research protocol involving greater than minimal risk, there should be an independent assessment of each potential subject's decisional capacity? Is this necessary? Would the benefits outweigh the costs? Besides financial costs, what are some of the practical consequences of this recommendation?

2. Do you agree with the British Working Party's recommendation that decisional capacity be made by the potential subject's own physician if the physician is not involved in the research protocol, and otherwise made by an independent party acceptable to the IRB?

3. Would widespread implementation of the *T.D.* court's holding compelling a formal judicial assessment of incompetence for every potential research subject receiving services in a licensed facility be practical and desirable? Do you agree with critics of this decision

that it could effectively shut down research on mental illness? What might be the implications of this approach for research involving the participation of demented older persons in nursing and assisted living facilities?

Surrogate Decision Making

Marshall B. Kapp, *id.*:

When a prospective research subject lacks mental capacity to personally consent to or refuse participation in a research protocol, the investigator ordinarily looks to a surrogate decision maker to act on behalf of the incapacitated potential subject. Who qualifies as a surrogate for this purpose has, in theory, depended on individual states' laws pertaining to guardianship/ conservatorship, the permissible scope of advance medical directives, and family surrogacy in the medical sphere. In practice, even in the absence of clearly delineated legal authority, investigators normally rely on available "next of kin" as a matter of longstanding custom to decide about research participation. Among the problems noted regarding the current surrogate decision making practice are possible conflicts of interest between surrogate and subject, discordance of preferences between surrogate and subject (for example, because possible benefits like "improvement in the quality of life" often are very subjective, the cumbersomeness of relying on surrogates, and in an increasing number of situations the unavailability of a capable and willing person to act as a conscientious and timely surrogate.

In 1964, the Declaration of Helsinki softened the previous absolute ban on surrogate consent to research participation by allowing the legal guardians of incompetent persons to provide consent on their behalf, at least for protocols offering a realistic likelihood of direct benefit to the individual subjects. NBAC in its recommendations distinguishes among different categories of research.

The categories of research identified by NBAC are:

- Protocols involving only minimal risk
- Protocols involving greater than minimal risk but offering a prospect of direct benefit to subjects
- Protocols involving greater than minimal risk and no prospect of direct benefit to that study's human subjects.

Most research seeking to enroll the mentally impaired probably falls into the latter category. NBAC would impose varying requirements regarding surrogate consent depending on the category of protocol involved.

Marshall B. Kapp, *id.*:

> Central to [its] recommendations are the concepts of PA [Prospective Authorization] and the LAR [Legally Authorized Representative]. Under the NBAC proposal, a capable person may give PA to future research participation. PA may be either of the instruction (e.g., living will) or the proxy (e.g., durable power of attorney) type. For an instruction type of PA to be valid, NBAC would require that the risks and benefits of the specific class of research involved must have been explained to the prospective subject while he or she was still decisionally capable; moreover, the greater the risk of the research, the more specific PA should be.
>
> In the NBAC formulation, an LAR may enroll a subject in a research protocol after the subject has become decisionally incapacitated, provided:
>
> - The LAR uses substituted judgment (i.e., makes the choice that the subject would have made if currently able to make and express his or her own autonomous decision about research participation;
> - The LAR monitors the subject's recruitment for, participation in, and withdrawal from the study; and
> - The LAR is chosen by the subject or is a relative or friend.
>
> According to NBAC, the LAR for research purposes should be the same friend or relative of the prospective subject who is recognized under state law for purposes of clinical, therapeutic decision making.
>
> The NBAC recommendations in many respects represent a proposed codification of ideas that are widely promoted already. Regarding recognition of a proxy type of PA for research purposes, for example, Moreno et al. have argued:
>
> The possibility of enrollment of an incompetent subject in research involving interventions that are potentially beneficial to the individual patient-subject and in research that involves minimal incremental risk should be part of the durable power of attorney for health care authority for several reasons: it is an expression of patient autonomy, it is an opportunity for the surrogate to act for the potential benefit of the now incompetent subject, and it might benefit future patients and therefore society in general.

Others support this idea as well, with the American Geriatrics Society agreeing with NBAC that "[s]urrogates should be allowed to refuse to enroll potential subjects or to withdraw a subject from an ongoing trial on the basis that the surrogate believes that the research protocol is not in the best interests of the subject or is not what the subject intended, even if that decision would conflict with the subject's advance directive."

On another note, NBAC's recommendation 7, that "Any potential or actual subject's objection to enrollment or to continued participation in a research protocol must be heeded in all circumstances," that is, guaranteeing to even incapacitated persons the right to veto their LAR's consent to research participation, embodies the prevailing ethical consensus. According to the American Geriatrics Society, "In general, the refusal of a (potential) subject, even if that subject has lost decision-making capacity, should be followed."

However, despite a vigorous defense by most NBAC members, some of that body's majority recommendations have been criticized. NBAC member Bernard Lo filed a partial dissent, saying that he would permit surrogate consent to enroll decisionally incapacitated persons in protocols involving a small increase over minimal risk if there were the meaningful possibility of significant benefit to the public in the future. The Alzheimer's Association position on dementia research, while largely consistent with the NBAC report, would permit, for greater than minimal risk research when there is no reasonable chance for benefit to the individual, enrollment of those persons who are capable of giving their own informed consent or have executed a research specific advance directive, and who have a proxy available to monitor the individual's involvement in the protocol.

At least one prominent psychiatrist has attacked NBAC's recommended requirement of both IRB and national review panel approval for research involving more than minimal risk with no real probability of benefit when the subject cannot personally consent, saying that "This represents an extraordinary shift of authority from the community in which the research is being conducted to a central body distant from both the subjects and the researchers." The same critic opines that, regarding NBAC's recommendation for independent assessment of potential subjects' decisional capacity for all research involving more than minimal risk, "Many psychiatric researchers consider these recommended procedures expensive, cumbersome, and clinically insensitive to the experience of impaired subjects, and some patient advocates fear that the implied mistrust of care givers may have a negative effect on the doctor-patient relationship." The American Psychiatric Association has expressed agreement with these sentiments, adding that regulations singling out persons with mental disorders for special attention risks unfairly stigmatizing those individuals.

On another point, NBAC essentially left empowerment of LARs for research purposes up to state law, through statutes pertaining to guardianship/conservatorship and durable powers of attorney. Support has been expressed for recognizing the authority of family members to function in the surrogate role, even absent a formal transfer of power by a court or the decisionally capable potential subject, at least for protocols reasonably holding out the possibility of direct benefit.

Some would place more stringent limitations on surrogate consent in the research context than those contained in the NBAC report. The then-Chairperson of the New York State Commission on Quality of Care for the Mentally Disabled would disallow any nontherapeutic research that exposes decisionally incapacitated human subjects to more than minimal risk, unless the person had explicitly authorized a proxy to consent to the specific type of research protocol involved.

"While competent adults are free to make martyrs of themselves in the cause of science, they do not have the license to make martyrs of other people by volunteering them for experiments that expose them to significant risks, especially when those experiments cannot do them any good. The authorization for such research must reliably and authentically find its source in the exercise of free will by the subject when competent."

In a 1996 decision [*T.D. v. New York State Office of Mental Health*] that has been soundly condemned as erecting an enormously unnecessary and unwise barrier to the conduct of useful research on problems encountered by mentally disabled persons, the New York Court of Appeals effectively precluded the conduct of biomedical and behavioral research, regardless of funding source, using any person residing in facilities either owned or licensed by OMH.

In reaction to this judicial overreaction to perceived ethical abuses in the preexisting research enterprise, the New York State Department of Health established an Advisory Work Group on Human Subject Research Involving the Protected Classes, which in early 1999 proposed, with adequate safeguards, allowing the conduct of research involving more than minimal risk on decisionally incapacitated subjects even in the absence of likely benefit to the subjects themselves. (Citations omitted)

Discussion Questions

1. What is your opinion regarding surrogate consent to research participation on behalf of a decisionally impaired older person?

Should the extent and limits of the surrogate's authority vary depending on the relative risks and benefits entailed in the particular research protocol? Should the authority of a surrogate be recognized in the research context absent a formal court order or proxy directive timely executed by the potential human subject?

2. Is PA realistic and desirable in the research context? What might health care and human service professionals do to help older persons to effectuate this concept in practice?

3. Who ought to serve as a LAR? What are the ideal qualities for someone fulfilling this role? Should the LAR be the same person who makes decisions about diagnostic and therapeutic matters for the decisionally incapacitated person?

4. Do you agree with NBAC and the American Geriatrics Society that even decisionally incapacitated individuals should be able to veto participation in a research study? What are the (especially nonverbal) ways in which such a veto might be expressed? Who should make the determination that a veto is being expressed? Can a LAR insist that the incapacitated individual be included in a research study?

Index